Suzanne S. Frucht

Worksheets for Medical Terminology:
Get Connected!

Custom Edition for Southeast Community College
Medical Assisting Program

Taken from:
Worksheets for Medical Terminology: Get Connected!
by Suzanne S. Frucht

Cover Art: Courtesy of Photodisc/Getty Images.

Taken from:

Worksheets for Medical Terminology: Get Connected!
by Suzanne S. Frucht
Copyright © 2012 by Pearson Education, Inc.
Upper Saddle River, New Jersey 07458

All rights reserved. No part of this book may be reproduced, in any form or by any means, without permission in writing from the publisher.

This special edition published in cooperation with Pearson Learning Solutions.

All trademarks, service marks, registered trademarks, and registered service marks are the property of their respective owners and are used herein for identification purposes only.

Pearson Learning Solutions, 501 Boylston Street, Suite 900, Boston, MA 02116
A Pearson Education Company
www.pearsoned.com

Printed in the United States of America

4 5 6 7 8 9 10 V092 16 15 14 13

000200010271288757

CB

ISBN 10: 1-256-51399-7
ISBN 13: 978-1-256-51399-5

Contents

Chapter 1 Introduction to Medical Terminology 1

Chapter 2 Suffixes 12

Chapter 3 Prefixes 23

Chapter 4 Anatomical Terminology 33

Chapter 5 Dermatology: Integumentary System 56

Chapter 6 Orthopedics: Musculoskeletal System 83

Chapter 7 Cardiology: Cardiovascular System 108

Chapter 8 Hematology: Blood 135

Chapter 9 Immunology: Immune Systems 159

Chapter 10 Pulmonology: Respiratory System 183

Chapter 11 Gastroenterology: Digestive System 211

Chapter 12 Urology and Nephrology: Urinary System and Male Reproductive System 236

Chapter 13 Obstetrics and Gynecology: Female Reproductive System 265

Chapter 14 Neurology: Nervous System 293

Chapter 15 Endocrinology: Endocrine System 319

Chapter 16 Ophthalmology: The Eye 343

Chapter 17 Otorhinolaryngology: The Ear, Nose, and Throat 370

Chapter 1
Introduction to Medical Terminology

Learning Objectives

After completing this chapter, students will be able to:

1. Identify the three types of medical terms.
2. Explain the differences between prefixes, suffixes, word roots, and combining vowels.
3. Form combining forms.
4. Explain how to analyze (building and interpreting) medical terms.
5. Describe how to pluralize medical terms.
6. Understand how to pronounce medical terms.

Worksheet 1A
Med Term Analysis

Directions: The medical terms given below have been divided into word parts. For each term: list its word parts and give the category and its meaning for each part (using the glossary at the back of your text or a medical dictionary). Then define the term.

	Word Parts	Category	Meaning
1. oste/o/arthr/itis	osteo	word root	bone
	o	N/A	N/A
	arthr	word root	joint
	itis	suffix	inflammation
Term means:	bone + joint inflammation		
2. hepat/o/megaly	hepat	word root	liver
	o	N/A	N/A
	megaly	suffix	enlarge
Term means:	enlarged liver		
3. cardi/o/my/o/pathy	cardi	word root	heart
	o	N/A	N/A
	my	word root	muscle
	o	N/A	N/A
	pathy	suffix	disease
Term means:	disease of heart muscle		
4. inter/vertebr/al	inter	prefix	between
	vertebr	word root	vertebra
	al	suffix	pertaining to
Term means:	pertaining to between vertebra		
5. rhin/o/plasty	rhin	word root	nose
	o	N/A	N/A
	plasty	suffix	surgical repair
Term means:	surgical repair of the nose		

(Continued)

	Word Parts	Category	Meaning
6. electr/o/therapy	electr	word root	electricity
	o	N/A	N/A
	therapy	suffix	treatment
Term means:	treatment with electricity		
7. carcin/o/genic	carcin	word root	cancer
	o	N/A	N/A
	genic	suffix	producing
Term means:	cancer producing		
8. gastr/ectomy	gastr	word root	stomach
	ectomy	suffix	surgical removal
Term means:	surgical removal of stomach		
9. sub/cutane/ous	sub	prefix	under, below
	cutane	word root	skin
	ous	suffix	pertaining to
Term means:	pertaining to beneath the skin		
10. dys/pepsia	dys	prefix	painful, difficult, abnormal
	pepsia	suffix	digestion
Term means:	abnormal digestion		

Worksheet 1B
More Practice Building Medical Terms

Directions: Use the word parts list below to build a medical term for each definition. This exercise is a little different from the one in your text because many of the word parts are used more than once to illustrate how using the same word parts in different combinations produces terms with very different meanings.

Word Parts	Category	Meaning
-al	suffix	pertaining to
-ary	suffix	pertaining to
bronch	word root	bronchus
crani	word root	skull
-ectomy	suffix	surgical removal
intra-	prefix	within
-itis	suffix	inflammation
-logy	suffix	study of
neur	word root	nerve
o	combining vowel	(none)
-plasty	suffix	surgical repair
pulmon	word root	lung
-scope	suffix	instrument for viewing
tonsill	word root	tonsils

1. surgical removal of tonsils — tonsill / ectomy
2. study of the lungs — pulmon / o / logy
3. pertaining to within the skull — crani / intra / al
4. study of nerves — neur / o / logy
5. surgical repair of the skull — crani / o / plasty
6. instrument for viewing the bronchus — bronch / o / scope
7. inflammation of the tonsils — tonsill / itis
8. inflammation of nerves — neur / itis
9. pertaining to within the lungs — pulmon / intra / ary
10. surgical repair of a bronchus — bronch / o / plasty

Worksheet 1C
Making Plurals

Directions: For each singular term below, write the plural form.

1. carcinoma carcinomata
2. criterion criteria
3. bronchus bronchi
4. deformity deformities
5. larynx larynges
6. papilla papillae
7. cortex cortices
8. bacterium bacteria
9. fungus fungi
10. orthosis orthoses

Name _____ Date _____ Score _____

Chapter 1
Labeling Quiz

Directions: Label each organ with its name.

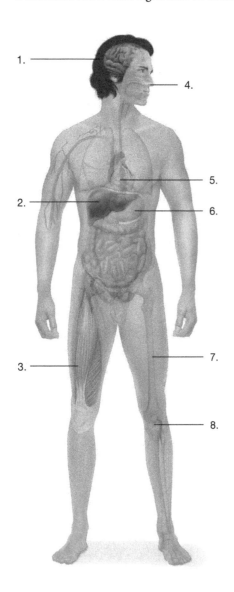

1. Cephal/o: head
2. hepat/o: liver
3. my/o: muscle
4. rhin/o: nose
5. cardi/o: heart
6. gastr/o: stomach
7. oste/o: bone
8. arthr/o: joint

Name _____   Date _____   Score _____

Chapter 1 Quiz

True/False

__T__ 1. The word root is the foundation of a medical term.

__F__ 2. The most common combining vowel is i.

__F__ 3. Prefixes indicate such information as disease.

__F__ 4. Combining vowels are translated as *pertaining to*.

__T__ 5. Suffixes provide such information as a surgical procedure.

__F__ 6. A combining form is a word root and its suffix.

__F__ 7. The only word part found in every medical term is a word root.

__T__ 8. An eponym is based on a person's name.

__T__ 9. A singular term ending in -um is made plural by dropping the -um and adding -a.

__T__ 10. If a term begins with pn, pronounce only the n.

Fill-in-the-Blank

1. In the term gastr/itis, the word root is __gastr__.
2. In the term carcin/oma, -oma is a __suffix__.
3. In the term my/o/gram, the combining vowel is __o__.
4. In the term oste/o/pathy, oste is a __word root__.
5. In the term rhin/o/plasty, rhin/o is a __combining form__.
6. In the term sub/cutane/ous, the prefix is __sub__.
7. In the term cardi/o/logy, the suffix is __logy__.
8. The term oste/o/arthr/itis contains __two__ word roots.
9. In the term dys/uria, dys is a __prefix__.
10. In the term hepat/o/megaly, the combining form is __hepat/o__.

Chapter 1 Answer Keys

Worksheet 1A Answer Key

1. oste, word root, bone; o, combining vowel, no meaning; arthr, word root, joint; -itis, suffix, inflammation; term means inflammation of bones and joints
2. hepat, word root, liver; o, combining vowel, no meaning; -megaly, suffix, enlarged; term means enlarged liver
3. cardi, word root, heart; o, combining vowel, no meaning; my, word root, muscle; o, combining vowel, no meaning; -pathy, suffix, disease; term means disease of heart muscle
4. inter-, prefix, between; vertebr, word root, vertebra; -al, suffix, pertaining to; term means pertaining to between verbebrae
5. rhin, word root, nose; o, combining vowel, no meaning; -plasty, suffix, surgical repair; term means surgical repair of the nose
6. electr, word root, electricity; o, combining vowel, no meaning; -therapy, suffix, treatment; term means treatment with electricity
7. carcin, word root, cancer; o, combining form, no meaning; -genic, suffix, producing; term means cancer producing
8. gastr, word root, stomach; -ectomy, suffix, surgical removal; term means surgical removal of the stomach
9. sub-, prefix, below; cutane, word root, skin; -ous, suffix, pertaining to; term means pertaining to below the skin
10. dys-, prefix, abnormal; -pepsia, suffix, digestion; term means abnormal digestion

Worksheet 1B Answer Key

1. tonsillectomy
2. pulmonology
3. intracranial
4. neurology
5. cranioplasty
6. bronchoscope
7. tonsillitis
8. neuritis
9. intrapulmonary
10. bronchoplasty

Worksheet 1C Answer Key

1. carcinomata
2. criteria
3. bronchi
4. deformities
5. larynges
6. papillae
7. cortices
8. bacteria
9. fungi
10. orthoses

Chapter 1 Labeling Quiz Answer Key

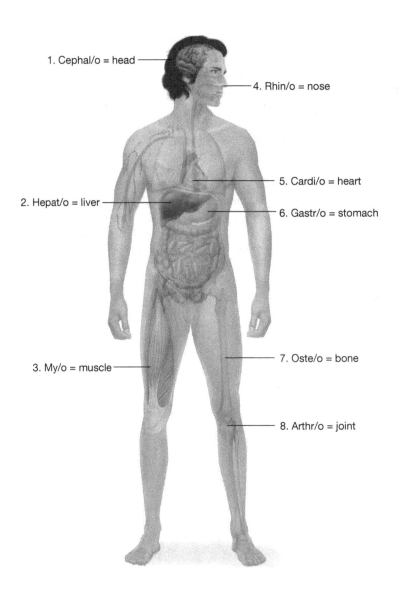

1. Cephal/o = head
2. Hepat/o = liver
3. My/o = muscle
4. Rhin/o = nose
5. Cardi/o = heart
6. Gastr/o = stomach
7. Oste/o = bone
8. Arthr/o = joint

Chapter 1 Quiz Answer Key

True/False

1. True
2. False
3. False
4. False
5. True
6. False
7. False
8. True
9. True
10. True

Fill-in-the-Blank

1. gastr
2. suffix
3. o
4. word root
5. combining form
6. sub-
7. -logy
8. two
9. prefix
10. hepat/o

Chapter 2
Suffixes

Learning Objectives

After completing this chapter, students will be able to:

1. Explain the role of suffixes in building medical terms.
2. Use suffixes to indicate diseases or abnormal conditions.
3. Use suffixes to indicate surgical procedures.
4. Use suffixes to indicate diagnostic procedures.
5. Use general suffixes.
6. Use suffixes to indicate medical specialties or personnel.
7. Use suffixes to convert word roots into nouns or adjectives.

Use this word list to focus your studying for the chapter test.

Arthritis
Bronchitis
Cardiac
Colostomy
Dermatitis
Dermatology
Esophageal
Gastric
Hepatic
Hepatitis
Neurology
Pulmonary
Rhinorrhea
Rhinoplasty
Uterine
Venous

Worksheet 2A
Using Suffixes

Directions: Write out the meaning for each suffix. Then locate two new terms using the suffix from later chapters in your text or a medical dictionary (do not use the examples given in this chapter).

Suffixes	Meaning	New Term	Meaning
1. -algia	pain		
2. -asthenia	weakness		
3. -cele	protrusion		
4. -dynia	pain		
5. -cytosis	abdominal cell condition		
6. -ectasis	dilated		
7. -edema	swelling		
8. -emesis	vomiting		
9. -emia	blood condition		
10. -itis	inflammation		
11. -lith	stone		

(Continued)

Suffixes	Meaning	New Term	Meaning
12. -lysis	to destroy		
13. -lytic	destruction		
14. -malacia	abnormal softening		
15. -megaly	enlarged		
16. -oma	tumor, mass		
17. -pathy	disease		
18. -penia	too few		
19. -phobia	fear		
20. -plegia	paralysis		
21. -ptosis	drooping		
22. -rrhage	abnormal flow condition		
23. -rrhea	discharge, flow		
24. -rrhexis	rupture		

(Continued)

Suffixes	Meaning	New Term	Meaning
25. -sclerosis	hardening		
26. -spasm	involuntary muscle contraction		
27. -stasis	stopping		
28. -stenosis	narrowing		
29. -uria	urine condition		
30. -clasia	surgical breaking		
31. -desis	surgical fusing		
32. -ectomy	surgical removal		
33. -ostomy	surgically create an opening		
34. -otomy	cutting into		
35. -pexy	surgical fixation		
36. -plasty	surgical repair		
37. -rrhaphy	suture		

(*Continued*)

Suffixes	Meaning	New Term	Meaning
38. -tripsy	Surgical crushing		
39. -centesis	Puncture to withdraw fluid		
40. -gram	Record or picture		
41. -graphy	Process of recording		
42. -meter	Instrument for measuring		
43. -metry	Process of measuring		
44. -scope	Instrument for viewing		
45. -scopy	Process of visually examining		
46. -cyte	Cell		
47. -derma	Skin condition		
48. -esthesia	Feeling, sensation		
49. -kinesia	Movement		
50. -opia	Vision		

(Continued)

Suffixes	Meaning	New Term	Meaning
51. -osmia	sense of smell		
52. -oxia	oxygen		
53. -partum	child birth		
54. -pepsia	digestion		
55. -phagia	eating, swallowing		
56. -phasia	speech		
57. -pnea	breathing		
58. -poiesis	formation		
59. -therapy	treatment		
60. -thorax	chest		

Worksheet 2B
Word Search

Directions: Find and circle the answer for each fill-in-the-blank question in the word search puzzle.

1. The suffix -edema means Swelling.
2. The suffix -itis means inflammation.
3. The suffix -pathy means disease.
4. The suffix -stenosis means narrowing.
5. The suffix -tripsy means surgical crushing.
6. The suffix -gram means record or picture.
7. The suffix -cyesis means pregnancy.
8. The suffix -globin means protein.
9. The suffix -ole means small.
10. The suffix -ician means specialist.

18 Chapter 2/SUFFIXES © 2012 Pearson Education, Inc.

Name _____ Date _____ Score _____

Chapter 2 Quiz

Directions: Define the suffix in the spaces provided.

1. -cele Protrusion
2. -plasty Surgical repair
3. -sclerosis hardening
4. -iatrist Physician
5. -osis abnormal condition
6. -derma Skin condition
7. -eal pertaining to
8. -uria urine condition
9. -ectomy Surgical removal
10. -stenosis narrowing
11. -logy study of
12. -phasia speech
13. -stasis stopping
14. -centesis puncture to withdraw fluid
15. -dipsia thirst
16. -porosis porous
17. -cytosis abnormal cell condition (too many)
18. -pnea breathing
19. -manometer instrument for measuring pressure
20. -genic producing
21. -kinesia movement
22. -tic pertaining to
23. -otomy cutting into
24. -cyte cell
25. -scope instrument for viewing

Chapter 2 Answer Keys

Worksheet 2A Answer Key

1. pain
2. weakness
3. hernia, protrusion
4. pain
5. abnormal cell condition
6. dilated, stretched out
7. swelling
8. vomiting
9. condition of the blood
10. inflammation
11. stone
12. destruction
13. destruction
14. abnormal softening
15. enlargement, large
16. tumor, mass
17. disease
18. too few
19. fear
20. paralysis
21. drooping
22. bursting forth
23. discharge, flow
24. rupture
25. hardened condition
26. involuntary muscle contraction
27. stopping
28. narrowing
29. condition of the urine
30. surgical breaking
31. surgical fixation
32. surgical removal, excision
33. surgically create an opening
34. cutting into, incision
35. surgical fixation
36. surgical repair
37. suture
38. crushing
39. puncture to withdraw fluid
40. record or picture
41. process of recording
42. instrument for measuring
43. process of measuring
44. instrument for viewing
45. process of visually examining
46. cell
47. skin condition
48. feeling, sensation
49. movement
50. vision
51. sense of smell
52. oxygen
53. birth, labor
54. digestion
55. eating, swallowing
56. speech
57. breathing
58. formation
59. treatment
60. chest

Worksheet 2B Answer Key

1. swelling
2. inflammation
3. disease
4. narrowing
5. crushing
6. record
7. pregnancy
8. protein
9. small
10. specialist

```
X  T  N  A  R  R  O  W  I  N  G  P
W  T  G  R  F  V  G  M  N  R  T  R
R  D  N  R  W  V  Q  X  F  Z  S  E
P  N  I  E  T  O  R  P  L  M  I  G
X  R  L  C  M  Y  E  X  A  W  L  N
N  K  L  T  R  S  R  R  M  B  A  A
Q  G  E  R  A  U  E  N  M  R  I  N
L  L  W  E  C  C  S  J  A  R  C  C
L  L  S  B  O  X  V  H  T  M  E  Y
K  I  A  R  H  J  M  M  I  P  P  R
D  C  D  M  J  T  M  D  O  N  S  Y
K  N  N  D  S  K  N  J  N  L  G  N
```

Chapter 2 Quiz Answer Key

1. hernia, protrusion
2. surgical repair
3. hardened condition
4. physician
5. abnormal condition
6. skin condition
7. pertaining to
8. condition of the urine
9. surgical removal, excision
10. narrowing
11. study of
12. speech
13. stopping
14. puncture to withdraw fluid
15. thirst
16. porous
17. abnormal cell condition (too many)
18. breathing
19. instrument for measuring pressure
20. producing
21. movement
22. pertaining to
23. cutting into, incision
24. cell
25. instrument for viewing

Chapter 3
Prefixes

Learning Objectives

After completing this chapter, students will be able to:

1. Explain the role of prefixes in building medical terms.
2. Use prefixes to indicate diseases or abnormal conditions.
3. Use prefixes to indicate directions or body positions.
4. Use prefixes to indicate numbers or quantity measurements.
5. Use prefixes to indicate time.
6. Use prefixes to build additional medical terms.

Use this word list to focus your studying for the chapter test.

Anuria
Apnea
Bilateral
Bradycardia
Dysuria
Intracellular
Endocarditis
Epidermal
Extracellular
Pericarditis
Polyuria
Postoperative
Tachycardia
Unilateral

Worksheet 3A
Using Prefixes

Directions: Write out the meaning for each prefix. Then locate two new terms using the prefix from later chapters in your text or a medical dictionary (do not use the examples given in this chapter).

Prefixes	Meaning	New Term	Meaning
1. a-	without		
2. an-	without		
3. anti-	against		
4. brady-	slow		
5. de-	without		
6. dys-	painful, difficult, abnormal		
7. pachy-	thick		
8. tachy-	fast		
9. ante-	before, in front of		
10. endo-	within, inner		
11. epi-	above		

(Continued)

Prefixes	Meaning	New Term	Meaning
12. ex-	outward		
13. extra-	outside of		
14. hypo-	below		
15. infra-	below		
16. inter-	between		
17. intra-	within		
18. para-	beside, two like parts of a pair		
19. peri-	around		
20. retro-	behind		
21. sub-	beneath, under		
22. supra-	above		
23. trans-	across		
24. bi-	two		

(*Continued*)

Prefixes	Meaning	New Term	Meaning
25. di-	two		
26. hemi-	half		
27. hyper-	excessive		
28. micro-	small		
29. mono-	one		
30. multi-	many		
31. nulli-	none		
32. pan-	all		
33. poly-	many		
34. primi-	first		
35. quadri-	four		
36. tri-	three		
37. ultra-	excess		

(Continued)

Prefixes	Meaning	New Term	Meaning
38. uni-	one		
39. neo-	new		
40. post-	after		
41. pre-	before		
42. auto-	self		
43. eu-	normal, good		
44. hetero-	different		
45. homo-	same		
46. per-	through		

Worksheet 3B
Word Search

Directions: Find and circle the answer for each fill-in-the-blank question in the word search puzzle.

1. The prefix brady- means slow ✓
2. The prefix pachy- means thick ✓
3. The prefix inter- means between ✓
4. The prefix supra- means above ✓
5. The prefix nulli- means none ✓
6. The prefix primi- means first ✓
7. The prefix tri- means three ✓
8. The prefix neo- means new ✓
9. The prefix pre- means before ✓
10. The prefix hetero- means different ✓

28   Chapter 3/PREFIXES   © 2012 Pearson Education, Inc.

Name _____ Date _____ Score _____

Chapter 3 Prefixes Quiz

Directions: Define the prefix in the spaces provided.

1. a- without
2. anti- against
3. dys- painful, difficult, abnormal
4. tachy- fast
5. endo- within, inner
6. hypo- below
7. sub- beneath, under
8. trans- across
9. epi- above
10. intra- below
11. bi- two
12. pan- all
13. poly- many
14. hemi- half
15. ultra- excess
16. inter- between
17. post- after
18. pre- before
19. neo- none
20. auto- self
21. homo- same
22. per- through
23. brady- slow
24. eu- normal, good
25. pachy- thick

Chapter 3 Answer Keys

Worksheet 3A Answer Key

1. without
2. without
3. against
4. slow
5. without
6. painful, difficult
7. thick
8. fast
9. in front of, before
10. within, inner
11. above, upon
12. outward
13. outside of
14. below, under, insufficient, less than normal
15. below, under
16. between
17. inside, within
18. alongside, near
19. around, near
20. backward, behind
21. beneath, under
22. above
23. across, through
24. two
25. two
26. half
27. excessive, more than normal
28. small
29. one
30. many
31. none
32. all
33. many, much
34. first
35. four
36. three
37. excess
38. one
39. new
40. after
41. before
42. self
43. normal, good
44. different
45. same
46. through

Worksheet 3B Answer Key

1. slow
2. thick
3. between
4. above
5. none
6. first
7. three
8. new
9. before
10. different

Chapter 3 Prefixes Quiz Answer Key

1. without
2. against
3. painful, difficult
4. fast
5. within
6. below, insufficient, less than normal
7. beneath, under
8. across, through
9. above, upon
10. inside, within
11. two
12. all
13. many
14. half
15. excess
16. between
17. after
18. before
19. new
20. self
21. same
22. through
23. slow
24. normal, good
25. thick

Chapter 4
Anatomical Terminology

Learning Objectives

After completing this chapter, students will be able to:

1. Visualize patients in the anatomical position.
2. Identify the planes and sections of the body.
3. Use correct directional terms.
4. Use anatomical terms to refer to body surface structures.
5. Place internal organs into the correct body cavity.
6. Use either anatomical divisions or clinical divisions to describe the abdominopelvic cavity.

Use this word list to focus your studying for the chapter test.

Abdominal	Midline
Abdominopelvic cavity	Pelvic cavity
Antecubital	Pleural cavity
Anterior	Posterior
Axillary	Proximal
Caudal	Spinal cavity
Cephalic	Superficial
Cranial cavity	Superior
Distal	Thoracic cavity
Dorsal	Umbilical
Epigastric	Ventral
Hypochondriac	Viscera
Hypogastric	
Iliac	**Abbreviations**
Inferior	
Inguinal	RUQ
Lateral	RLQ
Lumbar	LUQ
Medial	LLQ

Worksheet 4A
New Word Parts

Directions: Write out the meaning for each combining form, prefix, and suffix. Then locate a new term from the chapter that uses the word part.

Combining Forms	Meaning	Chapter Term	Meaning
1. abdomin/o	_____	_____	_____
2. anter/o	_____	_____	_____
3. brachi/o	_____	_____	_____
4. caud/o	_____	_____	_____
5. cephal/o	_____	_____	_____
6. cervic/o	_____	_____	_____
7. chondr/o	_____	_____	_____
8. crani/o	_____	_____	_____
9. cubit/o	_____	_____	_____
10. dist/o	_____	_____	_____
11. dors/o	_____	_____	_____
12. femor/o	_____	_____	_____
13. gastr/o	_____	_____	_____
14. genit/o	_____	_____	_____
15. glute/o	_____	_____	_____
16. infer/o	_____	_____	_____
17. inguin/o	_____	_____	_____
18. later/o	_____	_____	_____
19. lumb/o	_____	_____	_____
20. medi/o	_____	_____	_____
21. nas/o	_____	_____	_____
22. orbit/o	_____	_____	_____

(*Continued*)

Combining Forms	Meaning	Chapter Term	Meaning
23. or/o	_____	_____	_____
24. ot/o	_____	_____	_____
25. patell/o	_____	_____	_____
26. proxim/o	_____	_____	_____
27. pelv/o	_____	_____	_____
28. poster/o	_____	_____	_____
29. thorac/o	_____	_____	_____
30. scapul/o	_____	_____	_____
31. spin/o	_____	_____	_____
32. stern/o	_____	_____	_____
33. super/o	_____	_____	_____
34. ventr/o	_____	_____	_____
35. vertebr/o	_____	_____	_____

Suffixes

	Meaning	Chapter Term	Meaning
36. -al	_____	_____	_____
37. -ar	_____	_____	_____
38. -iac	_____	_____	_____
39. -ic	_____	_____	_____
40. -ior	_____	_____	_____

Prefixes

	Meaning	Chapter Term	Meaning
41. ante-	_____	_____	_____
42. epi-	_____	_____	_____
43. hypo-	_____	_____	_____
44. retro-	_____	_____	_____

Worksheet 4B
Directional Terms

Directions: First, define each of the following directional terms. Then give its opposite direction.

1. anterior   definition: _____

   opposite is: _____

2. caudal   definition: _____

   opposite is: _____

3. cephalic   definition: _____

   opposite is: _____

4. deep   definition: _____

   opposite is: _____

5. distal   definition: _____

   opposite is: _____

6. dorsal   definition: _____

   opposite is: _____

7. inferior   definition: _____

   opposite is: _____

8. lateral   definition: _____

   opposite is: _____

9. medial   definition: _____

   opposite is: _____

10. posterior   definition: _____

    opposite is: _____

11. prone   definition: _____

    opposite is: _____

12. proximal   definition: _____

    opposite is: _____

(Continued)

13. superficial   definition: _____

     opposite is: _____

14. superior   definition: _____

     opposite is: _____

15. supine   definition: _____

     opposite is: _____

16. ventral   definition: _____

     opposite is: _____

Worksheet 4C
Word Search

Directions: Find and circle the answer for each fill-in-the-blank question in the word search puzzle.

1. The _____ plane divides the body into left and right portions.

2. A _____ section is produced by a slice along the long axis of a structure.

3. _____ means "pertaining to the side."

4. _____ means to lie face down.

5. _____ refers to the neck region of the body.

6. _____ refers to the eye socket region of the body.

7. The _____ cavity contains the brain.

8. Each of the _____ cavities contains a lung.

9. The anatomical division of the abdominopelvic cavity known as the _____ region is the middle area of the upper row.

10. The _____ is a membrane covering that protects the abdominopelvic organs.

```
C  P  E  R  I  T  O  N  E  U  M  J  Z
T  R  N  P  K  R  H  M  B  J  K  L  F
K  P  W  L  B  L  F  Y  P  R  A  L  R
T  G  B  I  P  Q  N  J  M  N  C  A  C
L  A  T  E  R  A  L  Q  I  J  E  T  I
R  A  T  L  L  X  M  D  L  G  R  T  R
L  P  T  Z  J  A  U  P  L  K  V  I  T
R  C  R  Z  Y  T  R  V  M  Q  I  G  S
R  M  W  O  I  J  R  U  C  K  C  A  A
P  R  G  G  N  G  T  Q  E  Q  A  S  G
P  Y  N  J  Z  E  R  B  K  L  L  M  I
D  O  D  N  T  N  T  N  N  D  P  M  P
L  L  A  I  N  A  R  C  X  K  C  M  E
```

38 Chapter 4/ANATOMICAL TERMINOLOGY © 2012 Pearson Education, Inc.

Worksheet 4D
Professional Profile and Journal

Professional Profile

Diagnostic Imaging

Diagnostic imaging services produce images of internal body parts through the use of X-ray, ultrasound, magnetic resonance imaging (MRI), or radionuclide slides. These images are then used by physicians and other healthcare personnel in diagnosing and planning patient treatment. Diagnostic imaging services are found in acute care facilities, clinics, physicians' offices, and private imaging services.

Registered Radiologic Technologist (RRT)

- Performs imaging procedures as ordered by a physician including X-rays, computed tomography (CT), MRI, and fluoroscopy
- Operates at least two different types of imaging equipment
- Completes an accredited 1-year certificate program, a 2-year associate's degree, or a 4-year bachelor's degree radiologic program
- Passes registration examination

Diagnostic Medical Sonographer

- Performs ultrasound procedures as ordered by a physician
- Completes an accredited 1-year certificate program, a 2-year associate's degree, or a 4-year bachelor's degree

Nuclear Medicine Technologist

- Performs nuclear medicine scans as ordered by a physician
- Completes an accredited 1-year certificate program, a 2-year associate's degree, or a 4-year bachelor's degree
- Some states require licensure

For more information regarding these health careers, visit the following websites:

- American Registry of Radiologic Technologists at www.arrt.org
- Society of Diagnostic Medical Sonographers at www.sdms.org
- Society of Nuclear Medicine at www.snm.org

Professional Journal

In this exercise you will now have an opportunity to put the words you have learned into practice. Imagine yourself in the role of one of the diagnostic imaging personnel. If you refer back to the Professional Profile, you will see that these healthcare professionals are responsible for producing images of internal body structures using various types of technology. Use the 10 words listed below, or any other new terms from this chapter, to write sentences to describe the patients you saw today.

An example of a sentence is: *The patient's* **femoral** *X-ray revealed a fracture.*

1. anatomical position _____
2. transverse plane _____
3. cross-section _____
4. anterior _____
5. supine _____
6. cranial _____
7. upper extremity _____
8. pelvic _____
9. thoracic _____
10. left upper quadrant _____

Worksheet 4E
Locating Organs Using the Clinical Divisions

Directions: On the figure below, draw the lines to represent the clinical divisions of the abdominopelvic cavity. Then write the names of the organs that are located in each quadrant.

_____
Quadrant

_____
_____
_____
_____
_____
_____

_____
Quadrant

_____
_____
_____
_____
_____
_____

_____
Quadrant

Midline Organs:
_____
_____
_____

_____
Quadrant

Name _____ Date _____ Score _____

Chapter 4 Word Parts Quiz

Directions: Define the combining form, prefix, or suffix in the spaces provided.

1. nas/o _____
2. or/o _____
3. crani/o _____
4. brachi/o _____
5. thorac/o _____
6. orbit/o _____
7. anter/o _____
8. medi/o _____
9. femor/o _____
10. inguin/o _____
11. cubit/o _____
12. poster/o _____
13. infer/o _____
14. spin/o _____
15. proxim/o _____
16. dors/o _____
17. lumb/o _____
18. ventr/o _____
19. ot/o _____
20. pelv/o _____
21. cervic/o _____
22. super/o _____
23. later/o _____
24. epi- _____
25. retro- _____

Name _____ Date _____ Score _____

Chapter 4 Spelling Quiz

Directions: Write each term as your instructor pronounces it.

1. _____
2. _____
3. _____
4. _____
5. _____
6. _____
7. _____
8. _____
9. _____
10. _____
11. _____
12. _____
13. _____
14. _____
15. _____
16. _____
17. _____
18. _____
19. _____
20. _____

Name _____ Date _____ Score _____

Chapter 4 Labeling Quiz 1

Directions: Label the planes of the body.

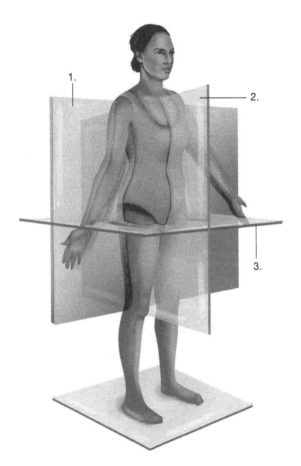

1. _____
2. _____
3. _____

44 Chapter 4/ANATOMICAL TERMINOLOGY © 2012 Pearson Education, Inc.

Name _____ Date _____ Score _____

Chapter 4 Labeling Quiz 2

Directions: Label the regions of the body.

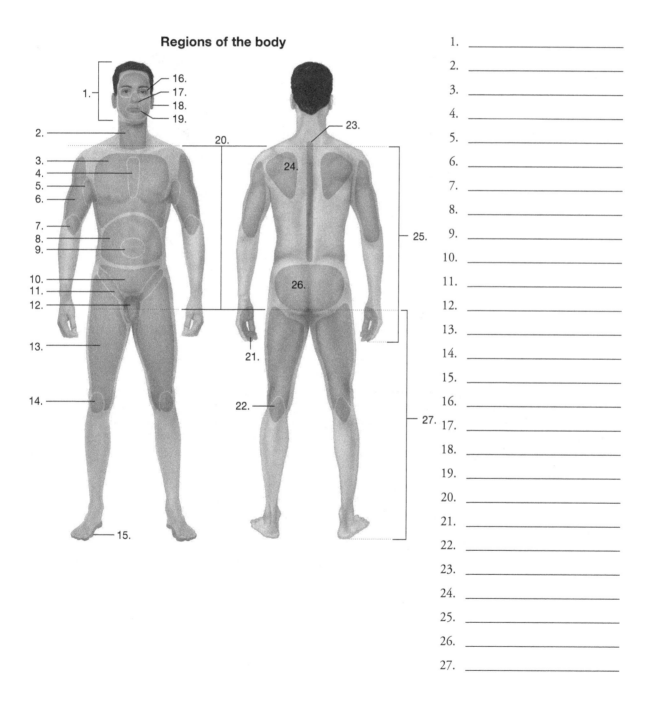

Regions of the body

1. _____
2. _____
3. _____
4. _____
5. _____
6. _____
7. _____
8. _____
9. _____
10. _____
11. _____
12. _____
13. _____
14. _____
15. _____
16. _____
17. _____
18. _____
19. _____
20. _____
21. _____
22. _____
23. _____
24. _____
25. _____
26. _____
27. _____

Name _____ Date _____ Score _____

Chapter 4 Labeling Quiz 3

Directions: Label the body cavities.

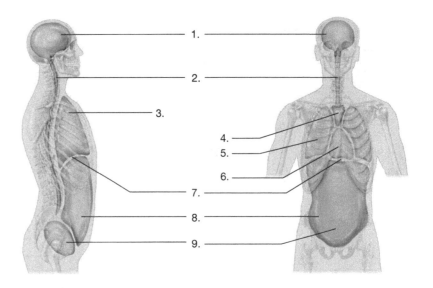

Lateral view **Anterior view**

1. _____ 6. _____

2. _____ 7. _____

3. _____ 8. _____

4. _____ 9. _____

5. _____

Name _____ Date _____ Score _____

Chapter 4 Word Building Quiz

Directions: Build a single medical term for each phrase below.

1. pertaining to vertebra _____
2. pertaining to the neck _____
3. pertaining to the groin _____
4. pertaining to the buttocks _____
5. pertaining to farthest away _____
6. pertaining to below _____
7. pertaining to above stomach _____
8. pertaining to the tail _____
9. pertaining to the front _____
10. pertaining to the pelvis _____
11. pertaining to the head _____
12. pertaining to the side _____
13. pertaining to the mouth _____
14. pertaining to the middle _____
15. pertaining to the skull _____
16. pertaining to nearest _____
17. pertaining to the abdomen _____
18. pertaining to the kneecap _____
19. pertaining to the femur _____
20. pertaining to above _____
21. pertaining to the chest _____
22. pertaining to the arm _____
23. pertaining to belly (side of body) _____
24. pertaining to the ear _____
25. pertaining to the spine _____

Name _____ Date _____ Score _____

Chapter 4 Quiz

Fill-in-the-Blank

1. In the anatomical position, the arms are _____.

2. The _____ plane divides the body into anterior and posterior portions.

3. The only horizontal plane is the _____ plane.

4. The opposite direction of distal is _____.

5. The direction term _____ means further below the surface.

6. The two dorsal cavities are the _____ and _____.

7. The protective membrane around the brain is called the _____.

8. The stomach is found in the _____ quadrant.

9. The _____ is the only major abdominopelvic organ that lies outside of the peritoneum.

10. When using the anatomical divisions, the middle row contains the left and right _____ area.

Word Building

Build a term that means:

1. pertaining to low back   _____

2. pertaining to skull   _____

3. pertaining to breast bone   _____

4. pertaining to kneecap   _____

5. pertaining to eye socket   _____

6. pertaining to buttocks   _____

7. pertaining to above   _____

8. pertaining to middle   _____

9. pertaining to neck   _____

10. pertaining to front   _____

Matching

_____ 1. superficial
_____ 2. popliteal
_____ 3. brachial
_____ 4. prone
_____ 5. scapular
_____ 6. antecubital
_____ 7. sagittal plane
_____ 8. axillary
_____ 9. cephalic
_____ 10. oral
_____ 11. ventral
_____ 12. LLQ
_____ 13. plantar
_____ 14. lateral
_____ 15. femoral
_____ 16. umbilical
_____ 17. hypochondriac
_____ 18. frontal plane
_____ 19. RUQ
_____ 20. lower extremity
_____ 21. trunk
_____ 22. supine
_____ 23. mediastinum
_____ 24. otic
_____ 25. inguinal

a. refers to the ear
b. underarm area
c. divides body into right and left portions
d. thigh bone
e. refers to the side
f. the torso
g. also called coronal
h. the navel
i. refers to the groin
j. to lie face up
k. the leg
l. contains gallbladder
m. nearer the surface
n. center region of chest
o. refers to being below the rib cartilage
p. to lie face down
q. refers to the sole of the foot
r. refers to the head
s. in front of elbow
t. refers to the shoulder blade
u. refers to the mouth
v. opposite of dorsal
w. contains sigmoid colon
x. refers to the arm
y. behind the knee

Chapter 4 Answer Keys

Worksheet 4A Answer Key

1. abdomen
2. front (side of body)
3. arm
4. tail
5. head
6. neck
7. cartilage
8. skull
9. elbow
10. farthest (away from beginning of structure)
11. back (side of body)
12. femur, thigh bone
13. stomach
14. genitals
15. buttocks
16. below, lower
17. groin
18. side
19. low back
20. middle
21. nose
22. eye socket
23. mouth
24. ear
25. patella, kneecap
26. nearest (to beginning of structure)
27. pelvis
28. back (side of body)
29. chest
30. scapula, shoulder blade
31. spine
32. sternum, breast bone
33. above, upper
34. belly (side of body)
35. vertebra, back
36. pertaining to
37. pertaining to
38. pertaining to
39. pertaining to
40. pertaining to
41. in front of
42. above
43. below
44. behind

Worksheet 4B Answer Key

1. pertaining to the front side of the body; opposite is posterior or dorsal
2. pertaining to the tail; opposite is cephalic or superior
3. pertaining to the head; opposite is caudal or inferior
4. further away from the surface; opposite is superficial
5. pertaining to farthest (away from beginning of structure); opposite is proximal
6. pertaining to back (side of the body); opposite is ventral or anterior
7. pertaining to below; opposite is superior or cephalic
8. pertaining to the side; opposite is medial
9. pertaining to the middle; opposite is lateral
10. pertaining to back (side of the body); opposite is anterior or ventral
11. to lie face down; opposite is supine
12. pertaining to nearest (to beginning of structure); opposite is distal
13. nearer the surface; opposite is deep
14. pertaining to above; opposite is inferior or caudal
15. to lie face up; opposite is prone
16. pertaining to belly (side of body); opposite is dorsal or posterior

Worksheet 4C Answer Key

1. sagittal
2. longitudinal
3. lateral
4. prone
5. cervical
6. orbital
7. cranial
8. pleural
9. epigastric
10. peritoneum

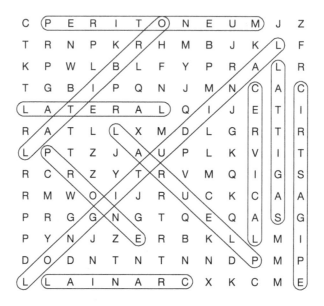

Worksheet 4D Answer Key

Student answers will vary.

Worksheet 4E Answer Key

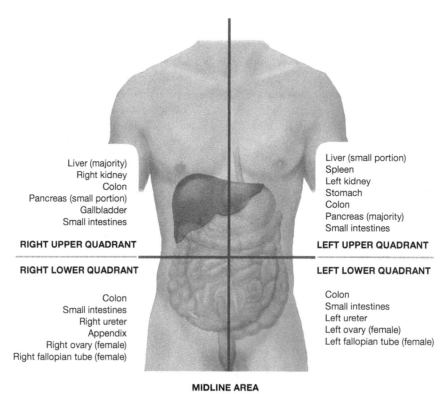

52 Chapter 4/ANATOMICAL TERMINOLOGY

Chapter 4 Word Parts Quiz Answer Key

1. nose
2. mouth
3. skull
4. arm
5. chest
6. eye socket
7. front (side of body)
8. middle
9. femur, thigh bone
10. groin
11. elbow
12. back (side of body)
13. below, lower
14. spine
15. nearest (to beginning of structure)
16. back (side of body)
17. low back
18. belly (side of body)
19. ear
20. pelvis
21. neck
22. above, upper
23. side
24. above
25. behind

Chapter 4 Spelling Quiz Answer Key

1. sagittal
2. coronal
3. longitudinal
4. caudal
5. proximal
6. ventral
7. antecubital
8. axillary
9. brachial
10. femoral
11. genital
12. plantar
13. popliteal
14. scapular
15. peritoneum
16. mediastinum
17. abdominopelvic
18. umbilical
19. inguinal
20. hypochondriac

Chapter 4 Labeling Quiz 1 Answer Key

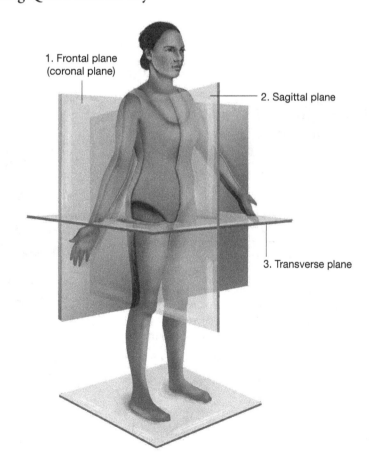

1. Frontal plane (coronal plane)
2. Sagittal plane
3. Transverse plane

Chapter 4 Labeling Quiz 2 Answer Key

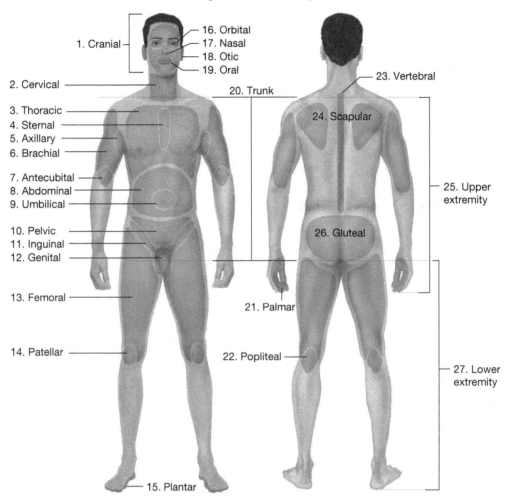

Chapter 4 Labeling Quiz 3 Answer Key

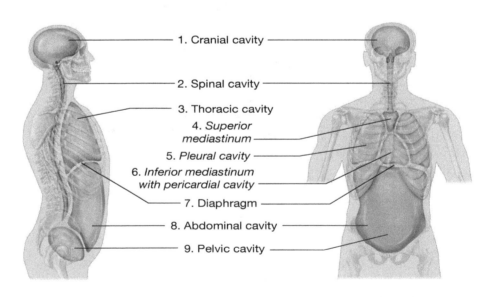

Lateral view **Anterior view**

Chapter 4 Word Building Quiz Answer Key

1. vertebral
2. cervical
3. inguinal
4. gluteal
5. distal
6. inferior
7. epigastric
8. caudal
9. anterior
10. pelvic
11. cephalic
12. lateral
13. oral
14. medial
15. cranial
16. proximal
17. abdominal
18. patellar
19. femoral
20. superior
21. thoracic
22. brachial
23. ventral
24. otic
25. spinal

Chapter 4 Quiz Answer Key

Fill-in-the-Blank

1. down to the side
2. frontal or coronal
3. transverse
4. proximal
5. deep
6. cranial, spinal
7. meninges
8. left upper
9. kidney
10. lumbar

Word Building

1. lumbar
2. cranial
3. sternal
4. patellar
5. orbital
6. gluteal
7. superior
8. medial
9. cervical
10. anterior

Matching

1. m
2. y
3. x
4. p
5. t
6. s
7. c
8. b
9. r
10. u
11. v
12. w
13. q
14. e
15. d
16. h
17. o
18. g
19. l
20. k
21. f
22. j
23. n
24. a
25. i

Chapter 5
Dermatology: Integumentary System

Learning Objectives

After completing this chapter, students will be able to:

1. Understand the functions of the skin.
2. Describe the medical specialty of dermatology.
3. Define dermatology-related combining forms, prefixes, and suffixes.
4. Identify the organs treated in dermatology.
5. Build dermatology medical terms from word parts.
6. Explain dermatology medical terms.
7. Use dermatology abbreviations.

Use this word list to focus your studying for the chapter test.

Abrasion	Erythroderma	Pyorrhea
Adenectomy	Hypodermic	Seborrhea
Adenitis	Impetigo	Subcutaneous
Adenoma	Intradermal	Transdermal
Adipose	Lesion	Ulcer
Cellulitis	Leukoderma	Urticaria
Cryosurgery	Lipectomy	Xanthoderma
Cutaneous	Lipoid	Wheal
Cyanosis	Lipoma	
Cyanotic	Melanoma	**Abbreviations**
Dermabrasion	Melanocyte	
Dermis	Necrosis	Bx
Dermatitis	Onychomycosis	C & S
Dermatologist	Percutaneous	Derm
Dermatology	Pruritus	I & D
Dermatopathy	Psoriasis	ID
Epidermis	Pyogenic	Subcu, Subq, SQ

Worksheet 5A
New Word Parts

Directions: Write out the meaning for each combining form, prefix, and suffix. Then locate a new term from the chapter that uses the word part.

Combining Forms	Meaning	Chapter Term	Meaning
1. aden/o			
2. adip/o			
3. cutane/o			
4. cyan/o			
5. dermat/o			
6. derm/o			
7. hidr/o			
8. kerat/o			
9. lip/o			
10. melan/o			
11. onych/o			
12. py/o			
13. seb/o			
14. trich/o			
15. ungu/o			

Prefixes

	Meaning	Chapter Term	Meaning
16. epi-			
17. pachy-			
18. per-			
19. sub-			
20. trans-			

(Continued)

Suffixes	Meaning	Chapter Term	Meaning
21. -derma	_____	_____	_____
22. -opsy	_____	_____	_____
23. -tome	_____	_____	_____

Worksheet 5B
Word Part Review

Directions: Write out the meaning for each combining form, prefix, and suffix.

Combining Forms   Meaning

1. bi/o _____
2. carcin/o _____
3. chem/o _____
4. cry/o _____
5. erythr/o _____
6. ichthy/o _____
7. leuk/o _____
8. myc/o _____
9. necr/o _____
10. scler/o _____
11. vesic/o _____
12. xanth/o _____
13. xer/o _____

Prefixes

14. an- _____
15. hyper- _____
16. hypo- _____
17. intra- _____

Suffixes

18. -al _____
19. -cle _____
20. -cyte _____

(Continued)

Suffixes	Meaning
21. -ectomy	_____
22. -genic	_____
23. -ia	_____
24. -ic	_____
25. -itis	_____
26. -logist	_____
27. -logy	_____
28. -malacia	_____
29. -megaly	_____
30. -oid	_____
31. -oma	_____
32. -ose	_____
33. -osis	_____
34. -ous	_____
35. -pathy	_____
36. -phagia	_____
37. -plasty	_____
38. -rrhea	_____
39. -sclerosis	_____
40. -tic	_____

Worksheet 5C
Word Surgery

Directions: Below are terms built from word parts. Analyze each term by listing and defining the word parts used to build it.

Medical Term   Word Part Meanings

1. cyanosis _____
2. dermatology _____
3. seborrhea _____
4. keratosis _____
5. trichophagia _____
6. subungual _____
7. carcinoma _____
8. ichthyoderma _____
9. hyperonychia _____
10. biopsy _____
11. pyogenic _____
12. dermatome _____
13. onychomalacia _____
14. melanocyte _____
15. lipoid _____
16. anhidrosis _____
17. adenopathy _____
18. adipoma _____
19. percutaneous _____
20. xanthoderma _____
21. dermatoplasty _____
22. transdermal _____
23. onychitis _____
24. dermatosclerosis _____
25. xeroderma _____

Worksheet 5D
Word Search

Directions: Find and circle the answer for each fill-in-the-blank question in the word search puzzle.

1. _____ is the medical specialty that treats conditions of the skin.

2. The term _____ describes a red skin condition.

3. A discharge of pus from a skin wound would be called _____.

4. _____ is a term to describe an enlarged gland.

5. _____ is the medical term meaning baldness.

6. The intentional destruction of tissue by an electric current or a laser is called _____.

7. _____ is a procedure used to remove acne scars.

8. A freckle and a birthmark are examples of a _____.

9. Tinea is a term to describe a _____ infection.

10. _____ means severe itching.

```
B N H N K J R M W D R G F F
N O F M L A G N U F R M N A
O I L P Y O R R H E A K T D
I T P Y D K Y Z F C P A L E
S A P G Q X C D U R M V G N
A Z T O M H A L P E N H T O
R I X L W S E L H G W M K M
B R L O T J U T O J R W J E
A E B T D K Y T D P Y K X G
M T C A F R P R I K E C R A
R U K M E J Q R Z R F C K L
E A Z R R H M Y Y J U R I Y
D C B E B G D R Y J Z R F A
T D C D R R K K N Q T P P R
```

Chapter 5/DERMATOLOGY: INTEGUMENTARY SYSTEM   © 2012 Pearson Education, Inc.

Worksheet 5E
Unscramble

Directions: Unscramble each medical term below. A definition for the term is given below each scrambled term.

1. u p p l e a _____

   solid raised skin lesion

2. a l a c r i v e l _____

   chicken pox

3. c y o s h e s m i c _____

   black and blue skin bruise

4. r a g g e n n e _____

   tissue necrosis

5. b t m i r e d n e e d _____

   removal of dead or damaged tissue from wound

6. g n h i s l s e _____

   herpes zoster infection

7. o e n y e a c t m d _____

   surgical removal of a gland

8. r e y h r h i d p o i s s _____

   abnormal condition of excessive sweating

9. m a d e r g t o o l y _____

   study of the skin

10. c u b e u s a t o u s n _____

    pertaining to under the skin

Worksheet 5F
Abbreviations

Directions: Write the full term that each abbreviation stands for.

1. BCC _____

2. BX, bx _____

3. C&S _____

4. decub _____

5. Derm _____

6. HSV _____

7. I&D _____

8. ID _____

9. MM _____

10. SG _____

11. SCC _____

12. STSG _____

13. Subcu, Subq _____

14. SQ _____

15. ung _____

Worksheet 5G
Case Study

Directions: Below is a case study presentation of a patient with a condition covered in this chapter. Read the case study and answer the questions below. Some questions will ask for information not included within this chapter. Use your text, a medical dictionary, or any other reference material you choose to answer these questions.

A 40-year-old female is seen in the dermatologist's office, upon the recommendation of her internist, for a workup for suspected MM on her left forearm. The suspicious lesion was a blackish skin growth approximately 1 cm in diameter. The dermatologist examined the patient and a tissue biopsy was performed. The biopsy confirmed that the growth was MM. Surgery was performed to remove the tumor. In addition, a 5 cm by 5 cm square of skin immediately surrounding the tumor was also moved. Because the removed skin included all three layers of skin, a skin graft was necessary to cover the open area. The donor site was the patient's thigh. Following recovery from surgery, the patient was referred to an oncologist for follow-up care.

1. What pathological condition does the internist think this patient may have? Look this condition up in a reference source and include a short description of it in your answer.

   _____
   _____

2. What diagnostic test did the dermatologist perform? Describe it in your own words.

   _____
   _____

3. Explain why a skin graft was necessary.

   _____
   _____

4. Explain why it was necessary to remove so much additional skin tissue along with the tumor.

   _____
   _____

5. What is the specialty of an oncologist?

   _____
   _____

6. What do you think the possible follow-up care might include?

   _____
   _____

Worksheet 5H
Web Destinations

Melanoma

The Skin Cancer Foundation web page regarding melanoma states:

> Melanoma is the most serious form of skin cancer. Even so, if diagnosed and removed while it is still thin and limited to the outermost skin layer, it is almost 100% curable. Once the cancer advances and metastasizes (spreads) to other parts of the body, it is hard to treat and can be deadly. During the past 10 years, the number of cases of melanoma has increased more rapidly than that of any other cancer. Over 51,000 new cases are reported to the American Cancer Society each year, and it is probable that a great many more occur and are not reported.

Visit this website at http://www.skincancer.org and left click on the Melanoma link. Write a summary of the information found there.

Indoor Tanning and UV Exposure

At its website, the Food and Drug Administration presents valuable consumer education information. This information may be used by individuals in making decisions that may affect their health. One area that receives a lot of attention is the amount of ultraviolet exposure persons receive when they visit tanning salons. Go to the following FDA Consumer website, http://www.fda.gov/fdac. In the Search box, type "indoor tanning." Select the article titled "Indoor Tanning: The Risks of Ultraviolet Rays." Use the information presented to address the following topics:

- The cancer risk from ultraviolet exposure
- The other risks associated with indoor tanning
- Tanning in children and teens
- The riskiest practices

Worksheet 5I
Professional Profile and Journal

Professional Profile

Nursing Service

Nursing service professionals assess patients, plan and carry out patient treatments, and evaluate the patient's response to treatment. Skilled nursing care includes intravenous therapy, administering medications and anesthesia, wound care, and patient education. Nursing service personnel are found in acute and long-term care facilities, clinics, physicians' offices, health maintenance organizations, home health agencies, public health agencies, and schools. See Medical Terminology Interactive for a video on Nurses.

Nurse Practitioner (NP)

- A registered nurse who receives advanced training in a specialized area of nursing such as family health, women's health, pediatric health, gerontological health, or acute care
- Meets all the requirements for becoming a registered nurse
- Completes advanced training and clinical experience in an accredited nurse practitioner program
- Passes national certification examination

Registered Nurse (RN, BSN, MSN)

- Assesses patient status and progress, provides patient care, administers medications, and provides patient education
- Graduates from an accredited 2-year associate, 4-year bachelor's, or 5-year master's degree nursing program
- Passes national licensing examination

Licensed Practical/Vocational Nurse (LPN or LVN)

- Trained in basic nursing techniques such as administering medications, dressing wounds, and collecting specimens for laboratory tests
- Works under the supervision of a physician or registered nurse
- Passes national licensing examination

Certified Nurse Aide (CNA)

- Trained in basic patient care such as taking vital signs, bathing, and feeding
- Works under supervision of RN or LPN
- Completes approved on-the-job certification program

For more information regarding these health careers, visit the following websites:

- American Nurses Association at www.nursingworld.org
- National Federation of Licensed Practical Nurses at www.nflpn.org
- National League for Nursing at www.nln.org

Professional Journal

In this exercise you will now have an opportunity to put the words you have learned into practice. Imagine yourself in the role of a registered nurse. If you refer back to the Professional Profile, you will see that this healthcare professional is responsible for assessing patient status and progress, providing patient care, administering medications, and providing patient education. Use the 10 words listed below to write sentences to describe the patients you saw today.

An example of a sentence is: *The patient underwent* **debridement** *to remove infected tissue from the skin wound.*

1. abrasion _____
2. ecchymosis _____
3. macule _____
4. culture and sensitivity _____
5. wheal _____
6. ulcer _____
7. malignant melanoma _____
8. tinea _____
9. varicella _____
10. second-degree burn _____

Name _____ Date _____ Score _____

Chapter 5 Word Parts Quiz

Directions: Define the combining form, prefix, or suffix in the spaces provided.

1. cutane/o _____
2. lip/o _____
3. py/o _____
4. ungu/o _____
5. seb/o _____
6. trich/o _____
7. aden/o _____
8. kerat/o _____
9. dermat/o _____
10. hidr/o _____
11. melan/o _____
12. cyan/o _____
13. onych/o _____
14. leuk/o _____
15. ichthy/o _____
16. scler/o _____
17. xer/o _____
18. bi/o _____
19. cry/o _____
20. -derma _____
21. -genic _____
22. -tome _____
23. epi- _____
24. pachy- _____

Name _____ Date _____ Score _____

Chapter 5 Spelling Quiz

Directions: Write each term as your instructor pronounces it.

1. _____
2. _____
3. _____
4. _____
5. _____
6. _____
7. _____
8. _____
9. _____
10. _____
11. _____
12. _____
13. _____
14. _____
15. _____
16. _____
17. _____
18. _____
19. _____
20. _____

Chapter 5 Labeling Quiz 1

Directions: Label the structures of the skin.

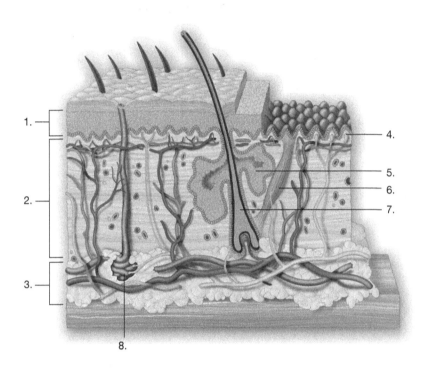

1. _____
2. _____
3. _____
4. _____
5. _____
6. _____
7. _____
8. _____

Chapter 5 Labeling Quiz 2

Directions: Label the structures of a nail.

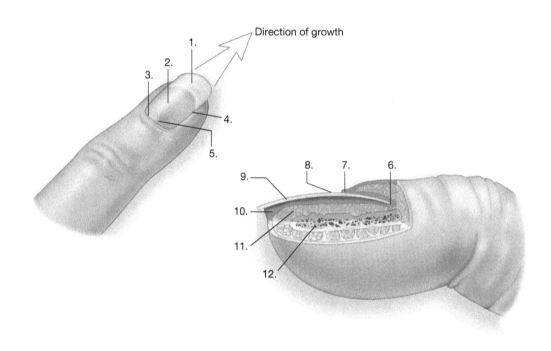

1. _____
2. _____
3. _____
4. _____
5. _____
6. _____
7. _____
8. _____
9. _____
10. _____
11. _____
12. _____

Name _____ Date _____ Score _____

Chapter 5 Labeling Quiz 3

Directions: Label the structures of hair.

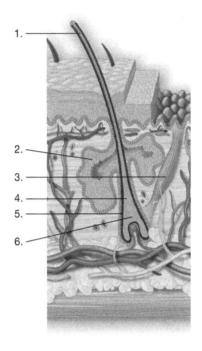

1. _____   4. _____

2. _____   5. _____

3. _____   6. _____

Name _____ Date _____ Score _____

Chapter 5 Word Building Quiz

Directions: Build a single medical term for each phrase below.

1. surgical repair of skin _____

2. abnormal condition with lack of sweat _____

3. nail eating _____

4. pus producing _____

5. pertaining to a nail _____

6. skin inflammation _____

7. study of skin _____

8. dry skin condition _____

9. hard skin condition _____

10. scaly skin condition _____

11. red skin condition _____

12. oil flow _____

13. enlarged gland _____

14. abnormal condition of excessive sweat _____

15. skin disease _____

16. one who studies the skin _____

17. pertaining to within the skin _____

18. pertaining to under skin _____

19. fat tumor _____

20. black cell _____

21. surgical removal of nail _____

22. nail softening _____

23. abnormal condition of hair fungus _____

24. pus skin condition _____

25. white skin condition _____

Name _____ Date _____ Score _____

Chapter 5 Quiz

Fill-in-the-Blank

1. The _____ is the outer layer of the skin.

2. The oily secretion of sebaceous glands is called _____.

3. The subcutaneous layer is composed primarily of _____.

4. The integument is another name for the _____.

5. The accessory organs of the skin are the _____, and _____.

6. Sweat glands are found in the _____ layer of the skin.

7. _____ is the pigment molecule that gives skin its color.

8. Hair and nails are composed of a hard protein called _____.

9. _____ repair, reconstruct, or improve damaged or missing body structures.

10. Sweat cools the skin by _____.

Word Building

Build a term that means:

1. skin disease   _____

2. black cell   _____

3. softening of nails   _____

4. oily discharge   _____

5. scaly skin   _____

6. abnormal condition of hair fungus   _____

7. abnormal condition of no sweat   _____

8. pertaining to within the skin   _____

9. skin inflammation   _____

10. hard skin   _____

Matching

_____ 1. furuncle
_____ 2. chemabrasion
_____ 3. ecchymosis
_____ 4. gangrene
_____ 5. herpes simplex
_____ 6. ulcer
_____ 7. vesicle
_____ 8. onychia
_____ 9. decubitus ulcer
_____ 10. erythema
_____ 11. varicella
_____ 12. alopecia
_____ 13. herpes zoster
_____ 14. papule
_____ 15. macule
_____ 16. fissure
_____ 17. pruritus
_____ 18. biopsy
_____ 19. cryosurgery
_____ 20. debridement
_____ 21. tinea
_____ 22. adipose
_____ 23. BCC
_____ 24. MM
_____ 25. C&S

a. tissue necrosis
b. remove tissue for diagnosis
c. open sore
d. skin cancer
e. redness of the skin
f. severe itching
g. solid, raised skin lesion
h. a boil
i. baldness
j. removal of dead tissue from a wound
k. lab test to identify bacteria
l. causes fever blisters
m. crack-like lesion on the skin
n. shingles
o. a chemical peel
p. fat tissue
q. chickenpox
r. fluid-filled raised spot
s. a "black & blue" bruise
t. cancer beginning in a melanocyte
u. flat discolored spot on the skin
v. inflamed nail bed
w. use of cold to freeze and destroy tissue
x. fungal infection
y. bedsore

Chapter 5 Answer Keys

Worksheet 5A Answer Key

1. gland
2. fat
3. skin
4. blue
5. skin
6. skin
7. sweat
8. keratin, hard, horn-like
9. fat
10. melanin, black
11. nail
12. pus
13. sebum, oil
14. hair
15. nail
16. above, upon
17. thick
18. through
19. beneath, under
20. across
21. skin condition
22. view of
23. instrument used to cut

Worksheet 5B Answer Key

1. life
2. cancer
3. chemical
4. cold
5. red
6. scaly
7. white
8. fungus
9. death
10. hard
11. bladder, sac
12. yellow
13. dry
14. without
15. excessive, above
16. below
17. inside, within
18. pertaining to
19. small
20. cell
21. surgical removal
22. producing
23. state, condition
24. pertaining to
25. inflammation
26. one who studies
27. study of
28. abnormal softening
29. enlargement, large
30. resembling
31. tumor, mass
32. pertaining to
33. abnormal condition
34. pertaining to
35. disease
36. eating or swallowing
37. surgical repair
38. flow, discharge
39. hardened condition
40. pertaining to

Worksheet 5C Answer Key

1. cyan/o = blue; -osis = abnormal condition
2. dermat/o = skin; -logy = study of
3. seb/o = oil; -rrhea = flow, discharge
4. kerat/o = hard, horny; -osis = abnormal condition
5. trich/o = hair; -phagia = eating
6. sub- = under; ungu/o = nail; -al = pertaining to
7. carcin/o = cancer; -oma = tumor
8. ichthy/o = dry, scaly; -derma = skin condition
9. hyper- = excessive; onych/o = nail; -ia = state, condition
10. bi/o = life; -opsy = view of
11. py/o = pus; -genic = producing
12. derm/o = skin; -tome = instrument to cut
13. onych/o = nail; -malacia = softening
14. melan/o = black; -cyte = cell
15. lip/o = fat; -oid = resembling
16. an- = lack of; hidr/o = sweat; -osis = abnormal condition
17. aden/o = gland; -pathy = disease
18. adip/o = fat; -oma = tumor
19. per- = through; cutane/o = skin; -ous = pertaining to
20. xanth/o = yellow; -derma = skin condition
21. dermat/o = skin; -plasty = surgical repair
22. trans- = across; derm/o = skin; -al = pertaining to
23. onych/o = nail; -itis = inflammation
24. dermat/o = skin; -sclerosis = hardened condition
25. xer/o = dry; -derma = skin condition

Worksheet 5D Answer Key

Fill-in-the-Blank
1. dermatology
2. erythema
3. pyorrhea
4. adenomegaly
5. alopecia
6. cauterization
7. dermabrasion
8. macule
9. fungal
10. pruritus

```
B N H N K J R M W D R G F F
N O F M L A G N U F R M N A
O I L P Y O R R H E A K T D
I T P Y D K Y Z F C P A L E
S A P G Q X C D U R M V G N
A Z T O M H A L P E N H T O
R I X L W S E L H G W M K M
B R L O T J U T O J R W J E
A E B T D K Y T D P Y K X G
M T C A F R P R I K E C R A
R U K M E J Q R Z R F C K L
E A Z R H M Y Y J U R I Y
D C B E B G D R Y J Z R F A
T D C D R R K K N Q T P P R
```

Worksheet 5E Answer Key

1. papule
2. varicella
3. ecchymosis
4. gangrene
5. debridement
6. shingles
7. adenectomy
8. hyperhidrosis
9. dermatology
10. subcutaneous

Worksheet 5F Answer Key

1. basal cell carcinoma
2. biopsy
3. culture and sensitivity
4. decubitus ulcer
5. dermatology
6. herpes simplex virus
7. incision and drainage
8. intradermal
9. malignant melanoma
10. skin graft
11. squamous cell carcinoma
12. split-thickness skin graft
13. subcutaneous
14. subcutaneous
15. ointment

Worksheet 5G Answer Key

1. MM—malignant melanoma
2. Tissue biopsy—small piece of tissue removed and examined under a microscope in order to make a diagnosis
3. Skin graft was necessary because surgery removed all three layers of skin
4. Malignant melanoma is an aggressive cancer that is prone to spreading
5. Treats cancer
6. Watching for the return of the cancer, chemotherapy, radiation therapy

Worksheet 5H Answer Key
Essay activity, student answers will vary.

Worksheet 5I Answer Key
Student answers will vary.

Chapter 5 Word Parts Quiz Answer Key

1. skin
2. fat
3. pus
4. nail
5. sebum
6. hair
7. gland
8. keratin, hard, horn-like
9. skin
10. sweat
11. melanin, black
12. blue
13. nail
14. white
15. scaly
16. hard
17. dry
19. life
20. cold
21. skin condition
22. producing
23. instrument to cut
24. above, upon
25. thick

Chapter 5 Spelling Quiz Answer Key

1. subcutaneous
2. erythema
3. petechiae
4. pruritus
5. urticaria
6. wheal
7. vesicle
8. decubitus ulcer
9. gangrene
10. impetigo
11. cyanosis
12. ichthyoderma
13. dermatopathy
14. intradermal
15. anhidrosis
16. onychectomy
17. seborrhea
18. trichomycosis
19. abscess
20. alopecia

Chapter 5 Labeling Quiz 1 Answer Key

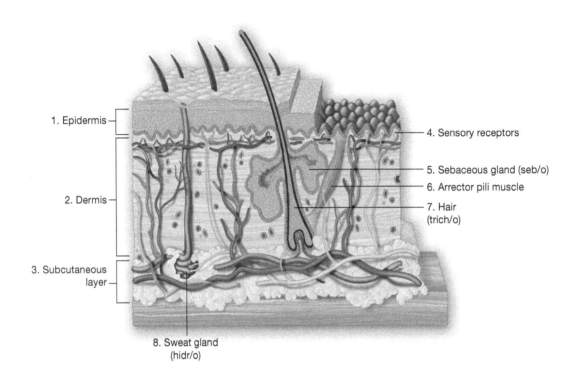

Chapter 5 Labeling Quiz 2 Answer Key

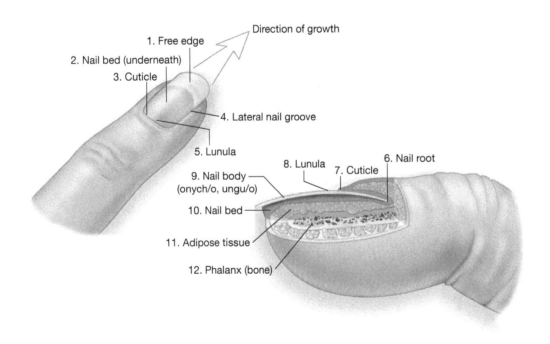

Chapter 5 Labeling Quiz 3 Answer Key

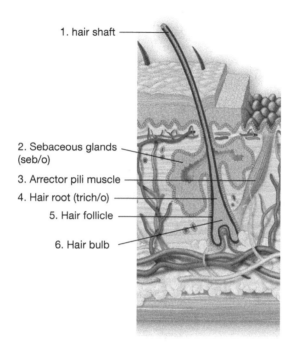

1. hair shaft
2. Sebaceous glands (seb/o)
3. Arrector pili muscle
4. Hair root (trich/o)
5. Hair follicle
6. Hair bulb

Chapter 5 Word Building Quiz Answer Key

1. dermatoplasty
2. anhidrosis
3. onychophagia
4. pyogenic
5. ungual
6. dermatitis
7. dermatology
8. xeroderma
9. scleroderma
10. ichthyoderma
11. erythroderma
12. seborrhea
13. adenomegaly
14. hyperhidrosis
15. dermatopathy
16. dermatologist
17. intradermal
18. subcutaneous or hypodermic
19. lipoma
20. melanocyte
21. onychectomy
22. onychomalacia
23. trichomycosis
24. pyoderma
25. leukoderma

Chapter 5 Quiz Answer Key

Fill-in-the-Blank

1. epidermis
2. sebum
3. fat
4. skin
5. hair, nails
6. dermis
7. melanin
8. keratin
9. plastic surgeons
10. evaporation

Word Building

1. dermatopathy
2. melanocyte
3. onychomalacia
4. seborrhea
5. ichthyoderma
6. trichomycosis
7. anhidrosis
8. intradermal
9. dermatitis
10. scleroderma

Matching

1. h
2. o
3. s
4. a
5. l
6. c
7. r
8. v
9. y
10. e
11. q
12. i
13. n
14. g
15. u
16. m
17. f
18. b
19. w
20. j
21. x
22. p
23. d
24. t
25. k

Chapter 6
Orthopedics: Musculoskeletal System

Learning Objectives

After completing this chapter, students will be able to:

1. Understand the function of the musculoskeletal system.
2. Describe the medical specialty of orthopedics.
3. Define orthopedic-related combining forms, prefixes, and suffixes.
4. Identify the organs treated in orthopedics.
5. Build orthopedic medical terms from word parts.
6. Explain orthopedic medical terms.
7. Use orthopedic abbreviations.

Use this word list to focus your studying for the chapter test.

Arthralgia	Femoral	Patellar	Ulnar
Arthritis	Fibular	Phalangeal	Vertebral
Arthrocentesis	Fixation	Prosthesis	
Arthroplasty	Humeral	Pubic	**Abbreviations**
Arthroscope	Iliac	Radial	
Arthroscopy	Intercostal	Radiography	C1, C2, etc
Atrophy	Intervertebral	Sacral	Ca
Bradykinesia	Intramuscular	Scapular	CTS
Bursitis	Mandibular	Scoliosis	DJD
Carpal	Maxillary	Spondylitis	EMG
Chondral	Metacarpal	Spondylosis	Fx
Chondritis	Metatarsal	Sprain	IM
Clavicular	Myeloma	Sternum	L1, L2, etc.
Closed fracture	Myopathy	Strain	MD
Coccygeal	Orthopedics	Substernal	NSAID
Costal	Orthopedist	Suprapubic	OA
Cranial	Osteoarthritis	Tarsal	Ortho
Craniotomy	Osteomalacia	Tendinitis	RA
Dyskinesia	Osteopathy	Tendinoplasty	T1, T2, etc.
Electromyogram	Osteoporosis	Tibial	

Worksheet 6A
New Word Parts

Directions: Write out the meaning for each combining form, prefix, and suffix. Then locate a new term from the chapter that uses the word part.

Combining Forms	Meaning	Chapter Term	Meaning
1. arthr/o	_____	_____	_____
2. burs/o	_____	_____	_____
3. carp/o	_____	_____	_____
4. chondr/o	_____	_____	_____
5. clavicul/o	_____	_____	_____
6. coccyg/o	_____	_____	_____
7. cost/o	_____	_____	_____
8. crani/o	_____	_____	_____
9. femor/o	_____	_____	_____
10. fibul/o	_____	_____	_____
11. humer/o	_____	_____	_____
12. ili/o	_____	_____	_____
13. ischi/o	_____	_____	_____
14. mandibul/o	_____	_____	_____
15. maxill/o	_____	_____	_____
16. metacarp/o	_____	_____	_____
17. metatars/o	_____	_____	_____
18. muscul/o	_____	_____	_____
19. my/o	_____	_____	_____
20. myel/o	_____	_____	_____
21. oste/o	_____	_____	_____
22. patell/o	_____	_____	_____
23. phalang/o	_____	_____	_____
24. pub/o	_____	_____	_____

(Continued)

Combining Forms	Meaning	Chapter Term	Meaning
25. radi/o			
26. sacr/o			
27. scapul/o			
28. spondyl/o			
29. stern/o			
30. tars/o			
31. ten/o			
32. tendin/o			
33. tibi/o			
34. uln/o			
35. vertebr/o			

Prefixes

	Meaning	Chapter Term	Meaning
36. per-			
37. sub-			
38. supra-			
39. inter-			
40. intra-			

Suffixes

	Meaning	Chapter Term	Meaning
41. -asthenia			
42. -clasia			
43. -desis			
44. -kinesia			
45. -porosis			
46. -rrhaphy			
47. -rrhexis			
48. -tome			
49. -trophy			

Worksheet 6B
Word Part Review

Directions: Write out the meaning for each combining form, prefix, and suffix.

Combining Forms Meaning

1. cutane/o _____
2. electr/o _____
3. fibr/o _____
4. kyph/o _____
5. lord/o _____
6. orth/o _____
7. path/o _____
8. scoli/o _____

Prefixes

9. a- _____
10. brady- _____
11. dys- _____
12. hyper- _____

Suffixes

13. -centesis _____
14. -algia _____
15. -malacia _____
16. -ectomy _____
17. -otomy _____
18. -plasty _____
19. -scope _____
20. -scopy _____
21. -gram _____
22. -graphy _____

Worksheet 6C
Word Surgery

Directions: Below are terms built from word parts. Analyze each term by listing and defining the word parts used to build it.

Medical Term	Word Part Meanings
1. subiliac	
2. carpal	
3. humeral	
4. clavicular	
5. fibular	
6. arthrogram	
7. arthroplasty	
8. supramaxillary	
9. bursitis	
10. chondromalacia	
11. intracranial	

(*Continued*)

Medical Term	Word Part Meanings
12. coccygeal	_____
13. pubic	_____
14. hyperkinesia	_____
15. muscular	_____
16. myopathy	_____
17. electromyography	_____
18. myelogenic	_____
19. myasthenia	_____
20. osteocyte	_____
21. osteoclasia	_____
22. osteochondroma	_____
23. spondylosis	_____
24. tenodesis	_____
25. tendinoplasty	_____

Worksheet 6D
Word Search

Directions: Find and circle the answer for each fill-in-the-blank question in the word search puzzle.

1. The bones are joined together by _____ to form the skeleton.

2. Orthopedic surgeons are also referred to as _____.

3. The anatomical name for the breast bone is the _____.

4. _____ is a term meaning to surgically break a joint.

5. _____ is a term meaning inside the skull.

6. A _____ fracture results in loss of height of a vertebral body.

7. _____ is a chronic condition with widespread aching and pain in the muscles and fibrous soft tissue.

8. A _____ fracture is commonly seen in children.

9. An abnormal increase in the normal outward curvature of the thoracic spine is called _____.

10. _____ means to realign the bones in a fracture or dislocation.

```
K A A I G L A Y M O R B I F I
S T R L V R Z L L N V S G C N
T K N T J R L J O J T Y R T T
N N C H H K X I V S D L W K R
E Z M I D R T K I W C M L S A
M R R W T C O D Z O T P F I C
A Q R R U S E C M M K R Q S R
G M F D X P N P L C M T R O A
I R E N O T R E F A T N D H N
L R N H T E F B E Y S P C P I
L G T Y S J P F B R W I B Y A
T R Y S M M B C P T G D A K L
O F I J L F S T E R N U M F N
W O L K T M H C Q C K G Y K M
N F X F K T Y Z G L R K J W K
```

Chapter 6/ORTHOPEDICS: MUSCULOSKELETAL SYSTEM

Worksheet 6E
Unscramble

Directions: Unscramble each medical term below. A definition for the term is given below each scrambled term.

1. m r a o f e l _____

   pertaining to the thigh

2. l a t e a l p r _____

   pertaining to the knee cap

3. c t a o r e s l t i n _____

   pertaining to between the ribs

4. b l a d i a n m u r _____

   pertaining to the lower jaw

5. p b u s a c u s r a l _____

   pertaining to below the shoulder blade

6. l u c v i l a r a c _____

   pertaining to the collar bone

7. l i s o c o i s s _____

   abnormal lateral curvature of the spine

8. p a r a i o r d h g y _____

   imaging procedure using x-rays

9. o c t u r a n r t e c _____

   abnormal shortening of muscle fibers

10. s r t o s i o h _____

    externally applied splint or brace

Worksheet 6F
Abbreviations

Directions: Write the full term that each abbreviation stands for.

1. AK _____
2. BDT _____
3. BE _____
4. BMD _____
5. C1 _____
6. Ca _____
7. CK _____
8. CTS _____
9. DJD _____
10. DTR _____
11. DXA _____
12. EMG _____
13. FX, Fx _____
14. HNP _____
15. IM _____
16. JRA _____
17. L2 _____
18. LE _____
19. LUE _____
20. MD _____
21. NSAID _____
22. OA _____
23. ORIF _____
24. Orth, ortho _____

(Continued)

25. RA _____

26. RLE _____

27. T3 _____

28. THA _____

29. TKR _____

30. UE _____

Worksheet 6G
Case Study

Directions: Below is a case study presentation of a patient with a condition covered in this chapter. Read the case study and answer the questions below. Some questions will ask for information not included within this chapter. Use your text, a medical dictionary, or any other reference material you choose to answer these questions.

Mary Pearl, age 60, has come into the orthopedic surgeon's office complaining of swelling, stiffness, and arthralgia, especially in her elbows, wrists, and hands. A bone scan revealed inflammation in multiple joints with cartilage degeneration. A diagnosis of rheumatoid arthritis was made. The physician ordered non-steroidal anti-inflammatory medication and hand/wrist orthoses.

1. What pathological condition does this patient have? Look this condition up in a reference source and include a short description of it.

2. What type of long-term damage may occur in a patient with rheumatoid arthritis?

3. Describe the other major type of arthritis mentioned in your textbook.

4. What diagnostic procedure did the physician order? Describe it in your own words. What were the results?

5. What medication was ordered? What benefit should the patient expect from this medication?

6. What are orthoses and what benefit should the patient expect from using them?

Worksheet 6H
Web Destinations

Osteoporosis

According to the National Osteoporosis Foundation's website, http://www.nof.org, "osteoporosis, or porous bone, is a disease characterized by low bone mass and structural deterioration of bone tissue, leading to bone fragility and an increased susceptibility to fractures of the hip, spine, and wrist." Explore this website and use the information presented to describe the prevalence, risk factors, symptoms, diagnosis, medications, prevention, and fractures associated with osteoporosis.

Muscular Dystrophy

As stated on the Muscular Dystrophy Association's (MDA) website, http://www.mda.org, "muscular dystrophies are genetic disorders characterized by progressive muscle wasting and weakness that begin with microscopic changes in the muscle. As muscles degenerate over time, the person's muscle strength declines."

Two common types of muscular dystrophy (MD) are Duchenne muscular dystrophy (DMD) and Becker muscular dystrophy (BMD). Visit the MDA website. Type "Duchenne and Becker" into the Search Our Site box. Select the *Facts About Duchenne & Becker Muscular Dystrophies* article from the list. Read about these two types of MD; then write an essay to describe what these two types of MD are, what causes them, what happens to the muscles, and how they are diagnosed.

Worksheet 6I
Professional Profile and Journal

Professional Profile

Physical Therapy and Occupational Therapy

Rehabilitation services consist of physical therapy and occupational therapy. These allied health personnel plan and carry out treatment programs to develop, restore, or maintain function. Rehabilitation services are found in acute and long-term facilities, rehabilitation centers, health maintenance organizations, schools, home health agencies, private practices, clinics, and mental health facilities.

Physical Therapy

Physical therapy specializes in programs for movement dysfunction and physical disabilities resulting from muscle, bone, joint, and nerve injuries or disease. They work with patients/clients to help them overcome these barriers to mobility.

Physical Therapist (PT or DPT)

- Graduates from an accredited 4-year bachelor's or 5-year graduate program in physical therapy
- Completes a 4-month clinical internship
- Passes a national licensing examination

Physical Therapy Assistant (PTA)

- Works under the supervision of a physical therapist
- Graduates from an accredited 2-year associate's degree physical therapy assistant program
- Passes a national licensing examination

Occupational Therapy

Occupational therapists specialize in rehabilitating patients/clients to perform activities that are essential for daily living. They develop a treatment plan and programs to restore personal care skills to persons with physical, mental, emotional, and/or developmental problems.

Occupational Therapist (OTR)

- Graduates from an approved 4-year college or university occupational therapy program
- Completes 6 months of clinical experience
- Passes a national certification examination

Certified Occupational Therapy Assistant (COTA)

- Works under the supervision of an occupational therapist
- Graduates from a 2-year approved occupational therapy assistant program
- Completes supervised clinical fieldwork
- Passes a national certification examination

For more information regarding these health careers, visit the following websites:

- American Occupational Therapy Association at www.aota.org
- American Physical Therapy Association at www.apta.org

Professional Journal

In this exercise you will now have an opportunity to put the words you have learned into practice. Imagine yourself in the role of a physical therapist. If you refer back to the Professional Profile, you will see that this healthcare professional is responsible for treating disorders involving the muscles, bones, and joints. Use the 10 words listed below, or any other new terms from this chapter, to write sentences to describe the patients you saw today.

An example of a sentence is: *Mrs. Jones'* **herniated nucleus pulposus** *was much improved after her treatment.*

1. spasm _____

2. arthritis _____

3. spina bifida _____

4. femur _____

5. lumbar vertebrae _____

6. deep tendon reflex _____

7. fibromyalgia _____

8. compound fracture _____

9. muscle atrophy _____

10. kyphosis _____

Name _____ Date _____ Score _____

Chapter 6 Word Parts Quiz

Directions: Define the combining form, prefix, or suffix in the spaces provided.

1. femor/o _____
2. my/o _____
3. chondr/o _____
4. ten/o _____
5. oste/o _____
6. arthr/o _____
7. spondyl/o _____
8. myel/o _____
9. burs/o _____
10. clavicul/o _____
11. metatars/o _____
12. coccyg/o _____
13. kyph/o _____
14. phalang/o _____
15. scoli/o _____
16. uln/o _____
17. lord/o _____
18. fibr/o _____
19. carp/o _____
20. -desis _____
21. -asthenia _____
22. -porosis _____
23. -kinesia _____
24. inter- _____
25. sub- _____

Name _____ Date _____ Score _____

Chapter 6 Spelling Quiz

Directions: Write each term as your instructor pronounces it.

1. _____
2. _____
3. _____
4. _____
5. _____
6. _____
7. _____
8. _____
9. _____
10. _____
11. _____
12. _____
13. _____
14. _____
15. _____
16. _____
17. _____
18. _____
19. _____
20. _____

Name _____ Date _____ Score _____

Chapter 6 Labeling Quiz

Directions: Label the bones of the skeleton.

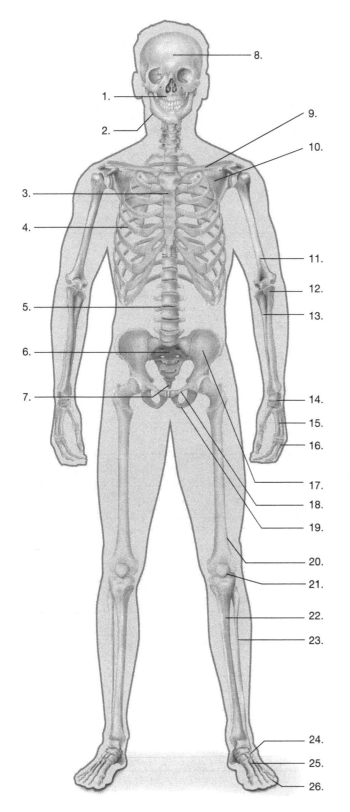

1. _____
2. _____
3. _____
4. _____
5. _____
6. _____
7. _____
8. _____
9. _____
10. _____
11. _____
12. _____
13. _____
14. _____
15. _____
16. _____
17. _____
18. _____
19. _____
20. _____
21. _____
22. _____
23. _____
24. _____
25. _____
26. _____

© 2012 Pearson Education, Inc.

Name _____ Date _____ Score _____

Chapter 6 Word Building Quiz

Directions: Build a single medical term for each phrase below.

1. pertaining to the ilium _____
2. pertaining to the ribs _____
3. pertaining to the wrist _____
4. pertaining to the collar bone _____
5. pertaining to the knee cap _____
6. instrument to visually examine a joint _____
7. cartilage softening _____
8. slow movement _____
9. pertaining to the upper jaw _____
10. muscle weakness _____
11. bone producing _____
12. ruptured muscle _____
13. pertaining to the pubis _____
14. puncture to withdraw fluid from a joint _____
15. instrument to cut bone _____
16. pertaining to within a muscle _____
17. bone cell _____
18. surgical repair of cartilage _____
19. muscle disease _____
20. red bone marrow tumor _____
21. surgical fixation of a tendon _____
22. pertaining to the tail bone _____
23. surgical breaking of a bone _____
24. record of muscle's electricity _____
25. surgical removal of a bursa _____

Name _____ Date _____ Score _____

Chapter 6 Quiz

Fill-in-the-Blank

1. Muscles are attached to the skeleton by _____.

2. The musculoskeletal system consists of bones, muscles, and _____.

3. The anatomical name for the shoulder blade is _____.

4. _____ joints are freely moving joints.

5. The function of a _____ is to reduce friction.

6. _____ muscle produces movement of internal organs.

7. Red bone marrow produces _____ cells.

8. Carpal tunnel syndrome is an example of a(n) _____.

9. _____ is a muscle enzyme found in skeletal and cardiac muscle.

10. In a _____ fracture one bone fragment is pushed into another.

Word Building

Build a term that means:

1. pertaining to fingers   _____

2. surgical repair of a joint   _____

3. excessive movement   _____

4. pertaining to the shin   _____

5. surgical removal of cartilage   _____

6. record of muscle electricity   _____

7. pertaining to the ankle   _____

8. bone softening   _____

9. tendon inflammation   _____

10. red bone marrow tumor   _____

Matching

____ 1. radius
____ 2. joint
____ 3. bone graft
____ 4. closed fracture
____ 5. bursa
____ 6. DXA
____ 7. orthosis
____ 8. ischium
____ 9. kyphosis
____ 10. cartilage
____ 11. MD
____ 12. comminuted fracture
____ 13. bone
____ 14. RA
____ 15. phalanges
____ 16. radiography
____ 17. osteogenic sarcoma
____ 18. compound fracture
____ 19. prosthesis
____ 20. fibula
____ 21. sprain
____ 22. HNP
____ 23. lordosis
____ 24. dislocation
____ 25. spina bifida

a. shock absorber
b. autoimmune joint disease
c. a birth defect
d. part of the pelvis
e. overstretched ligaments
f. open fracture
g. x-ray
h. fuses two bones together
i. ruptured disk
j. articulation
k. common type of bone cancer
l. substitute for missing body part
m. a forearm bone
n. a splint or brace
o. test for osteoporosis
p. humpback
q. bone is shattered
r. bones in joint no longer in contact
s. toes
t. swayback
u. simple fracture
v. progressive muscular degeneration
w. mineral store house
x. thinner lower leg bone
y. fluid-filled sac

Chapter 6 Answer Keys

Worksheet 6A Answer Key

1. joint
2. bursa
3. carpals (wrist)
4. cartilage
5. clavicle (collar bone)
6. coccyx (tailbone)
7. rib
8. skull
9. femur (thigh bone)
10. fibula (thinner lower leg bone)
11. humerus (upper arm bone)
12. ilium (part of pelvis)
13. ischium (part of pelvis)
14. mandible (lower jaw)
15. maxilla (upper jaw)
16. metacarpus (hand bones)
17. metatarsus (foot bones)
18. muscle
19. muscle
20. bone marrow
21. bone
22. patella (knee cap)
23. phalanges (fingers and toes)
24. pubis (part of pelvis)
25. radius (part of forearm)
26. sacrum
27. scapula (shoulder blade)
28. vertebra
29. sternum (breast bone)
30. tarsals (ankle)
31. tendon
32. tendon
33. tibia (shin, larger lower leg bone)
34. ulna (part of forearm)
35. vertebra
36. through
37. under
38. above
39. between
40. within
41. weakness
42. surgical breaking
43. surgical fixation
44. movement
45. porous
46. suture
47. rupture
48. instrument to cut
49. development

Worksheet 6B Answer Key

1. skin
2. electricity
3. fibrous
4. hump
5. bent backwards
6. straight
7. disease
8. crooked, bent
9. without
10. slow
11. difficult
12. excessive
13. puncture to withdraw fluid
14. pain
15. softening
16. surgical removal
17. cutting into
18. surgical repair
19. instrument for viewing
20. process of visually examining
21. record
22. process of recording

Worksheet 6C Answer Key

1. sub- = under; ili/o = ilium; -ac = pertaining to
2. carp/o = carpals, wrist; -al = pertaining to
3. humer/o = humerus; -al = pertaining to
4. clavicul/o = clavicle, collar bone; -ar = pertaining to
5. fibul/o = fibula; -ar = pertaining to
6. arthr/o = joint; -gram = record
7. arthr/o = joint; -plasty = surgical repair
8. supra- = above; maxill/o = maxilla, upper jaw; -ary = pertaining to
9. burs/o = bursa; -itis = inflammation
10. chondr/o = cartilage; -malacia = softening
11. intra- = within; crani/o = skull; -al = pertaining to
12. coccyg/o = coccyx, tailbone; -eal = pertaining to

13. pub/o = pubic bone; -ic = pertaining to
14. hyper- = excessive; -kinesia = movement
15. muscul/o = muscle; -ar = pertaining to
16. my/o = muscle; -pathy = disease
17. electr/o = electricity; my/o = muscle; -graphy = process of recording
18. myel/o = red bone marrow; -genic = producing
19. my/o = muscle; -asthenia = weakness
20. oste/o = bone; -cyte = cell
21. oste/o = bone; -clasia = surgical breaking
22. oste/o = bone; chondr/o = cartilage; -oma = tumor
23. spondyl/o = vertebra; -osis = abnormal condition
24. ten/o = tendon; -desis = surgical fixation
25. tendin/o = tendon; -plasty = surgical repair

Worksheet 6D Answer Key

Fill-in-the-blank

1. ligaments
2. orthopedists
3. sternum
4. arthroclasia
5. intracranial
6. compression
7. fibromyalgia
8. greenstick
9. kyphosis
10. reduction

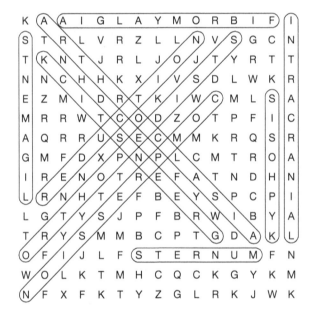

Worksheet 6E Answer Key

1. femoral
2. patellar
3. intercostal
4. mandibular
5. subscapular
6. clavicular
7. scoliosis
8. radiography
9. contracture
10. orthosis

Worksheet 6F Answer Key

1. above knee
2. bone density testing
3. below elbow
4. bone mineral density
5. first cervical vertebra
6. calcium
7. creatine kinase
8. carpal tunnel syndrome
9. degenerative joint disease
10. deep tendon reflex
11. dual-energy absorptiometry
12. electromyogram
13. fracture
14. herniated nucleus pulposus
15. intramuscular
16. juvenile rheumatoid arthritis

17. second lumbar vertebra
18. lower extremity
19. left upper extremity
20. muscular dystrophy
21. nonsteroidal anti-inflammatory drug
22. osteoarthritis
23. open reduction–internal fixation
24. orthopedics
25. rheumatoid arthritis
26. right lower extremity
27. third thoracic vertebra
28. total hip arthroplasty
29. total knee replacement
30. upper extremity

Worksheet 6G Answer Key

1. Rheumatoid arthritis
2. Crippling deformities
3. Osteoarthritis—Arthritis caused by loss of cartilage cushion covering bones in joint; most common in bearing weight joints; results in bone rubbing against bone
4. Bone scan—Nuclear medicine scan using radioactive dye to visualize bones; especially useful for finding stress fractures and bone cancer. Revealed inflammation in multiple joints with cartilage degeneration
5. Non-steroidal anti-inflammatory drugs (NSAIDs); pain relief and reduction in inflammation
6. Externally applied brace or splint; should prevent deformities

Worksheet 6H Answer Key
Essay activity, student answers will vary.

Worksheet 6I Answer Key
Student answers will vary.

Chapter 6 Word Parts Quiz Answer Key

1. femur
2. muscle
3. cartilage
4. tendon
5. bone
6. joint
7. vertebra
8. red bone marrow
9. bursa
10. clavicle
11. metatarsal
12. coccyx
13. hump
14. phalanges
15. crooked, bent
16. ulna
17. bent backwards
18. fibrous
19. carpals
20. surgical fixation
21. weakness
22. porous
23. movement
24. between
25. under

Chapter 6 Spelling Quiz Answer Key

1. coccygeal
2. phalanges
3. intracranial
4. prosthesis
5. pathologic
6. osteoporosis
7. electromyography
8. clavicular
9. arthroscopic
10. chondromalacia
11. dyskinesia
12. musculoskeletal
13. osteoarthritis
14. spondylosis
15. tendinous
16. fibromyalgia
17. scoliosis
18. radiography
19. comminuted
20. contracture

Chapter 6 Labeling Quiz Answer Key

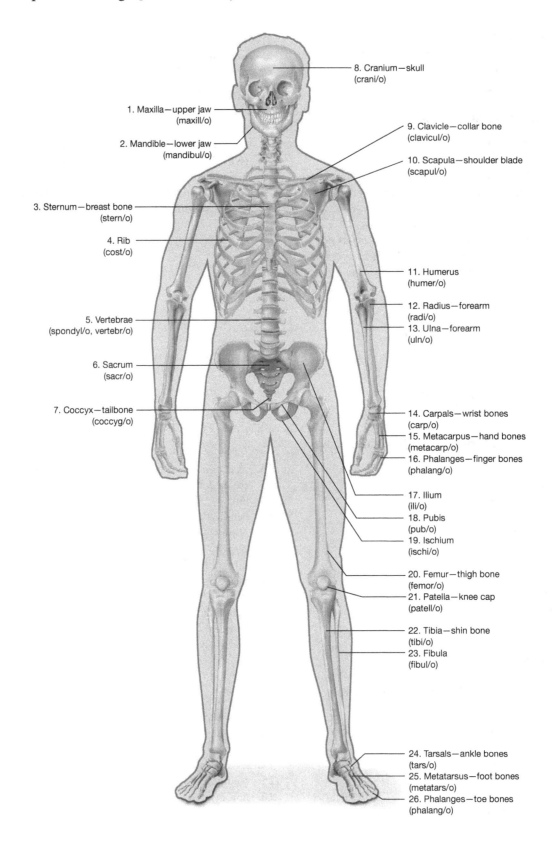

1. Maxilla—upper jaw (maxill/o)
2. Mandible—lower jaw (mandibul/o)
3. Sternum—breast bone (stern/o)
4. Rib (cost/o)
5. Vertebrae (spondyl/o, vertebr/o)
6. Sacrum (sacr/o)
7. Coccyx—tailbone (coccyg/o)
8. Cranium—skull (crani/o)
9. Clavicle—collar bone (clavicul/o)
10. Scapula—shoulder blade (scapul/o)
11. Humerus (humer/o)
12. Radius—forearm (radi/o)
13. Ulna—forearm (uln/o)
14. Carpals—wrist bones (carp/o)
15. Metacarpus—hand bones (metacarp/o)
16. Phalanges—finger bones (phalang/o)
17. Ilium (ili/o)
18. Pubis (pub/o)
19. Ischium (ischi/o)
20. Femur—thigh bone (femor/o)
21. Patella—knee cap (patell/o)
22. Tibia—shin bone (tibi/o)
23. Fibula (fibul/o)
24. Tarsals—ankle bones (tars/o)
25. Metatarsus—foot bones (metatars/o)
26. Phalanges—toe bones (phalang/o)

Chapter 6 Word Building Quiz Answer Key

1. iliac
2. costal
3. carpal
4. clavicular
5. patellar
6. arthroscope
7. chondromalacia
8. bradykinesia
9. maxillary
10. myasthenia
11. osteogenic
12. myorrhexis
13. pubic
14. arthrocentesis
15. osteotome
16. intramuscular
17. osteocyte
18. chondroplasty
19. myopathy
20. myeloma
21. tenodesis
22. coccygeal
23. osteoclasia
24. electromyogram
25. bursectomy

Chapter 6 Quiz Answer Key

Fill-in-the-Blank

1. tendons
2. joints
3. scapula
4. synovial
5. bursa
6. smooth
7. blood
8. repetitive motion disorder
9. creatine kinase
10. impacted

Word Building

1. phalangeal
2. arthroplasty
3. hyperkinesia
4. tibial
5. chondrectomy
6. electromyogram
7. tarsal
8. osteomalacia
9. tendinitis
10. myeloma

Matching

1. m
2. j
3. h
4. u
5. y
6. o
7. n
8. d
9. p
10. a
11. v
12. q
13. w
14. b
15. s
16. g
17. k
18. f
19. l
20. x
21. e
22. i
23. t
24. r
25. c

Chapter 7
Cardiology: Cardiovascular System

Learning Objectives

After completing this chapter, students will be able to:

1. Understand the functions of the cardiovascular system.
2. Describe the medical specialty of cardiology.
3. Define cardiology-related combining forms, prefixes, and suffixes.
4. Identify the organs treated in cardiology.
5. Build cardiology medical terms from word parts.
6. Explain cardiology medical terms.
7. Use cardiology abbreviations.

Use this word list to focus your studying for the chapter test.

Aneurysm	Coronary	Thrombogenic	CCU
Angiogram	Defibrillation	Thrombolysis	CPR
Angioplasty	Embolism	Thrombophlebitis	CV
Aortic	Endocarditis	Thrombosis	DVT
Arterial	Heart murmur	Ultrasonography	ECG
Arteriography	Heart valve stenosis	Valvular	ECHO
Arteriole	Hypertension	Vascular	EKG
Arteriosclerosis	Hypotension	Venipuncture	HR
Arrhythmia	Infarct	Venule	HTN
Atherosclerosis	Ischemia	Venous	ICU
Atrial	Myocardial		IV
Bradycardia	Occlusion	**Abbreviations**	MI
Cardiac catheterization	Pericardial		mmHg
Cardiologist	Phlebitis	ASHD	P
Cardiology	Phlebotomy	BP	PTCA
Cardiomegaly	Septum	Bpm	PVD
Cardiomyopathy	Stent	CABG	
Cardiorrhexis	Stress Test	CAD	
Cardiovascular	Tachycardia	Cath	

Worksheet 7A
New Word Parts

Directions: Write out the meaning for each combining form, prefix, and suffix. Then locate a new term from the chapter that uses the word part.

Combining Forms	Meaning	Chapter Term	Meaning
1. angi/o	_____	_____	_____
2. aort/o	_____	_____	_____
3. arteri/o	_____	_____	_____
4. arteriol/o	_____	_____	_____
5. ather/o	_____	_____	_____
6. atri/o	_____	_____	_____
7. cardi/o	_____	_____	_____
8. coron/o	_____	_____	_____
9. embol/o	_____	_____	_____
10. isch/o	_____	_____	_____
11. phleb/o	_____	_____	_____
12. steth/o	_____	_____	_____
13. thromb/o	_____	_____	_____
14. valv/o	_____	_____	_____
15. valvul/o	_____	_____	_____
16. varic/o	_____	_____	_____
17. vascul/o	_____	_____	_____
18. vas/o	_____	_____	_____
19. ven/o	_____	_____	_____
20. ventricul/o	_____	_____	_____
21. venul/o	_____	_____	_____

(Continued)

Prefixes	Meaning	Chapter Term	Meaning
22. brady-			
23. endo-			
24. peri-			
25. poly-			
26. tachy-			
27. trans-			
28. ultra-			

Suffixes

	Meaning	Chapter Term	Meaning
29. -ism			
30. -lysis			
31. -lytic			
32. -manometer			
33. -ole			
34. -sclerosis			
35. -spasm			
36. -stenosis			
37. -ule			

Worksheet 7B
Word Part Review

Directions: Write out the meaning for each combining form, prefix, and suffix.

Combining Forms   Meaning

1. cutane/o _____
2. electr/o _____
3. esophag/o _____
4. my/o _____
5. pulmon/o _____
6. son/o _____
7. sphygm/o _____

Prefixes

8. a- _____
9. hyper- _____
10. hypo- _____
11. inter- _____
12. intra- _____
13. per- _____

Suffixes

14. -dynia _____
15. -ectomy _____
16. -emia _____
17. -genic _____
18. -gram _____
19. -graphy _____
20. -ia _____
21. -itis _____

(Continued)

Suffixes	Meaning
22. -logist	_____
23. -logy	_____
24. -megaly	_____
25. -oma	_____
26. -osis	_____
27. -otomy	_____
28. -pathy	_____
29. -plasty	_____
30. -rraphy	_____
31. -rrhexis	_____
32. -scope	_____

Worksheet 7C
Word Surgery

Directions: Below are terms built from word parts. Analyze each term by listing and defining the word parts used to build it.

Medical Term	Word Part Meanings
1. angioma	
2. polyangiitis	
3. aortoplasty	
4. arteriorrhaphy	
5. arteriole	
6. atherosclerosis	
7. atrioventricular	
8. cardiogram	
9. cardiomegaly	
10. cardiomyopathy	
11. embolectomy	

(Continued)

Medical Term	Word Part Meanings
12. phlebotomy	_____
13. phlebography	_____
14. stethoscope	_____
15. thrombophlebitis	_____
16. thrombogenic	_____
17. thrombolysis	_____
18. valvule	_____
19. varicosis	_____
20. cardiovascular	_____
21. venous	_____
22. ischemia	_____
23. electrocardiogram	_____
24. vasospasm	_____
25. interventricular	_____

Worksheet 7D
Word Search

Directions: Find and circle the answer for each fill-in-the-blank question in the word search puzzle.

1. A specialist in studying the heart. _____
2. A localized widening of an artery. _____
3. An irregular heartbeat. _____
4. Abnormally slow heartbeat. _____
5. Surgical removal of the inner lining of an artery. _____
6. Abnormal quivering of heart. _____
7. A decrease in blood pressure. _____
8. An area of tissue necrosis. _____
9. Blockage of a blood vessel. _____
10. A blood pressure cuff. _____

```
S A R R H Y T H M I A B C T R W
P K B D B C V V Q Y K Y B Z D L
H F D E M R X Y H R G J X H B W
Y I N N M A K L D Q B N F B M
G B W D T C G D B H R T I N S L
M R M A S N K C Y H M N R Y F N
O I B R I X B J Y C F V R B O T
M L H T G Q F H M A A U B I V X
A L Y E O X N M R L E R S T L T
N A Q R L C G C N N M N D H T T
O T Y E O G T D A K E J P I N L
M I R C I Q H C P T R H Y Y A M
E O M T D X N L O D P G N V V J
T N N O R F Z P J D Y N W F F L
E Q V M A C Y T K H G N P J R L
R D T Y C H T N O I S U L C C O
```

Chapter 7/CARDIOLOGY: CARDIOVASCULAR SYSTEM

Worksheet 7E
Unscramble

Directions: Unscramble each medical term below. A definition for the term is given below each scrambled term.

1. a a i h h m r r t y _____

   irregular heart beat

2. l y r d i p o u c m a n o r a _____

   pertaining to heart and lungs

3. a e i i m h s c _____

   loss of blood supply from occlusion

4. o l b n i l i a t i f r _____

   abnormal quivering of heart

5. y r e s o n e i n t p h _____

   high blood pressure

6. r r a a c y a b d i d _____

   abnormally slow heart rate

7. a s d i c m o p a r s _____

   involuntary heart muscle spasm

8. r r o o c a y n _____

   pertaining to the heart

9. l r e a r i t r o c e o s i s s _____

   hardening of an artery

10. m k a c e a e r p _____

    electrical device to stimulate the heart to beat

Worksheet 7F
Abbreviations

Directions: Write the full term that each abbreviation stands for.

1. CP _____
2. CPR _____
3. CSD _____
4. CV _____
5. DVT _____
6. ECG _____
7. EKG _____
8. HR _____
9. HTN _____
10. ICD _____
11. ICU _____
12. IV _____
13. MI _____
14. mmHg _____
15. PTCA _____
16. PVD _____
17. SK _____
18. TEE _____
19. V-fib _____
20. V-tach _____

Worksheet 7G
Case Study

Directions: Below is a case study presentation of a patient with a condition covered in this chapter. Read the case study and answer the questions below. Some questions will ask for information not included within this chapter. Use your text, a medical dictionary, or any other reference material you choose to answer these questions.

Mr. Thomas is a 62-year-old man who has been diagnosed with an acute myocardial infarction with the following symptoms and history. His chief complaint is a persistent, crushing chest pain that radiates to his left arm, jaw, neck, and shoulder blade. He describes the pain, which he has had for the past 12 hours, as a "squeezing" sensation around his heart. He also reports nausea and dyspnea. He has a low-grade temperature, and his blood pressure is within a normal range at 130/82. He states that he smokes two packs of cigarettes a day, is overweight by 50 pounds, and has a family history of hypertension and coronary heart disease. He leads a relatively sedentary life style.

1. What is the common name for Mr. Thomas' condition? Look this condition up in a reference source and include a short description of it.

   _____

   _____

2. What is the medical term for this patient's chief complaint?

   _____

   _____

3. List and define each of the patient's additional symptoms in your own words. These terms appear in other chapters of your text.

   _____

   _____

4. Mr. Thomas does not have hypertension. According to your text, what is the blood pressure that is usually considered high?

   _____

   _____

5. Review the diagnostic heart tests described in this chapter. Which ones could be ordered to diagnose heart abnormalities or damage?

   _____

   _____

6. What are Mr. Thomas' risk factors for heart disease? Which can he change?

   _____

   _____

Worksheet 7H
Web Destinations

Myocardial Infarction

According to the American Heart Association (AHA), the warning signs of a heart attack include:

a. Uncomfortable pressure, fullness, squeezing, or pain in the center of the chest that lasts more than a few minutes or goes away and comes back
b. Pain that spreads to the shoulders, neck, or arms
c. Chest discomfort with lightheadedness, fainting, sweating, nausea, or shortness of breath
d. Atypical chest, stomach, or abdominal pain
e. Nausea or dizziness (without chest pain)
f. Shortness of breath and difficulty breathing (without chest pain)
g. Unexplained anxiety, weakness, or fatigue.
h. Palpitations, cold sweat, or paleness

Visit the following AHA website at http://www.americanheart.org.

1. Type "Heart Attack Prevention" into the search box. Select the article titled "Prevention and Treatment of Heart Attack."
2. Click on the link called "Learn the ABCs of heart attack prevention" and summarize the modifiable risk factors for heart disease.
3. Next, type "Heart Damage Detection" into the search box and select the article with the same name. From this information, describe electrocardiograms, Holter monitor, 12 lead electrocardiograms, echocardiography, and cardiac catheterization.
4. Finally, type "PTCA" into the search box and select the article entitled "Percutaneous Coronary Interventions (previously called Angioplasty, Percutaneous Transluminal Coronary [PTCA], or Balloon Angioplasty)." Use the information from this article to add a more detailed description of this procedure.

Cardiomyopathy

The medical term cardiomyopathy is used to describe a group of diseases affecting the muscle layer of the heart. For information regarding cardiomyopathy, visit the National Heart, Lung, and Blood Institute's (NHLBI) website at http://www.nhlbi.nih.gov. Type "Cardiomyopathy" into the search box and select the article titled "What is Cardiomyopathy?". Use the information from this page and the links in the left hand navigation bar to describe cardiomyopathy, its signs and symptoms, and how it is diagnosed and treated.

Worksheet 7I
Professional Profile and Journal

Professional Profile

Cardiovascular Professionals

Cardiology technologists, electrocardiogram technicians, and cardiac sonographers are all involved in the diagnosis and treatment of heart and blood vessel disease. The results of the tests and procedures they conduct are vitally important for the diagnosis and treatment of cardiovascular disease. These healthcare professionals are found wherever procedures to study the functioning of the cardiovascular system are performed. This includes hospitals, physicians' offices, cardiac rehabilitation programs, and diagnostic centers. See Medical Terminology Interactive for a video on Electrocardiogram Technicians.

Cardiology Technologist

- Assists with invasive heart procedures
- Includes cardiac catheterizations and angioplasty procedures
- Must complete an accredited 2- to 4-year program

Electrocardiogram Technician

- Conducts tests to record the electrical activity of the heart
- Includes electrocardiography (EKGs), Holter monitoring, and stress testing
- May complete a 1-year certification program or receive on-the-job training

Cardiac Sonographer

- Uses ultrasound to produce a moving image of the heart for diagnostic purposes
- Graduates from a 1-year certification, 2-year associate's degree, or 4-year baccalaureate program

For more information regarding these health careers, visit the following websites:

- Alliance of Cardiovascular Professionals at www.acp-online.org
- American Society of Echocardiography at www.asecho.org

Professional Journal

In this exercise you will now have an opportunity to put the words you have learned into practice. Imagine yourself in the role of a cardiology technologist, electrocardiogram technician, or a cardiac sonographer. These healthcare professionals are responsible for performing diagnostic tests and treatments such as invasive heart procedures, EKGs, and echocardiograms. Use the 10 words listed below, or any other new terms from this chapter, to write sentences to describe the patients you and the whole cardiology team saw today.

An example of a sentence is: *Mr. Brown's heart rate was so slow he will require a* **pacemaker implantation**.

1. aneurysm _____

2. heart murmur _____

3. cardiac catheterization _____

4. electrocardiogram _____

5. arrhythmia _____

6. mitral valve prolapse _____

7. cardiomegaly _____

8. stent _____

9. fibrillation _____

10. coronary artery disease _____

Name _____ Date _____ Score _____

Chapter 7 Word Parts Quiz

Directions: Define the combining form, prefix, or suffix in the spaces provided.

1. arteri/o _____
2. phleb/o _____
3. thromb/o _____
4. vascul/o _____
5. steth/o _____
6. varic/o _____
7. valvul/o _____
8. isch/o _____
9. ather/o _____
10. arteriol/o _____
11. atri/o _____
12. ventricul/o _____
13. coron/o _____
14. angi/o _____
15. cardi/o _____
16. sphygm/o _____
17. son/o _____
18. electr/o _____
19. my/o _____
20. -sclerosis _____
21. -lysis _____
22. -genic _____
23. -manometer _____
24. brady- _____
25. trans- _____

Name _____ Date _____ Score _____

Chapter 7 Spelling Quiz

Directions: Write each term as your instructor pronounces it.

1. _____
2. _____
3. _____
4. _____
5. _____
6. _____
7. _____
8. _____
9. _____
10. _____
11. _____
12. _____
13. _____
14. _____
15. _____
16. _____
17. _____
18. _____
19. _____
20. _____

Name _____ Date _____ Score _____

Chapter 7 Labeling Quiz 1

Directions: Label the parts of the cardiovascular system.

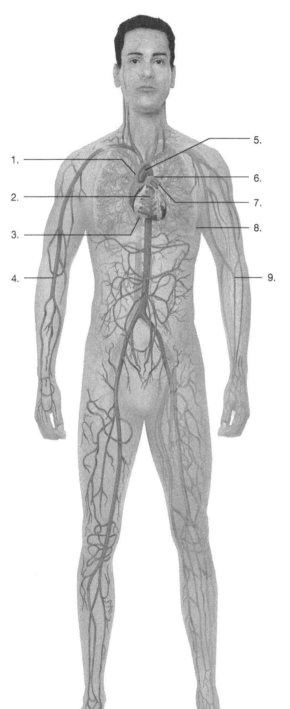

1. _____
2. _____
3. _____
4. _____
5. _____
6. _____
7. _____
8. _____
9. _____

Name _____ Date _____ Score _____

Chapter 7 Labeling Quiz 2

Directions: Label the structures of the heart.

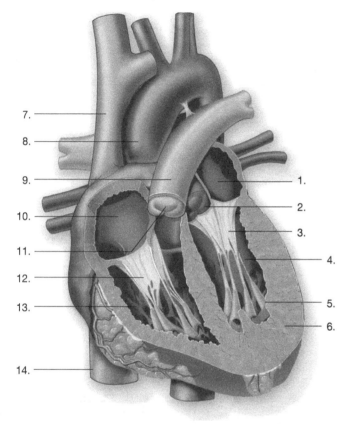

1. _____
2. _____
3. _____
4. _____
5. _____
6. _____
7. _____
8. _____
9. _____
10. _____
11. _____
12. _____
13. _____
14. _____

Name _____ Date _____ Score _____

Chapter 7 Word Building Quiz

Directions: Build a single medical term for each phrase below.

1. surgical repair of a vessel _____

2. narrowing of an artery _____

3. surgical removal of embolus _____

4. condition of being held back _____

5. producing a clot _____

6. abnormal condition of having a varicosity _____

7. pertaining to within a vein _____

8. hardening of plaque _____

9. pertaining to the heart _____

10. record of heart's electricity _____

11. vessel tumor _____

12. inflammation inside the heart _____

13. suture of an artery _____

14. pertaining to the aorta _____

15. small vein _____

16. enlarged heart _____

17. pertaining to heart muscle _____

18. pertaining to the heart and lungs _____

19. instrument to measure pulse _____

20. ruptured artery _____

21. destruction of a clot _____

22. fast heart condition _____

23. pertaining to between atria _____

24. cutting into a valve _____

25. heart pain _____

Name _____ Date _____ Score _____

Chapter 7 Quiz

Fill-in-the-Blank

1. _____ carry blood toward the heart and _____ carry blood away from the heart.

2. _____ are the smallest arteries and _____ are the smallest veins.

3. The build up of fatty deposits along the inner wall of a blood vessel is called a(n) _____.

4. The _____ is the largest artery in the body.

5. A(n) _____ is an upper heart chamber and a(n) _____ is a lower heart chamber.

6. The heart is composed of _____ tissue.

7. A(n) _____ is a floating clot.

8. A(n) _____ is a flap-like structure that closes to prevent backflow of blood.

9. Arteries going to the lungs carry _____ blood.

10. PVD typically occurs in arteries of the _____.

Word Building

Build a term that means:

1. inflammation of many vessels   _____

2. artery narrowing   _____

3. pertaining to in between atria   _____

4. cutting into a vein   _____

5. surgical repair of a valve   _____

6. one who studies the heart   _____

7. producing a clot   _____

8. hardening of plaque   _____

9. abnormal condition of having a varicosity   _____

10. pertaining to around the heart   _____

Matching

_____ 1. aneurysm
_____ 2. fibrillation
_____ 3. endarterectomy
_____ 4. hypotension
_____ 5. prolapse
_____ 6. myocardial infarction
_____ 7. ischemia
_____ 8. heart murmur
_____ 9. pacemaker
_____ 10. angina pectoris
_____ 11. sphygmomanometer
_____ 12. CABG
_____ 13. Doppler ultrasonography
_____ 14. congenital septal defect
_____ 15. cardiac enzymes
_____ 16. streptokinase
_____ 17. CAD
_____ 18. auscultation
_____ 19. bradycardia
_____ 20. endocardium
_____ 21. catheter
_____ 22. HTN
_____ 23. stress test
_____ 24. cardiac arrest
_____ 25. stenosis

a. abnormal heart sound
b. heart bypass surgery
c. heart attack
d. a "clot-buster"
e. chest pain
f. uses a treadmill
g. abnormal quivering of heart muscle
h. high blood pressure
i. present from birth
j. blood test for heart damage
k. listening to body sounds
l. loss of blood flow due to blockage
m. complete stoppage of all heart activity
n. stiff heart valve
o. inner lining of the heart
p. surgery that removes plaque
q. localized widened artery
r. thin tube passed through veins
s. creates a moving image
t. floppy heart valve
u. also called arteriosclerotic heart disease
v. blood pressure cuff
w. electrical device to stimulate heart
x. slow heart rate
y. low blood pressure

Chapter 7 Answer Keys

Worksheet 7A Answer Key

1. vessel
2. aorta
3. artery
4. arteriole
5. fatty substance, plaque
6. atrium
7. heart
8. heart
9. plug
10. to keep back
11. vein
12. chest
13. clot
14. valve
15. valve
16. dilated vein
17. blood vessel
18. blood vessel
19. vein
20. ventricle
21. venule
22. slow
23. within
24. around
25. many
26. fast
27. across
28. excess
29. condition
30. destruction
31. destruction
32. instrument to measure pressure
33. small
34. hardening
35. involuntary muscle contraction
36. narrowing
37. small

Worksheet 7B Answer Key

1. skin
2. electricity
3. esophagus
4. muscle
5. lung
6. sound
7. pulse
8. without
9. excessive
10. insufficient
11. between
12. within
13. through
14. pain
15. surgical removal
16. blood condition
17. producing
18. record
19. process of recording
20. condition
21. inflammation
22. one who studies
23. study of
24. enlarged
25. tumor
26. abnormal condition
27. cutting into
28. disease
29. surgical repair
30. suture
31. rupture
32. instrument for viewing

Worksheet 7C Answer Key

1. angi/o = vessel; -oma = tumor
2. poly- = many; angi/o = vessel; -itis = inflammation
3. aort/o = aorta; -plasty = surgical repair
4. arteri/o = artery; -rrhaphy = suture
5. arteri/o = artery; -ole = small
6. ather/o = fatty substance, plaque; -sclerosis = hardening
7. atri/o = atrium; ventricul/o = ventricle; -ar = pertaining to
8. cardi/o = heart; -gram = record
9. cardi/o = heart; -megaly = enlarged
10. cardi/o = heart; my/o = muscle; -pathy = disease
11. embol/o = plug, embolus; -ectomy = surgical removal
12. phleb/o = vein; -otomy = cutting into
13. phleb/o = vein; -graphy = process of recording
14. steth/o = chest; -scope = instrument for viewing
15. thromb/o = clot; phleb/o = vein; -itis = inflammation

16. thromb/o = clot; -genic = producing
17. thromb/o = clot; -lysis = destruction
18. valv/o = valve; -ule = small
19. varic/o = dilated vein, varicosity; -osis = abnormal condition
20. cardi/o = heart; vascul/o = blood vessel; -ar = pertaining to
21. ven/o = vein; -ous = pertaining to
22. isch/o = hold back; -emia = blood condition
23. electr/o = electricity; cardi/o = heart; -gram = record
24. vas/o = blood vessel; -spasm = involuntary muscle contraction
25. inter- = between; ventricul/o = ventricle; -ar = pertaining to

Worksheet 7D Answer Key

1. cardiologist
2. aneurysm
3. arrhythmia
4. bradycardia
5. endarterectomy
6. fibrillation
7. hypotension
8. infarct
9. occlusion
10. sphygmomanometer

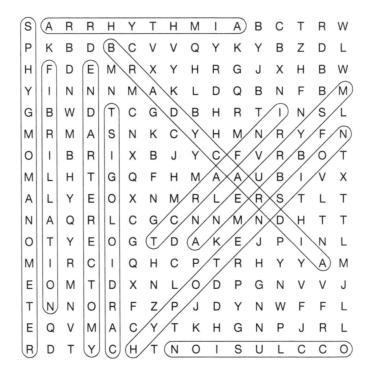

Worksheet 7E Answer Key

1. arrhythmia
2. cardiopulmonary
3. ischemia
4. fibrillation
5. hypertension
6. bradycardia
7. cardiospasm
8. coronary
9. arteriosclerosis
10. pacemaker

Worksheet 7F Answer Key

1. chest pain
2. cardiopulmonary resuscitation
3. congenital septal defect
4. cardiovascular

5. deep vein thrombosis
6. electrocardiogram
7. electrocardiogram
8. heart rate
9. hypertension
10. implantable cardioverter defibrillator
11. intensive care unit
12. intravenous
13. myocardial infarction
14. millimeters of mercury
15. percutaneous transluminal coronary angioplasty
16. peripheral vascular disease
17. streptokinase
18. transesophageal echocardiogram
19. ventricular fibrillation
20. ventricular tachycardia

Worksheet 7G Answer Key

1. heart attack
2. angina pectoris
3. nausea—feeling the urge to vomit; dyspnea—difficulty breathing
4. systolic pressure over 140 mmHg and/or diastolic pressure over 90 mmHg
5. cardiac catheterization, cardiac enzymes, Doppler ultrasonography, electrocardiography, Holter monitor, stress test, transesophageal echocardiography
6. smoking, overweight, family history, sedentary lifestyle; he can change smoking, overweight and sedentary lifestyle

Worksheet 7H Answer Key

Essay activity, student answers will vary.

Worksheet 7I Answer Key

Student answers will vary.

Chapter 7 Word Parts Quiz Answer Key

1. artery
2. vein
3. clot
4. blood vessel
5. chest
6. dilated vein
7. valve
8. to keep back
9. fatty substance, plaque
10. arteriole
11. atrium
12. ventricle
13. heart
14. vessel
15. heart
16. pulse
17. sound
18. electricity
19. muscle
20. hardening
21. destruction
22. producing
23. instrument to measure pressure
24. slow
25. across

Chapter 7 Spelling Quiz Answer Key

1. pericardial
2. interventricular
3. atherosclerosis
4. cardiorrhexis
5. phlebotomy
6. ischemia
7. sphygmomanometer
8. fibrillation
9. infarction
10. catheterization
11. aneurysm
12. auscultation
13. stethoscope
14. cardiopulmonary
15. endarterectomy
16. intravascular
17. tachycardia
18. venipuncture
19. embolectomy
20. polyangiitis

Chapter 7 Labeling Quiz 1 Answer Key

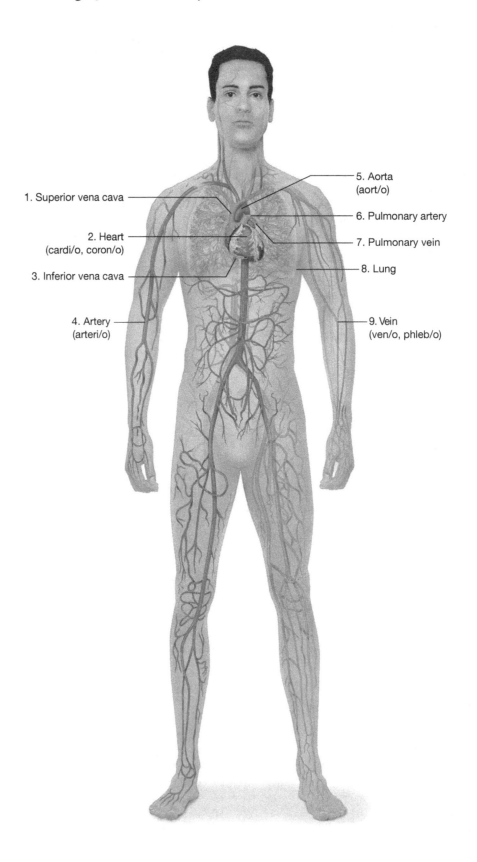

1. Superior vena cava
2. Heart (cardi/o, coron/o)
3. Inferior vena cava
4. Artery (arteri/o)
5. Aorta (aort/o)
6. Pulmonary artery
7. Pulmonary vein
8. Lung
9. Vein (ven/o, phleb/o)

Chapter 7 Labeling Quiz 2 Answer Key

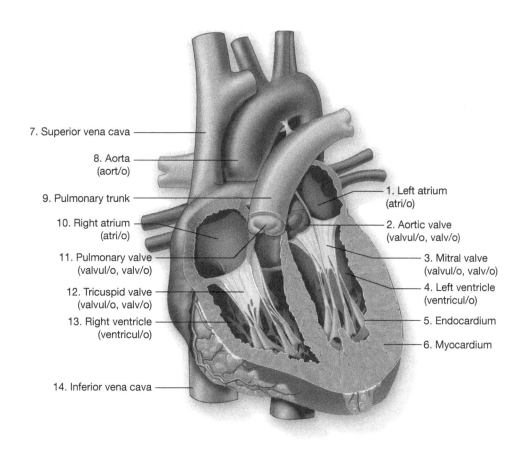

Chapter 7 Word Building Quiz Answer Key

1. angioplasty
2. arteriostenosis
3. embolectomy
4. ischemia
5. thrombogenic
6. varicosis
7. intravenous
8. atherosclerosis
9. coronary, cardiac
10. electrocardiogram
11. angioma
12. endocarditis
13. arteriorrhaphy
14. aortic
15. venule
16. cardiomegaly
17. myocardial
18. cardiopulmonary
19. sphygmomanometer
20. arteriorrhexis
21. thrombolysis, thrombolytic
22. tachycardia
23. interatrial
24. valvotomy
25. cardiodynia

Chapter 7 Quiz Answer Key

Fill-in-the-Blank

1. veins; arteries
2. arterioles; venules
3. plaque
4. aorta
5. atrium; ventricle
6. cardiac muscle
7. embolus
8. valve
9. deoxygenated
10. legs

Word Building

1. polyangiitis
2. arteriostenosis
3. interatrial
4. phlebotomy
5. valvoplasty
6. cardiologist
7. thrombogenic
8. atherosclerosis
9. varicosis
10. pericardial

Matching

1. q
2. g
3. p
4. y
5. t
6. c
7. l
8. a
9. w
10. e
11. v
12. b
13. s
14. i
15. j
16. d
17. u
18. k
19. x
20. o
21. r
22. h
23. f
24. m
25. n

Chapter 8
Hematology: Blood

Learning Objectives

After completing this chapter, students will be able to:

1. Understand the function of blood.
2. Describe the medical specialty of hematology.
3. Define hematology-related combining forms, prefixes, and suffixes.
4. Identify the components of blood.
5. Build hematology medical terms from word parts.
6. Explain hematology medical terms.
7. Use hematology abbreviations.

Use this word list to focus your studying for the chapter test.

Anemia	Hemolysis	Lymphocyte	**Abbreviations**
Anticoagulant	Hemophilia	Phlebotomy	
Blood transfusion	Hemorrhage	Plasma	CBC
Embolus	Hemostasis	Platelets	Diff
Erythrocyte	Hyperglycemia	Polycythemia	ESR
Erythrocytosis	Hyperlipemia	Septicemia	Hct
Erythropoiesis	Hypoglycemia	Thrombectomy	Hgb
Hematologist	Leukemia	Thrombocyte	PT
Hematology	Leukocyte	Thrombocytopenia	RBC
Hematoma	Leukocytosis	Thrombolysis	WBC
Hemoglobin	Leukopenia	Thrombosis	

Worksheet 8A
New Word Parts

Directions: Write out the meaning for each combining form, prefix, and suffix. Then locate a new term from the chapter that uses the word part.

Combining Forms	Meaning	Chapter Term	Meaning
1. bas/o	_____	_____	_____
2. coagul/o	_____	_____	_____
3. eosin/o	_____	_____	_____
4. erythr/o	_____	_____	_____
5. hem/o	_____	_____	_____
6. hemat/o	_____	_____	_____
7. lymph/o	_____	_____	_____
8. leuk/o	_____	_____	_____
9. neutr/o	_____	_____	_____
10. thromb/o	_____	_____	_____

Prefixes

11. anti-	_____	_____	_____
12. auto-	_____	_____	_____
13. mono-	_____	_____	_____
14. pan-	_____	_____	_____

Suffixes

15. -cyte	_____	_____	_____
16. -cytosis	_____	_____	_____
17. -emia	_____	_____	_____
18. -globin	_____	_____	_____

(Continued)

Suffixes	Meaning	Chapter Term	Meaning
19. -penia			
20. -phil			
21. -plasm			
22. -poiesis			
23. -rrhage			
24. -stasis			

Worksheet 8B
Word Part Review

Directions: Write out the meaning for each combining form, prefix, and suffix.

Combining Forms   Meaning

1. cyt/o   _____

2. embol/o   _____

3. glyc/o   _____

4. lip/o   _____

5. path/o   _____

6. phleb/o   _____

7. septic/o   _____

Prefixes

8. a-   _____

9. an-   _____

10. hyper-   _____

11. hypo-   _____

12. poly-   _____

Suffixes

13. -ectomy   _____

14. -ia   _____

15. -logist   _____

16. -logy   _____

17. -lysis   _____

18. -meter   _____

19. -metry   _____

20. -oma   _____

21. -osis   _____

22. -otomy   _____

Worksheet 8C
Word Surgery

Directions: Below are terms built from word parts. Analyze each term by listing and defining the word parts used to build it.

Medical Term	Word Part Meanings
1. erythrocyte	
2. monocyte	
3. leukocytosis	
4. thrombocytosis	
5. anemia	
6. hypoglycemia	
7. hematoma	
8. hematocytopenia	
9. hematology	
10. hematopoiesis	
11. hemoglobin	
12. hemolysis	
13. hemocytometer	

(*Continued*)

Medical Term	Word Part Meanings
14. pancytopenia	_____
15. neutropenia	_____
16. eosinophil	_____
17. basophil	_____
18. thrombectomy	_____
19. thrombosis	_____
20. septicemia	_____

Worksheet 8D
Word Search

Directions: Find and circle the answer for each fill-in-the-blank question in the word search puzzle.

1. The term _____ means having too much sugar in the blood.

2. The term _____ means having too few red blood cells.

3. A(n) _____ is a substance that prevents clot formation.

4. A(n) _____ is a blood test to measure the volume of red blood cells within the total volume of blood.

5. _____ is a cancer of leukocyte-forming red bone marrow.

6. _____ is commonly called blood poisoning.

7. _____ is commonly called a floating clot.

8. _____ is commonly called a bruise.

9. A venipuncture may also be called _____.

10. _____ is an inherited condition in which the blood fails to clot.

```
H  M  R  J  T  R  A  A  N  V  N  N  N
T  H  K  R  N  A  I  M  L  C  W  P  K
I  J  L  R  A  I  M  O  N  F  L  L  V
R  S  W  Y  L  N  E  T  N  H  K  X  S
C  E  J  M  U  E  C  A  C  E  C  U  C
O  P  A  O  G  P  Y  M  B  M  L  R  F
T  T  I  T  A  O  L  E  M  O  T  M  F
A  I  M  O  O  R  G  H  B  P  N  M  W
M  C  E  B  C  H  R  M  F  H  Q  J  H
E  E  K  E  I  T  E  Q  R  I  K  H  F
H  M  U  L  T  Y  P  J  T  L  G  R  K
N  I  E  H  N  R  Y  H  Z  I  X  Z  W
L  A  L  P  A  E  H  H  T  A  X  K  X
```

© 2012 Pearson Education, Inc.   Chapter 8/HEMATOLOGY: BLOOD   141

Worksheet 8E
Unscramble

Directions: Unscramble each medical term below. A definition for the term is given below each scrambled term.

1. t n f s u n o i s r a u a t o _____

   using one's own blood to replace lost blood

2. p l a i m e o h h i _____

   inherited lack of one blood clotting factor

3. m t a m o a e h _____

   a bruise

4. o t r m b s o i s h _____

   abnormal condition of clots

5. g l u o t a e c a _____

   formation of blood clot

6. m t y r o t m e h a y c o t e _____

   process of measuring blood cells

7. m e p r h l i e i a p y _____

   having an excessive amount of fat in the blood

8. t h p a o o i e i s e m s _____

   the formation of blood

9. l m e o n h o b i g _____

   blood protein that transports oxygen

10. p u r t o i l h e n _____

    type of white blood cell attracted to neutral stain

Worksheet 8F
Abbreviations

Directions: Write the full term that each abbreviation stands for.

1. basos _____
2. BMT _____
3. CBC _____
4. diff _____
5. eosins, eos _____
6. ESR, SR, sed rate _____
7. HCT, Hct, crit _____
8. Hgb, Hb, HGB _____
9. lymphs _____
10. monos _____
11. PA _____
12. PMN, polys _____
13. PT, pro-time _____
14. RBC _____
15. Rh+ _____
16. Rh- _____
17. segs _____
18. SMAC _____
19. WBC _____

Worksheet 8G
Case Study

Directions: Below is a case study presentation of a patient with a condition covered in this chapter. Read the case study and answer the questions below. Some questions will ask for information not included within this chapter. Use your text, a medical dictionary, or any other reference material you choose to answer these questions.

A 2-year-old boy is being seen by a hematologist. The child's symptoms include the sudden onset of high fevers, epistaxis, petechiae, and ecchymosis after minor traumas. A CBC revealed erythropenia and thrombocytopenia and leukocytosis. The physician has ordered a bone marrow aspiration to confirm the suspected diagnosis of acute lymphocytic leukemia. If the diagnosis is positive, the child will be placed immediately on intensive chemotherapy. The physician has informed the parents that treatment produces remission in 90% of children with ALL, especially those between the ages of 2 and 8.

1. What pathological condition does the hematologist suspect? Look this condition up in a reference source and include a short description of it.

2. List and define each of the patient's presenting symptoms in your own words. (Note: see Chapter 17 in your text for a definition of epistaxis.)

3. What is a CBC? Explain the results.

4. What diagnostic test did the physician perform? Describe it in your own words.

5. If the suspected diagnosis is correct, explain the treatment that will begin.

6. Remission is not a term found in this text. Use a medical dictionary or other reference source to define this term.

Worksheet 8H
Web Destinations

Leukemia

The American Cancer Society's Childhood Leukemia webpage states:

> Leukemia is a cancer of the white blood cells. This type of cancer starts in the bone marrow but can then spread to the blood, lymph nodes, the spleen, liver, central nervous system, and other organs. In contrast, other types of cancer can start in these organs and then spread to the bone marrow (or elsewhere). Those cancers are not leukemia. Both children and adults can develop leukemia.
>
> Leukemia is a complex disease with many different types and subtypes. The kind of treatment given and the outlook for the child with leukemia vary greatly according to the exact type and other, individual factors.

Visit this website at http://www.cancer.org. Type "Overview leukemia children" into the search box and select the article titled "Overview: Leukemia—Children's." From this page there are many links to further information about childhood leukemia. Go through these links and summarize the following information: What is childhood leukemia? What are the different types of leukemia? What are the risk factors? How is childhood leukemia diagnosed? How is childhood leukemia treated?

Sickle Cell Anemia

Sickle cell anemia is an inherited condition resulting in abnormal red blood cells. To learn more about this disease visit the American Sickle Cell Anemia Association's (ASCAA) website at http://www.ascaa.org. Left click on the FAQ's link and summarize the information from the links found on this webpage to write a description of this condition, its cause, its signs and symptoms, diagnosis, and treatment.

Worksheet 8I
Professional Profile and Journal

Professional Profile

Clinical Laboratory Science

Clinical laboratory scientists perform a variety of tests using laboratory equipment, microscopes, and computers. These laboratory tests include chemical analyses on body tissues, blood, and other body fluids; growing bacterial cultures; and typing and cross-matching blood for transfusions. Medical laboratory technologists play a key role in patient care because physicians study and use the results of these tests to make their diagnoses. Medical laboratories are found in acute-care facilities, physicians' offices, clinics, private laboratories, public health facilities, and research facilities. See Medical Terminology Interactive for a video on Clinical Laboratory Technicians.

Medical Technologist (MT) or Clinical Laboratory Scientist (CLS)

- Performs laboratory tests as ordered by a physician
- Graduates from an accredited 4-year college or university program
- Passes a national certification exam

Medical Laboratory Technician (MLT) or Clinical Laboratory Technician (CLT)

- Works under the supervision of a medical technologist
- Graduates from an accredited 2-year laboratory technician program at a community college or vocational education program
- Passes a national certification exam

Phlebotomist

- A specialist in drawing venous blood
- Does not conduct laboratory tests
- Completes a vocational education program or on-the-job training program
- Certification exam is available

For more information regarding these health careers, visit the following websites:

- American Medical Technologists at www.amt1.com
- American Society for Clinical Laboratory Science at www.ascls.org
- American Society for Clinical Pathology at www.ascp.org

Professional Journal

In this exercise you will now have an opportunity to put the words you have learned into practice. Imagine yourself in the role of a Clinical Laboratory Scientist. This healthcare professional is responsible for performing a variety of tests using laboratory equipment, microscopes, and computers. Use the 10 words listed below, or any other new terms from this chapter, to write sentences to describe the patients you saw today.

An example of a sentence is: *The results from the* **CBC** *confirmed that the patient has* **pancytopenia**.

1. aplastic anemia _____

2. blood culture and sensitivity _____

3. bone marrow aspiration _____

4. phlebotomy _____

5. SMAC _____

6. erythropenia _____

7. leukocytosis _____

8. leukemia _____

9. thrombolytic therapy _____

10. hyperlipemia _____

Name _____ Date _____ Score _____

Chapter 8 Word Parts Quiz

Directions: Define the combining form, prefix, or suffix in the spaces provided.

1. bas/o _____
2. coagul/o _____
3. eosin/o _____
4. erythr/o _____
5. hem/o _____
6. hemat/o _____
7. lymph/o _____
8. leuk/o _____
9. neutr/o _____
10. thromb/o _____
11. glyc/o _____
12. lip/o _____
13. path/o _____
14. phleb/o _____
15. septic/o _____
16. -cytosis _____
17. -emia _____
18. -globin _____
19. -penia _____
20. -phil _____
21. -poiesis _____
22. -stasis _____
23. -rrhage _____
24. an- _____
25. pan- _____

148 Chapter 8/HEMATOLOGY: BLOOD

Name _____ Date _____ Score _____

Chapter 8 Spelling Quiz

Directions: Write each term as your instructor pronounces it.

1. _____
2. _____
3. _____
4. _____
5. _____
6. _____
7. _____
8. _____
9. _____
10. _____
11. _____
12. _____
13. _____
14. _____
15. _____
16. _____
17. _____
18. _____
19. _____
20. _____

Name _____ Date _____ Score _____

Chapter 8 Labeling Quiz

Directions: Label the components of whole blood.

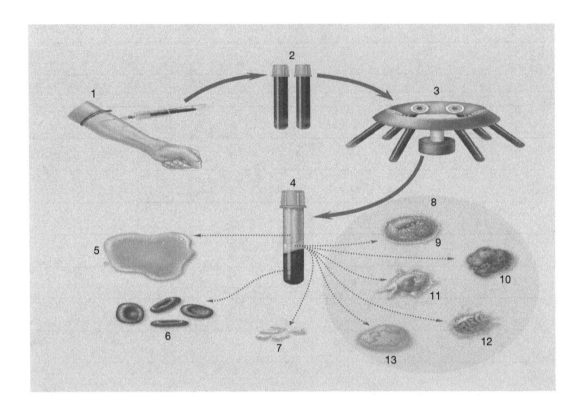

1. _____
2. _____
3. _____
4. _____
5. _____
6. _____
7. _____
8. _____
9. _____
10. _____
11. _____
12. _____
13. _____

Name _____ Date _____ Score _____

Chapter 8 Word Building Quiz

Directions: Build a single medical term for each phrase below.

1. white cell _____

2. abnormal condition in red cells _____

3. condition of being without blood _____

4. blood condition with insufficient sugar _____

5. blood formation _____

6. too few clotting cells _____

7. attracted to rosy red _____

8. blood protein _____

9. one cell _____

10. formation of white (cells) _____

11. bursting forth of blood _____

12. destruction of a clot _____

13. blood mass _____

14. cutting into a vein _____

15. process of measuring blood cells _____

16. surgical removal of a clot _____

17. clotting cell _____

18. stopping of blood _____

19. study of blood disease _____

20. blood condition with excessive fat _____

Name _____ Date _____ Score _____

Chapter 8 Quiz

Fill-in-the-Blank

1. The cells in whole blood are collectively referred to as the _____.

2. The blood clotting process is called _____.

3. _____ are blood cells that provide protection against pathogens.

4. A physician who specializes in blood transfusions is called a(n) _____.

5. _____ anemia is a severe form of anemia caused by a loss of functioning red bone marrow.

6. An erythrocyte sedimentation rate is a blood test that indicates the presence of _____ in the body.

7. _____ is the protein in red blood cells that carries oxygen.

8. A(n) _____ is a blood test that measures the volume of red blood cells present in the total volume of blood.

9. _____ anemia results from an insufficient amount of vitamin B12.

10. Blood that has the formed elements and clotting factors removed is called _____.

Word Building

Build a term that means:

1. red cell _____

2. blood condition with insufficient sugar _____

3. too few clotting cells _____

4. stopping of blood _____

5. attracted to rosy red _____

6. blood formation _____

7. instrument for measuring blood cells _____

8. destruction of a clot _____

9. abnormal condition in white cells _____

10. one who studies blood _____

Matching

_____ 1. pernicious anemia
_____ 2. thrombolytic therapy
_____ 3. septicemia
_____ 4. polycythemia vera
_____ 5. WBC differential
_____ 6. phlebotomy
_____ 7. sickle cell anemia
_____ 8. leukemia
_____ 9. hemophilia
_____ 10. embolus
_____ 11. RBC
_____ 12. leukopoiesis
_____ 13. hematoma
_____ 14. coagulate
_____ 15. formed elements
_____ 16. hormones
_____ 17. SMAC
_____ 18. hyperlipemia
_____ 19. Pro time
_____ 20. thalassemia
_____ 21. blood C&S
_____ 22. anticoagulant
_____ 23. platelets
_____ 24. basophil
_____ 25. sed rate

a. blood test for inflammatory diseases
b. the process for forming white blood cells
c. carried by the plasma
d. measures how long for blood clot to form
e. refers to all the cells in the blood
f. checks blood for bacterial growth
g. substance to prevent clots
h. caused by vitamin B12 deficiency
i. formation of a blood clot
j. cancer in red bone marrow
k. determines number of each type of leukocyte
l. computerized machine for testing blood
m. too much fat in the blood
n. venipuncture
o. WBC attracted to basic dyes
p. blood poisoning
q. inherited; unable to correctly make hemoglobin
r. erythrocyte
s. a floating clot
t. initiate blood clotting process
u. blood is unable to clot properly
v. treatment to dissolve clots
w. blood is too thick
x. a bruise
y. occurs exclusively in persons of African descent

Chapter 8 Answer Keys

Worksheet 8A Answer Key

1. base
2. clotting
3. rosy red
4. red
5. blood
6. blood
7. lymph
8. white
9. neutral
10. clot
11. against
12. self
13. one
14. all
15. cell
16. abnormal cell condition (too many)
17. blood condition
18. protein
19. too few
20. attracted to
21. formation
22. formation
23. bursting forth
24. stopping

Worksheet 8B Answer Key

1. cell
2. plug
3. sugar
4. fat
5. disease
6. vein
7. infection
8. without
9. without
10. excessive
11. insufficient
12. many
13. surgical removal
14. condition
15. one who studies
16. study of
17. destruction
18. instrument for measuring
19. process of measuring
20. mass
21. abnormal condition
22. cutting into

Worksheet 8C Answer Key

1. erythr/o = red; -cyte = cell
2. mono- = one; -cyte = cell
3. leuk/o = white; -cytosis = abnormal cell condition
4. thromb/o = clot; -cytosis = abnormal cell condition
5. an- = without; -emia = blood condition
6. hypo- = insufficient; glyc/o = sugar; -emia = blood condition
7. hemat/o = blood; -oma = mass
8. hemat/o = blood; cyt/o = cell; -penia = too few
9. hemat/o = blood; -logy = study of
10. hemat/o = blood, -poiesis = formation
11. hem/o = blood; -globin = protein
12. hem/o = blood; -lysis = destruction
13. hem/o = blood; cyt/o = cell; -meter = instrument for measuring
14. pan- = all; cyt/o = cell; -penia = too few
15. neutr/o = neutral, -penia = too few
16. eosin/o = rosy red; -phil = attracted to
17. bas/o = basic; -phil = attracted to
18. thromb/o = clot; -ectomy = surgical removal
19. thromb/o = clot; -osis = abnormal condition
20. septic/o = infection; -emia = blood condition

Worksheet 8D Answer Key

1. hyperglycemia
2. erythropenia
3. anticoagulant
4. hematocrit
5. leukemia
6. septicemia
7. embolus
8. hematoma
9. phlebotomy
10. hemophilia

Worksheet 8E Answer Key

1. autotransfusion
2. hemophilia
3. hematoma
4. thrombosis
5. coagulate
6. hematocytometry
7. hyperlipemia
8. hematopoiesis
9. hemoglobin
10. neutrophil

Worksheet 8F Answer Key

1. basophils
2. bone marrow transplant
3. complete blood count
4. differential
5. eosinophils
6. erythrocyte sedimentation rate
7. hematocrit
8. hemoglobin
9. lymphocytes
10. monocytes
11. pernicious anemia
12. polymorphonuclear neutrophil
13. prothrombin time
14. red blood cell, red blood count
15. Rh-positive
16. Rh-negative
17. segmented neutrophils
18. sequential multiple analyzer computer
19. white blood cell, white blood count

Worksheet 8G Answer Key

1. Acute lymphocytic leukemia
2. High fever; epistaxis—nose bleed; petechiae—pinpoint bruises; ecchymosis—large black and blue bruises
3. CBC—complete blood count, a comprehensive blood test; erythropenia—too few red blood cells; thrombocytopenia—too few platelets; leukocytosis—too many white blood cells
4. Bone marrow aspiration—sample of bone marrow is removed by aspiration with a needle and examined for diseases
5. Chemotherapy—treating a disease by using chemicals that have a toxic effect on the body, especially cancerous cells
6. Remission—a period during which the symptoms of a disease or disorder leave; may be temporary

Worksheet 8H Answer Key

Essay activity, student answers will vary.

Worksheet 8I Answer Key

Student answers will vary.

156 Chapter 8/HEMATOLOGY: BLOOD © 2012 Pearson Education, Inc.

Chapter 8 Word Parts Quiz Answer Key

1. base
2. clotting
3. rosy red
4. red
5. blood
6. blood
7. lymph
8. white
9. neutral
10. clot
11. sugar
12. fat
13. disease
14. vein
15. infection
16. abnormal cell condition (too many)
17. blood condition
18. protein
19. too few
20. attracted to
21. formation
22. stopping
23. bursting forth
24. without
25. all

Chapter 8 Spelling Quiz Answer Key

1. hematopoiesis
2. erythrocyte
3. eosinophil
4. anticoagulant
5. leukopenia
6. hemoglobin
7. septicemia
8. leukemia
9. pernicious
10. thalassemia
11. hematocrit
12. phlebotomy
13. polycythemia
14. prothrombin
15. thrombolysis
16. hyperglycemia
17. hematologist
18. pancytopenia
19. hemocytometer
20. hematopathology

Chapter 8 Labeling Quiz Answer Key

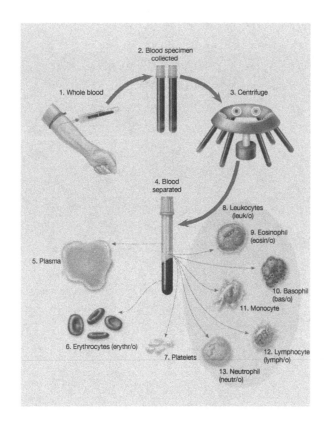

Chapter 8 Word Building Quiz Answer Key

1. leukocyte
2. erythrocytosis
3. anemia
4. hypoglycemia
5. hematopoiesis
6. thrombocytopenia
7. eosinophil
8. hemoglobin
9. monocyte
10. leukopoiesis
11. hemorrhage
12. thrombolysis
13. hematoma
14. phlebotomy
15. hemocytometry
16. thrombectomy
17. thrombocyte
18. hemostasis
19. hematopathology
20. hyperlipemia

Chapter 8 Quiz Answer Key

Fill-in-the-Blank
1. formed elements
2. hemostasis
3. leukocytes
4. hematologist
5. aplastic
6. inflammation; inflammatory disease
7. hemoglobin
8. hematocrit
9. pernicious
10. serum

Word Building
1. erythrocyte
2. hypoglycemia
3. thrombocytopenia
4. hemostasis
5. eosinophil
6. hematopoiesis
7. hemocytometer
8. thrombolysis, thrombolytic
9. leukocytosis
10. hematologist

Matching
1. h
2. v
3. p
4. w
5. k
6. n
7. y
8. j
9. u
10. s
11. r
12. b
13. x
14. i
15. e
16. c
17. l
18. m
19. d
20. q
21. f
22. g
23. t
24. o
25. a

Chapter 9
Immunology: Immune Systems

Learning Objectives

After completing this chapter, students will be able to:

1. Understand the function of the immune system and lymphatic systems.
2. Describe the medical specialty of immunology.
3. Define immunology-related combining forms, prefixes, and suffixes.
4. Identify the organs treated in immunology.
5. Build immunology medical terms from word parts.
6. Explain immunology medical terms.
7. Use immunology abbreviations.

Worksheet 9A
New Word Parts

Directions: Write out the meaning for each combining form, prefix, and suffix. Then locate a new term from the chapter that uses the word part.

Combining Forms	Meaning	Chapter Term	Meaning
1. adenoid/o	_____	_____	_____
2. immun/o	_____	_____	_____
3. lymph/o	_____	_____	_____
4. lymphaden/o	_____	_____	_____
5. lymphangi/o	_____	_____	_____
6. path/o	_____	_____	_____
7. phag/o	_____	_____	_____
8. splen/o	_____	_____	_____
9. thym/o	_____	_____	_____
10. tonsill/o	_____	_____	_____

Prefixes

	Meaning	Chapter Term	Meaning
11. anti-	_____	_____	_____
12. auto-	_____	_____	_____

Suffixes

	Meaning	Chapter Term	Meaning
13. -ectasis	_____	_____	_____
14. -edema	_____	_____	_____
15. -gen	_____	_____	_____
16. -globulin	_____	_____	_____
17. -iasis	_____	_____	_____
18. -ist	_____	_____	_____
19. -oid	_____	_____	_____

(Continued)

Suffixes	Meaning	Chapter Term	Meaning
20. -pexy	_____	_____	_____
21. -therapy	_____	_____	_____
22. -toxic	_____	_____	_____

Worksheet 9B
Word Part Review

Directions: Write out the meaning for each combining form, prefix, and suffix.

Combining Forms   Meaning

1. cortic/o   _____
2. cyt/o   _____
3. system/o   _____

Prefixes

4. mono-   _____

Suffixes

5. -itis   _____
6. -logist   _____
7. -cyte   _____
8. -ectomy   _____
9. -genic   _____
10. -gram   _____
11. -graphy   _____
12. -logy   _____
13. -malacia   _____
14. -megaly   _____
15. -oma   _____
16. -osis   _____
17. -pathy   _____
18. -plasty   _____
19. -rrhaphy   _____
20. -stasis   _____

Worksheet 9C
Word Surgery

Directions: Below are terms built from word parts. Analyze each term by listing and defining the word parts used to build it.

Medical Term	Word Part Meanings
1. adenoiditis	
2. immunologist	
3. immunoglobulin	
4. lymphatic	
5. pathogen	
6. lymphadenosis	
7. phagocyte	
8. splenomalacia	
9. immunotherapy	
10. lymphangiectasis	
11. tonsillitis	

(*Continued*)

Medical Term	Word Part Meanings
12. lymphedema	_____
13. splenoid	_____
14. lymphangiogram	_____
15. thymic	_____
16. lymphadenectomy	_____
17. tonsillar	_____
18. lymphangiopathy	_____
19. pathology	_____
20. lymphoma	_____

Worksheet 9D
Word Search

Directions: Find and circle the answer for each fill-in-the-blank question in the word search puzzle.

1. Many functions of the immune system are carried out by cells called _____.

2. The _____ gland is an organ of the lymphatic system.

3. AIDS is the later stage of a(n) _____ infection.

4. A(n) _____ is a hypersensitivity to a common substance.

5. A(n) _____ disease results when the body's own immune system attacks healthy body cells.

6. _____ occurs when the immune system is unable to respond properly to pathogens.

7. _____ is the tissue response to injury.

8. The _____ test is a type of allergy testing.

9. _____ is the severe itching associated with hives.

10. Another term for vaccination is _____.

```
Y K R M M Q Y Z N K W I V L R K
C F Q H J A G N R L N D Q G K X
N T Z J F U M C M F D M R V K P
E Q M Y G T K M L S N C K K W R
I Z B Q Q O R A U E M W N Y R R
C P T C Y I M N R T K L M B F S
I L J T K M L L T Y K G R D U M
F C N L A M W V I C V X H M R N
E K A T D U H N C O T N Y B G F
D T I L Q N K B A H M H N N R R
O O V Y L E K L R P T V L M D T
N K P G H E G N I M H I V Y F D
U R T R G R R V A Y G N V H B G
M F L Z P N Y G F L R L N R C R
M H C T A R C S Y M R N G C N L
I N O I T A Z I N U M M I L G L
```

Worksheet 5E
Unscramble

Directions: Unscramble each medical term below. A definition for the term is given below each scrambled term.

1. i x o t t o y c c _____

   cell capable of killing pathogens or diseased cells

2. l a s t o p o i g t h _____

   one who studies disease

3. g y l r e a l _____

   hypersensitivity to common substance

4. n l m o c u n o e o i s s _____

   acute viral infection of lymphoid tissue

5. l n m i a n f a o i t m _____

   tissue response to injury

6. n p r o p u t o i s c i t _____

   infection in patients with compromised immune systems

7. c a n c n i a v i o t _____

   exposure to weakened pathogen to stimulate immunity

8. t a o h g n p e _____

   causes disease

9. e l e n p s _____

   organ that removes worn out erythrocytes

10. s e t l p o h c y m y _____

    white blood cells important to the immune system

Worksheet 9F
Abbreviations

Directions: Write the full term that each abbreviation stands for.

1. AIDS _____
2. ANA _____
3. ARC _____
4. ELISA _____
5. HD _____
6. HIV _____
7. Ig _____
8. KS _____
9. mono _____
10. NHL _____
11. PCP _____
12. SCIDS _____
13. T & A _____

Worksheet 9G
Case Study

Directions: Below is a case study presentation of a patient with a condition covered in this chapter. Read the case study and answer the questions below. Some questions will ask for information not included within this chapter. Use your text, a medical dictionary, or any other reference material you choose to answer these questions.

Patient is a 36-year-old businessman who was first seen in the office with complaints of feeling generally "run down," ascites, intermittent diarrhea, and weight loss. He states he has been aware of these symptoms for approximately six months, but admits it may have been "coming on" for closer to one year. A screening test for mononucleosis was negative. A chest X-ray was negative for pneumonia or bronchitis, but did reveal enlarged nodules in the left thoracic cavity. In spite of a 35-pound weight loss, he has abdominal swelling and splenomegaly detected with abdominal palpation. Abdominal ultrasound confirmed generalized splenomegaly and a 3-cm tumor in the spleen. A lymphangiogram identified the thoracic nodules to be enlarged lymph nodes. Biopsies taken from the splenic tumor and thoracic lymph nodes confirmed the diagnosis of non-Hodgkin lymphoma. The patient underwent splenectomy for removal of the primary tumor. He will be referred to an oncologist to begin treatment for the lymphadenomas.

1. What complaints caused the patient to go to the doctor?

2. One of these terms in your first answer has not yet been defined. Look it up in the Gastroenterology chapter and define the term.

3. Which tests were negative? What does the term negative mean in this situation?

4. Which tests revealed pathology?

5. What surgical procedure did he undergo?

6. What type of doctor was he referred to following surgery? Why?

Worksheet 9H
Web Destinations

Allergies

As stated at www.webmed.com/allergies, "At least one out of every 5 Americans suffers from allergies." Visit the website above; type "allergies overview" in the search box. Select the article titled "Allergies: Overview & Facts" from the list. Read through the information presented and write a summary covering:

- What are allergies
- Causes of allergies
- Risk factors for allergies
- Prevention of allergies
- Allergy treatment

HIV/AIDS

HIV/AIDS is a serious health topic that has a lot of misinformation circulating throughout our population. This makes it doubly important to be informed regarding this topic. Go to the Centers for Disease Control and Prevention HIV/AIDS site at www.cdc.gov/hiv. Type "basic information" in the search box and select the article entitled "Basic Information / Topics / CDC HIV/AIDS. Read through the information on this site and write a summary covering:

- What is HIV
- What is AIDS
- How HIV is and is not transmitted
- Risk factors for HIV transmission
- Prevention
- Symptoms
- HIV testing

Worksheet 9I
Professional Profile and Journal

Professional Profile

Medical Care

Physicians oversee patient care. They examine patients, diagnose diseases, order treatments, perform surgery, and educate patients on health issues. Physician assistants (PAs) and certified medical assistants (CMAs) assist physicians in direct patient care. PAs perform many of the tasks previously performed only by physicians. CMAs have a variety of duties ranging from front office management to routine medical duties. See Medical Terminology Interactive for a video on Physicians Assistants.

Doctor of Medicine (MD)

- Also known as allopathic physician
- Graduates from an approved 4-year medical school
- Passes national board examination and completes 3- to 8-year residency

Doctor of Osteopathy (DO)

- Osteopathic physician emphasizes the role of the musculoskeletal system in the health of the body
- Graduates from an approved 4-year osteopathic school
- Passes national board examination and completes internship and residency

Physician Assistant (PA)

- Performs tasks such as conducting physical examinations, ordering tests and treatments, making diagnoses, counseling patients, assisting in surgery, and writing prescriptions
- Works under the supervision of a physician
- Graduates from 2-year physician assistant program
- Passes national certification examination

Certified Medical Assistant (CMA)

- Duties may include record keeping, billing, preparing insurance forms, taking vital signs, and stocking examination rooms
- Works under the supervision of a physician
- Completes an accredited 1-year certificate or 2-year associate's degree clinical medical assistant program and passes a certification exam

For more information regarding these health careers, visit the following websites:

- American Academy of Physician Assistants at www.aapa.org
- American Association of Colleges of Osteopathic Medicine at www.aacom.org
- American Association of Medical Assistants at www.aama-ntl.org
- Association of American Medical Colleges at www.aamc.org

Professional Journal

In this exercise you will now have an opportunity to put the words you have learned into practice. Imagine yourself in the role of a physician assistant. If you refer back to the Professional Profile, you will see that this care professional is responsible for conducting physical examinations, ordering tests and treatments, and making diagnoses. Use the 10 words listed below to write sentences to describe the patients you saw today.

An example of a sentence is: *Due to her compromised immune system, the patient was provided detailed patient education on* **opportunistic infections**.

1. anaphylactic shock _____

2. hives _____

3. AIDS-related complex _____

4. allergy _____

5. inflammation _____

6. corticosteroids _____

7. Hodgkin disease _____

8. SCIDS _____

9. autoimmune disease _____

10. Kaposi sarcoma _____

Name _____ Date _____ Score _____

Chapter 9 Word Parts Quiz

Directions: Define the combining form, prefix, or suffix in the spaces provided.

1. immun/o _____
2. lymphaden/o _____
3. splen/o _____
4. adenoid/o _____
5. tonsill/o _____
6. lymphangi/o _____
7. thym/o _____
8. lymph/o _____
9. phag/o _____
10. path/o _____
11. cyt/o _____
12. system/o _____
13. anti- _____
14. auto- _____
15. -toxic _____
16. -therapy _____
17. -ectasis _____
18. -rrhaphy _____
19. -ist _____
20. -malacia _____
21. -pexy _____
22. -oid _____
23. -edema _____
24. -genic _____
25. -globulin _____

Name _____ Date _____ Score _____

Chapter 9 Spelling Quiz

Directions: Write each term as your instructor pronounces it.

1. _____
2. _____
3. _____
4. _____
5. _____
6. _____
7. _____
8. _____
9. _____
10. _____
11. _____
12. _____
13. _____
14. _____
15. _____
16. _____
17. _____
18. _____
19. _____
20. _____

Name _____ Date _____ Score _____

Chapter 9 Labeling Quiz

Directions: Label the organs of the immune system.

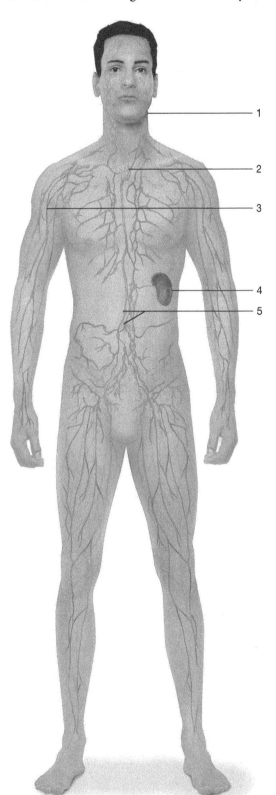

1. _____

2. _____

3. _____

4. _____

5. _____

174   Chapter 9/IMMUNOLOGY: IMMUNE SYSTEMS   © 2012 Pearson Education, Inc.

Name _____   Date _____   Score _____

Chapter 9 Word Building Quiz

Directions: Build a single medical term for each phrase below.

1. inflammation of adenoids _____

2. stopping lymph _____

3. cell poison _____

4. surgical removal of tonsils _____

5. thymus gland tumor _____

6. process of recording lymph nodes _____

7. pertaining to systems _____

8. suture of the spleen _____

9. one who studies disease _____

10. protection protein _____

11. dilated lymph vessel _____

12. eating cell _____

13. lymph cell tumor _____

14. surgical repair of lymph vessel _____

15. surgical removal of tonsils _____

16. abnormal condition of the lymph nodes _____

17. immunity treatment _____

18. resembling the spleen _____

19. lymph vessel record _____

20. disease of lymph nodes _____

Name _____ Date _____ Score _____

Chapter 9 Quiz

Fill-in-the-Blank

1. Anything that damages the body is called a(n) _____.

2. Lymphatic tissue located in the throat is called the _____.

3. Pain, redness, swelling and feeling hot to the touch are all signs of _____.

4. The _____ destroys worn out blood cells.

5. _____ are an example of phagocytic cells.

6. Lymph nodes are commonly called _____.

7. The latter stage of HIV infection is called _____.

8. The _____ is necessary early in life for proper development of the immune system.

9. SLE and sarcoidosis are examples of _____.

10. A(n) _____ test is considered more precise than ELISA.

Word Building

Build a term that means:

1. surgical removal of adenoids   _____

2. producing protection   _____

3. lymph swelling   _____

4. lymph node disease   _____

5. record of lymph vessels   _____

6. one who studies disease   _____

7. eating cell   _____

8. enlarged spleen   _____

9. pertaining to thymus gland   _____

10. inflammation of tonsils   _____

Matching

_____ 1. an opportunistic infection
_____ 2. mononucleosis
_____ 3. ELISA
_____ 4. inflammation
_____ 5. Kaposi sarcoma
_____ 6. hives
_____ 7. corticosteroids
_____ 8. vaccination
_____ 9. anaphylactic shock
_____ 10. T&A
_____ 11. scratch test
_____ 12. ARC
_____ 13. antinuclear antibody titer
_____ 14. cytotoxic cells
_____ 15. elephantiasis
_____ 16. immunodeficiency
_____ 17. SLE
_____ 18. sarcoidosis
_____ 19. allergy
_____ 20. autoimmune disease
_____ 21. lymphocyte
_____ 22. adenoids
_____ 23. SCIDS
_____ 24. immunosuppressant
_____ 25. antihistamines

a. life threatening allergy attack
b. a genetic condition
c. pharyngeal tonsils
d. immune system attacks body's normal tissue
e. immune system attacks connective tissue
f. fibrous lesions form in organs
g. medication to block immune system
h. *Pneumocystis carinii* pneumonia
i. cells that attack and kill pathogens
j. medication for allergy attacks
k. immunocompromised
l. lab test for AIDS
m. hypersensitivity to a common substance
n. tissue response to injury
o. skin cancer seen in AIDS patients
p. type of leukocyte
q. a test for allergies
r. blood test for autoimmune diseases
s. a surgical procedure
t. immunization
u. results from blocked lymph vessels
v. wheals
w. early stage of HIV infection
x. acute viral infection of lymphoid tissue
y. strong anti-inflammatory properties

Chapter 9 Answer Keys

Worksheet 9A Answer Key

1. adenoids
2. protection
3. lymph
4. lymph node
5. lymph vessel
6. disease
7. eating
8. spleen
9. thymus
10. tonsils
11. against
12. self
13. dilated
14. swelling
15. that which produces
16. protein
17. abnormal condition
18. specialist
19. resembling
20. surgical fixation
21. treatment
22. poison

Worksheet 9B Answer Key

1. cortex
2. cell
3. system
4. one
5. inflammation
6. one who studies
7. cell
8. surgical removal
9. producing
10. record
11. process of recording
12. study of
13. softening
14. enlarged
15. tumor
16. abnormal condition
17. disease
18. surgical repair
19. suture
20. stopping

Worksheet 9C Answer Key

1. adenoid/o = adenoids; -itis = inflammation
2. immun/o = immunity; -logist = one who studies
3. immun/o = protection; -globulin = protein
4. lymph/o = lymph; -atic = pertaining to
5. path/o = disease; -gen = that which produces
6. lymphaden/o = lymph node
7. phag/o = eating; -cyte = cell
8. splen/o = spleen; -malacia = softening
9. immun/o = immunity; -therapy = treatment
10. lymphangi/o = lymph vessel
11. tonsill/o = tonsils; -itis = inflammation
12. lymph/o = lymph; -edema = swelling
13. splen/o = spleen; -oid = resembling
14. lymphangi/o = lymph vessel
15. thym/o = thymus gland; -ic = pertaining to
16. lymphaden/o = lymph node
17. tonsill/o = tonsils; -ar = pertaining to
18. lymphangi/o = lymph vessel
19. path/o = disease; -logy = study of
20. lymph/o = lymph; -oma = tumor

Worksheet 9D Answer Key

1. lymphocytes
2. thymus
3. HIV
4. allergy
5. autoimmune
6. immunodeficiency
7. inflammation
8. scratch
9. urticaria
10. immunization

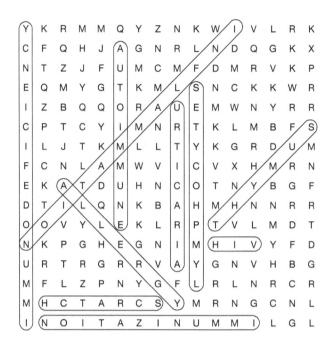

Worksheet 9E Answer Key

1. cytotoxic
2. pathologist
3. allergy
4. mononucleosis
5. inflammation
6. opportunistic
7. vaccination
8. pathogen
9. spleen
10. lymphocytes

Worksheet 9F Answer Key

1. acquired immunodeficiency syndrome
2. antinuclear antibody titer
3. AIDS-related complex
4. enzyme-linked immunosorbent assay
5. Hodgkin disease
6. human immunodeficiency virus (causes AIDS)
7. immunoglobulins (IgA, IgD, IgE, IgG, IgM)
8. Kaposi sarcoma
9. mononucleosis
10. non-Hodgkin lymphoma
11. *Pneumocystis carinii* pneumonia
12. severe combined immunodeficiency syndrome
13. tonsillectomy and adenoidectomy

Worksheet 9G Answer Key

1. Feeling run down, ascites, intermittent diarrhea, and weight loss
2. Ascites—accumulation of fluid in the abdominal cavity
3. Mononucleosis test; chest x-ray for pneumonia and bronchitis; negative means the condition being tested for is not present
4. Chest x-ray showed enlarged nodules in the chest; abdominal ultrasound showed splenomegaly and a tumor; lymphangiogram showed enlarged lymph nodes; biopsies revealed non-Hodgkin lymphoma
5. Splenectomy
6. Referred to an oncologist to begin cancer treatment

Worksheet 9H Answer Key

Essay activity, student answers will vary.

Worksheet 9I Answer Key

Student answers will vary.

Chapter 9 Word Parts Quiz Answer Key

1. protection
2. lymph node
3. spleen
4. adenoids
5. tonsils
6. lymph vessels
7. thymus gland
8. lymph
9. eating
10. disease
11. cell
12. system
13. against
14. self
15. poison
16. treatment
17. dilated
18. suture
19. specialist
20. softening
21. surgical fixation
22. resembling
23. swelling
24. producing
25. protein

Chapter 9 Spelling Quiz Answer Key

1. adenoiditis
2. sarcoidosis
3. immunotherapy
4. lymphatic
5. splenomegaly
6. lymphangiography
7. vaccination
8. lymphadenopathy
9. anaphylactic
10. urticaria
11. immunodeficiency
12. pathogens
13. antihistamine
14. corticosteroids
15. cytotoxic
16. elephantiasis
17. mononucleosis
18. erythematosus
19. immunosuppressant
20. antinuclear

Chapter 9 Word Building Quiz Answer Key

1. adenoiditis
2. lymphostasis
3. cytotoxic
4. tonsillectomy
5. thymoma
6. lymphadenography
7. systemic
8. splenorrhaphy
9. pathologist
10. immunoglobulin
11. lymphangiectasis
12. phagocyte
13. lymphocytoma
14. lymphangioplasty
15. tonsillectomy
16. lymphadenosis
17. immunotherapy
18. splenoid
19. lymphangiogram
20. lymphadenopathy

Chapter 9 Quiz Answer Key

Fill-in-the-Blank

1. pathogen
2. tonsils
3. inflammation
4. spleen
5. monocytes
6. lymph glands
7. AIDS
8. thymus gland
9. autoimmune diseases
10. Western blot

Word Building

1. adenoidectomy
2. immunogenic
3. lymphedema
4. lymphadenopathy
5. lymphangiogram
6. pathologist
7. phagocyte
8. splenomegaly
9. thymic
10. tonsillitis

Chapter 9 Labeling Quiz Answer Key

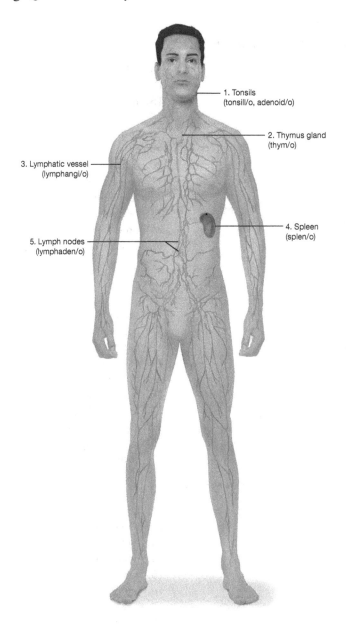

Matching

1. h
2. x
3. l
4. n
5. o
6. v
7. y
8. t
9. a
10. s
11. q
12. w
13. r
14. i
15. u
16. k
17. e
18. f
19. m
20. d
21. p
22. c
23. b
24. g
25. j

Chapter 10
Pulmonology: Respiratory System

Learning Objectives

After completing this chapter, students will be able to:

1. Understand the functions of the respiratory system.
2. Describe the medical specialty of pulmonology.
3. Define pulmonology-related combining forms, prefixes, and suffixes.
4. Identify the organs treated in pulmonology.
5. Build pulmonology medical terms from word parts.
6. Explain pulmonology medical terms.
7. Use pulmonology abbreviations.

Use this word list to focus your studying for the chapter test.

Alveolar	Hypoventilation	Tachypnea	CXR
Apnea	Hypoxia	Thoracic	ET
Asthma	Lobar	Thoracotomy	LLL
Bradypnea	Lobectomy	Thoracocentesis	LUL
Bronchial	Mediastinal	Tracheal	O2
Bronchitis	Orthopnea	Tracheostomy	PA view
Bronchodilator	Oximetry	Tracheotomy	PE
Bronchogenic	Pleural	Tuberculosis	PFT
Bronchoscopy	Pleurisy	Ventilator	PPD
Bronchospasm	Pleurocentesis		R
Croup	Pneumonectomy	**Abbreviations**	RLL
Cyanosis	Pneumonia		RML
Dyspnea	Pneumothorax	ABG's	RUL
Emphysema	Pulmonary embolism	AP view	SIDS
Endotracheal	Pulmonologist	CF	SOB
Eupnea	Purulent	CO2	TB
Hemoptysis	Spirometer	COPD	TPR
Hyperventilation	Sputum cytology	C & S	

Worksheet 10A
New Word Parts

Directions: Write out the meaning for each combining form, prefix, and suffix. Then locate a new term from the chapter that uses the word part.

Combining Forms	Meaning	Chapter Term	Meaning
1. alveol/o	_____	_____	_____
2. bronch/o	_____	_____	_____
3. bronchi/o	_____	_____	_____
4. bronchiol/o	_____	_____	_____
5. coni/o	_____	_____	_____
6. cyan/o	_____	_____	_____
7. lob/o	_____	_____	_____
8. mediastin/o	_____	_____	_____
9. ox/i	_____	_____	_____
10. pleur/o	_____	_____	_____
11. pneum/o	_____	_____	_____
12. pneumon/o	_____	_____	_____
13. pulmon/o	_____	_____	_____
14. spir/o	_____	_____	_____
15. thorac/o	_____	_____	_____
16. trache/o	_____	_____	_____

Prefixes

	Meaning	Chapter Term	Meaning
17. endo-	_____	_____	_____
18. eu-	_____	_____	_____

Suffixes

	Meaning	Chapter Term	Meaning
19. -centesis	_____	_____	_____
20. -ectasis	_____	_____	_____
21. -graph	_____	_____	_____

(*Continued*)

Suffixes	Meaning	Chapter Term	Meaning
22. -graphy	_____	_____	_____
23. -ia	_____	_____	_____
24. -meter	_____	_____	_____
25. -metry	_____	_____	_____
26. -ostomy	_____	_____	_____
27. -oxia	_____	_____	_____
28. -pnea	_____	_____	_____
29. -ptysis	_____	_____	_____
30. -thorax	_____	_____	_____

Worksheet 10B
Word Part Review

Directions: Write out the meaning for each combining form, prefix, and suffix.

Combining Forms   Meaning

1. angi/o   _____

2. arteri/o   _____

3. atel/o   _____

4. carcin/o   _____

5. cardi/o   _____

6. cyt/o   _____

7. embol/o   _____

8. fibr/o   _____

9. hem/o   _____

10. orth/o   _____

11. py/o   _____

Prefixes

12. a-   _____

13. an-   _____

14. brady-   _____

15. dys-   _____

16. hyper-   _____

17. hypo-   _____

18. tachy-   _____

Suffixes

19. -ectomy   _____

20. -genic   _____

21. -gram   _____

(Continued)

Suffixes	Meaning
22. -itis	_____
23. -logist	_____
24. -logy	_____
25. -ole	_____
26. -osis	_____
27. -otomy	_____
28. -plasty	_____
29. -scope	_____
30. -scopy	_____
31. -spasm	_____

Worksheet 10C
Word Surgery

Directions: Below are terms built from word parts. Analyze each term by listing and defining the word parts used to build it.

Medical Term	Word Part Meanings
1. bronchitis	_____
2. anoxia	_____
3. tachypnea	_____
4. pneumothorax	_____
5. pulmonary	_____
6. lobectomy	_____
7. hemoptysis	_____
8. spirograph	_____
9. mediastinotomy	_____
10. thoracostomy	_____
11. tracheal	_____

(*Continued*)

Medical Term	Word Part Meanings
12. bronchoscope	_____
13. atelectasis	_____
14. pneumoconiosis	_____
15. pyothorax	_____
16. endotracheal	_____
17. bronchiectasis	_____
18. thoracic	_____
19. pneumonotomy	_____
20. dyspnea	_____
21. alveolar	_____
22. pleurocentesis	_____
23. oximeter	_____
24. orthopnea	_____
25. cyanosis	_____

Worksheet 10D
Word Search

Directions: Find and circle the answer for each fill-in-the-blank question in the word search puzzle.

1. The body must have a constant supply of oxygen to produce _____ for the body.
2. _____ is also called suffocation.
3. _____ is a viral infection in children with a characteristic harsh cough.
4. _____ results in the destruction of alveolar walls.
5. Breathing too fast and too deep is called _____.
6. When phlegm is coughed up and expelled through the mouth it is called _____.
7. _____ is the inflammation of the pleura.
8. _____ may result in a collapsed lung.
9. The term _____ means containing pus.
10. A whistling or wheezing breath sound is called _____.

```
L  D  K  T  X  Z  M  C  R  O  U  P  J  H  R  N
T  V  V  W  K  B  N  Y  A  M  V  M  K  Y  X  L
C  G  X  J  V  N  W  I  X  N  L  R  C  P  A  Y
Q  V  X  M  F  T  X  P  G  G  Q  F  I  E  R  G
K  X  P  Z  K  Y  P  Q  K  H  R  H  M  R  O  R
L  K  L  W  H  T  R  Q  H  B  C  B  G  V  H  E
D  F  K  P  E  H  G  G  M  N  L  H  D  E  T  N
R  R  S  W  K  M  M  Z  O  T  K  T  F  N  O  E
M  A  T  J  K  M  P  H  V  Q  T  Z  M  T  M  R
J  N  K  N  N  K  R  H  S  J  G  Q  V  I  U  V
N  T  C  L  E  X  Q  P  Y  M  K  Q  F  L  E  F
J  Q  X  C  B  L  U  R  M  S  K  K  P  A  N  K
H  N  R  M  W  T  U  M  W  R  E  G  L  T  P  C
K  V  V  U  H  X  R  V  L  W  M  C  I  K  J
Y  D  Q  M  Y  S  I  R  U  E  L  P  A  O  G  C
T  T  R  D  N  J  Z  V  N  P  D  L  F  N  Y  L
```

190 Chapter 10/PULMONOLOGY: RESPIRATORY SYSTEM © 2012 Pearson Education, Inc.

Worksheet 10E
Unscramble

Directions: Unscramble each medical term below. A definition for the term is given below each scrambled term.

1. h h n r c i o _____

   abnormal whistling sound

2. b l c t r s s e i o u u _____

   infectious disease caused by the tubercle bacillus

3. h p y s m m a e e _____

   condition resulting from the destruction of alveolar walls

4. p m b c r h n s s a o o _____

   involuntary muscle spasm in a bronchus

5. l i y o v n t a i o p h e n t _____

   breathing too slow and too shallow

6. n a l f u n i z e _____

   viral infection with chills, fever, body aches, and dry cough

7. n i n m e u p o a _____

   death may occur as alveoli fill up with fluid

8. r e o n i t v a t l _____

   mechanical device that assists breathing

9. s c o a s i n y _____

   abnormal condition of being blue

10. p e s n a d y _____

    labored breathing

Worksheet 10F
Abbreviations

Directions: Write the full term that each abbreviation stands for.

1. ABGs _____
2. ARF _____
3. AP view _____
4. ARD _____
5. ARDS _____
6. Broncho _____
7. BS _____
8. CF _____
9. CO_2 _____
10. COLD _____
11. COPD _____
12. CPR _____
13. C&S _____
14. CTA _____
15. CXR _____
16. DOE _____
17. ET _____
18. flu _____
19. HMD _____
20. IPPB _____
21. IRDS _____
22. LLL _____
23. LUL _____
24. O_2 _____

(Continued)

25. PA view _____
26. PE _____
27. PFT _____
28. PPD _____
29. R _____
30. RD _____
31. RDS _____
32. RLL _____
33. RML _____
34. RR _____
35. RUL _____
36. SARS _____
37. SIDS _____
38. SOB _____
39. TB _____
40. TPR _____

Worksheet 10G
Case Study

Directions: Below is a case study presentation of a patient with a condition covered in this chapter. Read the case study and answer the questions below. Some questions will ask for information not included within this chapter. Use your text, a medical dictionary, or any other reference material you choose to answer these questions.

An 88-year-old female was seen in the physician's office complaining of SOB, dizziness, orthopnea, elevated temperature, and a productive cough. Lung auscultation revealed rales over the R bronchus. CXR revealed fluid in the RUL. The patient was sent to the hospital with an admitting diagnosis of pneumonia. Vital signs upon admission were: temperature 102°F, pulse 100 and rapid, respirations 24 and labored, blood pressure 180/110. She was treated with IV antibiotics and IPPB. She responded well to treatment and was released home to her family with oral antibiotics on the third day.

1. What is this patient's admitting diagnosis? Look this condition up in a reference source and include a short description of it.

   _____
   _____

2. List and define each of the patient's presenting symptoms in your own words.

   _____
   _____

3. Define auscultation and CXR. Describe what each revealed in your own words.

   _____
   _____

4. What does the term "vital signs" mean? Describe the patient's vital signs in your own words.

   _____
   _____

5. Describe the treatments she received while in the hospital in your own words.

   _____
   _____

6. Explain the change in her medication when she was discharged home.

   _____
   _____

Worksheet 10H
Web Destinations

Chronic Obstructive Pulmonary Disease (COPD)

The American Lung Association's website describes COPD the following way:

> Chronic obstructive pulmonary disease (COPD) is a term referring to two lung diseases, chronic bronchitis and emphysema, which are characterized by obstruction to airflow that interferes with normal breathing. Both of these conditions frequently co-exist, hence physicians prefer the term COPD.

Visit this website at http://www.lungusa.org. Type "COPD Fact Sheet" in the search box and select the article by the same name. Use this information to describe these two diseases, chronic bronchitis and emphysema, and how they are treated.

Asthma

The Asthma and Allergy Foundation of America's asthma website reports that each day, 14 people die from asthma. However, with proper treatment and management, most people should be able to keep their asthma under control to avoid life-threatening asthma attacks. It is important that all people with asthma follow their doctor's instructions and keep their emergency medications current and handy.

Visit this website at http://www.aafa.org and click on the Asthma tab. Read the information presented under each link in this tab and prepare a summary about what asthma is, who is at risk, what causes an asthma attack, and how asthma is treated.

Worksheet 10I
Professional Profile and Journal

Professional Profile

Respiratory Therapy

Respiratory therapists assist patients with respiratory illness and cardiopulmonary disorders. They carry out a wide variety of duties that include performing tests to assess pulmonary function, monitoring oxygen and carbon dioxide levels in the blood, administering breathing treatments, and educating the public on respiratory issues. Often, respiratory therapists are called in to handle emergency situations. They may be responsible for treating victims in distress, such as premature babies and drowning victims. Respiratory therapy services are found in acute and long-term care facilities, health maintenance organizations, and home health agencies. See Medical Terminology Interactive for a video on Respiratory Therapists.

Registered Respiratory Therapist (RRT)

- Develops and implements respiratory care plans, performs diagnostic tests, provides respiratory treatments, and participates in patient education
- Provides respiratory therapy as ordered by a physician
- Graduates from an accredited 2-year associate or 4-year bachelor's degree respiratory therapy program
- Completes clinical training
- Passes the national registry examination

Certified Respiratory Therapist (CRT)

- Performs general respiratory care procedures
- Works under the supervision of a physician or registered respiratory therapist
- Completes an accredited 2-year associate degree respiratory therapy program
- Completes clinical training
- Passes the national technician certification examination

For more information regarding these health careers, visit the following websites:

American Association for Respiratory Care at www.aarc.org
National Board for Respiratory Care at www.nbrc.org

Professional Journal

In this exercise you will now have an opportunity to put the words you have learned into practice. Imagine yourself in the role of a registered respiratory therapist. This healthcare professional is responsible for performing diagnostic tests, providing respiratory treatments, and participating in patient education. Use the 10 words listed below, or any other new terms from this chapter, to write sentences to describe the patients you saw today.

An example of a sentence is: *Following the* **percussion** *treatment, the patient coughed up* **purulent sputum**.

1. oxygen _____

2. adult respiratory distress syndrome _____

3. asthma _____

4. pulmonary function test _____

5. CPR _____

6. cystic fibrosis _____

7. pneumothorax _____

8. dyspnea _____

9. ventilator _____

10. rhonchi _____

Name _____ Date _____ Score _____

Chapter 10 Word Parts Quiz

Directions: Define the combining form, prefix, or suffix in the spaces provided.

1. alveol/o _____
2. bronch/o _____
3. bronchi/o _____
4. bronchiol/o _____
5. coni/o _____
6. cyan/o _____
7. lob/o _____
8. mediastin/o _____
9. ox/i _____
10. pleur/o _____
11. pneum/o _____
12. pneumon/o _____
13. pulmon/o _____
14. spir/o _____
15. thorac/o _____
16. trache/o _____
17. atel/o _____
18. orth/o _____
19. -centesis _____
20. -pnea _____
21. -thorax _____
22. -ptysis _____
23. -oxia _____
24. dys- _____
25. tachy- _____

Name _____ Date _____ Score _____

Chapter 10 Spelling Quiz

Directions: Write each term as your instructor pronounces it.

1. _____
2. _____
3. _____
4. _____
5. _____
6. _____
7. _____
8. _____
9. _____
10. _____
11. _____
12. _____
13. _____
14. _____
15. _____
16. _____
17. _____
18. _____
19. _____
20. _____

Name _____ Date _____ Score _____

Chapter 10 Labeling Quiz 1

Directions: Label the respiratory system organs in the thoracic cavity.

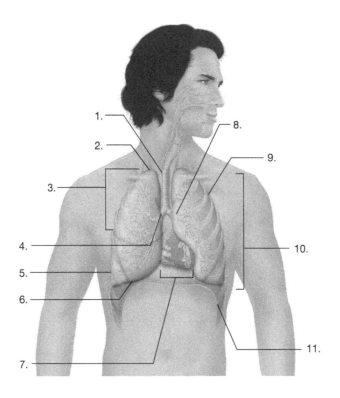

1. _____
2. _____
3. _____
4. _____
5. _____
6. _____
7. _____
8. _____
9. _____
10. _____
11. _____

Name _____ Date _____ Score _____

Chapter 10 Labeling Quiz 2

Directions: Label the microscopic structure of the lung.

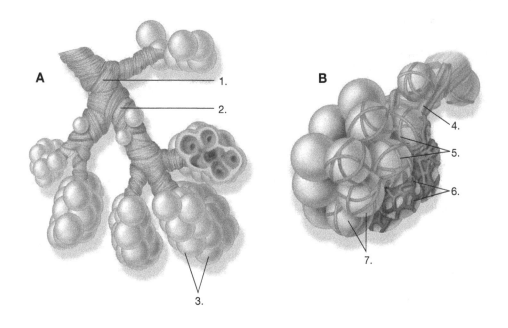

1. _____

2. _____

3. _____

4. _____

5. _____

6. _____

7. _____

Name _____ Date _____ Score _____

Chapter 10 Word Building Quiz

Directions: Build a single medical term for each phrase below.

1. inflammation of bronchus _____
2. abnormal condition of being blue _____
3. without oxygen _____
4. surgical removal of a lobe _____
5. small bronchus _____
6. pus in the chest _____
7. slow breathing _____
8. pertaining to the heart and lungs _____
9. process of measuring oxygen _____
10. instrument to record the lungs _____
11. spitting up blood _____
12. pertaining to the lungs _____
13. without breathing _____
14. abnormal condition of dust in the lungs _____
15. pertaining to the mediastinum _____
16. normal breathing _____
17. dilated bronchus _____
18. study of the lung _____
19. surgical repair of trachea _____
20. bronchus producing _____
21. cutting into the chest _____
22. pertaining to alveoli _____
23. instrument to measure breathing _____
24. pleural pain _____
25. create a new opening in the chest _____

Name _____ Date _____ Score _____

Chapter 10 Quiz

Fill-in-the-Blank

1. _____ is a lung tumor that originates in the bronchi.

2. Emphysema leads to overinflated _____.

3. _____ is a healthcare professional whose duties include administering oxygen therapy and measuring lung capacity.

4. The organs of the lower respiratory system include the: _____, _____, _____, and _____.

5. _____ means to inhale fluid or foreign object into the airways.

6. _____ is dangerous because the alveoli fill up with fluid.

7. A(n) _____ may result in a collapsed lung.

8. Pulmonary _____ injects dye into blood vessels of the lungs.

9. _____ uses gravity to promote drainage of lung secretions; treatment for CF.

10. Pulmonary _____ occurs when a blood clot blocks a branch of the pulmonary artery.

Word Building
Build a term that means:

1. dilated bronchus   _____
2. pertaining to a bronchiole   _____
3. record of bronchus   _____
4. surgical removal of lobe   _____
5. process of measuring oxygen   _____
6. puncture pleura to withdraw fluid   _____
7. slow breathing   _____
8. pus in chest   _____
9. instrument to measure breathing   _____
10. cutting into the trachea   _____

Matching

____ 1. pleura
____ 2. cystic fibrosis
____ 3. croup
____ 4. PFT
____ 5. oximeter
____ 6. rales
____ 7. trachea
____ 8. SARS
____ 9. hemoptysis
____ 10. ventilator
____ 11. ABGs
____ 12. cyanosis
____ 13. hypoxia
____ 14. orthopnea
____ 15. sputum cytology
____ 16. alveoli
____ 17. sputum C&S
____ 18. IRDS
____ 19. sweat test
____ 20. rhonchi
____ 21. hypopnea
____ 22. purulent
____ 23. pleural effusion
____ 24. sputum
____ 25. asphyxiation

a. fluid or gas in pleural cavity
b. tests for presence of cancerous cells
c. suffocation
d. test to identify and treat bacterial infection
e. air sacs
f. containing pus
g. test for cystic fibrosis
h. hyaline membrane disease
i. shallow breathing
j. wheezing breath sounds
k. genetic condition with thick mucus
l. breathe easier when sitting up
m. coughed up phlegm
n. having a blue color
o. crackling breath sound
p. protective sac around the lungs
q. worldwide epidemic in 2003
r. instrument to measure oxygen
s. respirator
t. using spirometer to test respiratory function
u. windpipe
v. having insufficient oxygen in the body
w. viral infection with harsh cough, found in children
x. spitting up blood
y. blood test for levels of O_2 and CO_2

Chapter 10 Answer Keys

Worksheet 10A Answer Key

1. alveolus; air sac
2. bronchus
3. bronchus
4. bronchiole
5. dust
6. blue
7. lobe
8. mediastinum
9. oxygen
10. pleura
11. lung, air
12. lung
13. lung
14. breathing
15. chest
16. trachea, windpipe
17. within
18. normal
19. puncture to withdraw fluid
20. dilated, expansion
21. instrument for recording
22. process of recording
23. state of
24. instrument to measure
25. process of measuring
26. create a new opening
27. oxygen
28. breathing
29. spitting
30. chest

Worksheet 10B Answer Key

1. vessel
2. artery
3. incomplete
4. cancer
5. heart
6. cell
7. plug
8. fibrous
9. blood
10. straight
11. pus
12. without
13. without
14. slow
15. abnormal, labored
16. excessive
17. insufficient
18. fast
19. surgical removal
20. producing
21. record
22. inflammation
23. one who studies
24. study of
25. small
26. abnormal condition
27. cutting into
28. surgical repair
29. instrument for viewing
30. process of visually examining
31. involuntary, strong muscle contraction

Worksheet 10C Answer Key

1. bronch/o = bronchus; -itis = inflammation
2. an- = without; -oxia = oxygen
3. tachy- = fast; -pnea = breathing
4. pneum/o = air; -thorax = chest
5. pulmon/o = lung; -ary = pertaining to
6. lob/o = lobe; -ectomy = surgical removal
7. hem/o = blood; -ptysis = spitting
8. spir/o = breathing; -graph = instrument to measure
9. mediastin/o = mediastinum; -otomy = cutting into
10. thorac/o = chest; -ostomy = create a new opening
11. trache/o = trachea; -al = pertaining to
12. bronch/o = bronchus; -scope = instrument for viewing
13. atel/o = incomplete; -ectasis = dilation
14. pneum/o = lung; coni/o = dust; -osis = abnormal condition
15. py/o = pus; -thorax = chest
16. endo- = within; trache/o = trachea; -al = pertaining to
17. bronchi/o = bronchus; -ectasis = dilated
18. thorac/o = chest; -ic = pertaining to
19. pneumon/o = lung; -otomy = cutting into
20. dys- = difficult, labored; -pnea = breathing
21. alveol/o = alveolus; -ar = pertaining to

22. pleur/o = pleura; -centesis = puncture to withdraw fluid
23. ox/i = oxygen; -meter = instrument for measuring
24. orth/o = straight; -pnea = breathing
25. cyan/o = blue; -osis = abnormal condition

Worksheet 10D Answer Key

1. energy
2. asphyxia
3. croup
4. emphysema
5. hyperventilation
6. sputum
7. pleurisy
8. pneumothorax
9. purulent
10. rhonchi

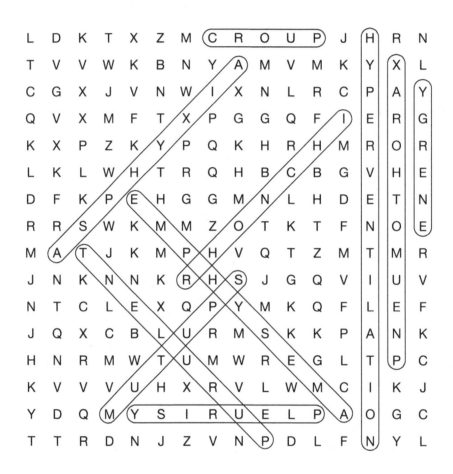

Worksheet 10E Answer Key

1. rhonchi
2. tuberculosis
3. emphysema
4. bronchospasm
5. hypoventilation
6. influenza
7. pneumonia
8. ventilator
9. cyanosis
10. dyspnea

Worksheet 10F Answer Key

1. arterial blood gases
2. acute respiratory failure
3. anteroposterior view in radiology
4. acute respiratory disease
5. adult respiratory distress syndrome
6. bronchoscopy
7. breath sounds
8. cystic fibrosis
9. carbon dioxide
10. chronic obstructive lung disease
11. chronic obstructive pulmonary disease
12. cardiopulmonary resuscitation
13. sputum culture and sensitivity
14. clear to auscultation
15. chest x-ray
16. dyspnea upon exertion
17. endotracheal
18. influenza
19. hyaline membrane disease
20. intermittent positive pressure breathing
21. infant respiratory distress syndrome
22. left lower lobe
23. left upper lobe
24. oxygen
25. posteroanterior view in radiology
26. pulmonary embolus
27. pulmonary function test
28. purified protein derivative (tuberculin test)
29. respirations
30. respiratory disease
31. respiratory distress syndrome
32. right lower lobe
33. right middle lobe
34. respiratory rate
35. right upper lobe
36. severe acute respiratory syndrome
37. sudden infant death syndrome
38. shortness of breath
39. tuberculosis
40. temperature, pulse, and respiration

Worksheet 10G Answer Key

1. Pneumonia—acute inflammatory condition of lung which can be caused by bacterial and viral infections, diseases, and chemicals; symptoms include severe dyspnea and death may result when alveoli fill with fluid
2. SOB—shortness of breath; dizziness; orthopnea—most comfortable breathing when sitting up; elevated temperature; productive cough—coughing up sputum
3. Auscultation—to listen to body sounds—revealed rales which is a crackling sound; CXR is a chest x-ray—revealed fluid in the right upper lobe of the lung
4. Vital signs are measurements of temperature, pulse, respiratory rate, and blood pressure used to assess a person's general state of health and the function of the heart and lungs; this patient's vital signs are: temperature 102°F, pulse 100 and rapid, respirations 24 and labored, blood pressure 180/110
5. IV antibiotics—medicine to kill bacteria given into the veins; IPPB—method of artificial ventilation using mask connected to machine that produces pressure to assist air to fill lungs
6. The IV antibiotics were changed to oral antibiotics—she started taking pills

Worksheet 10H Answer Key

Essay activity, student answers will vary.

Worksheet 10I Answer Key

Student answers will vary.

Chapter 10 Word Parts Quiz Answer Key

1. alveolus; air sac
2. bronchus
3. bronchus
4. bronchiole
5. dust
6. blue
7. lobe
8. mediastinum
9. oxygen
10. pleura

11. lung, air
12. lung
13. lung
14. breathing
15. chest
16. trachea, windpipe
17. incomplete
18. straight
19. puncture to withdraw fluid
20. breathing
21. chest
22. spitting
23. oxygen
24. difficult, labored
25. fast

Chapter 10 Spelling Quiz Answer Key

1. bronchioles
2. mediastinum
3. bronchiectasis
4. hemoptysis
5. orthopnea
6. rhonchi
7. asphyxiation
8. asthma
9. bronchodilator
10. resuscitation
11. emphysema
12. endotracheal
13. anoxia
14. pneumoconiosis
15. phlegm
16. pleurisy
17. pneumothorax
18. tuberculosis
19. ventilator
20. cardiopulmonary

Chapter 10 Labeling Quiz 1 Answer Key

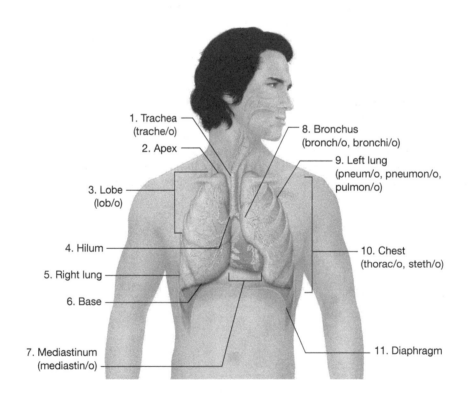

1. Trachea (trache/o)
2. Apex
3. Lobe (lob/o)
4. Hilum
5. Right lung
6. Base
7. Mediastinum (mediastin/o)
8. Bronchus (bronch/o, bronchi/o)
9. Left lung (pneum/o, pneumon/o, pulmon/o)
10. Chest (thorac/o, steth/o)
11. Diaphragm

Chapter 10 Labeling Quiz 2 Answer Key

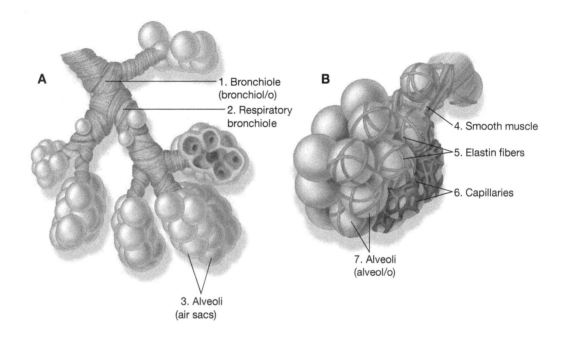

Chapter 10 Word Building Quiz Answer Key

1. bronchitis
2. cyanosis
3. anoxia
4. lobectomy
5. bronchiole
6. pyothorax
7. bradypnea
8. cardiopulmonary
9. oximetry
10. pneumograph
11. hemoptysis
12. pulmonary or pneumonic
13. apnea
14. pneumoconiosis
15. mediastinal
16. eupnea
17. bronchiectasis
18. pulmonology
19. tracheoplasty
20. bronchogenic
21. thoracotomy
22. alveolar
23. spirometer
24. pleurodynia or pleuralgia
25. thoracostomy

Chapter 10 Quiz Answer Key

Fill-in-the-Blank

1. bronchogenic carcinoma
2. alveoli
3. respiratory therapist
4. trachea, bronchi, lungs, pleura
5. aspirate
6. pneumonia
7. pneumothorax
8. angiography
9. postural drainage
10. embolism

Word Building

1. bronchiectasis
2. bronchiolar
3. bronchogram
4. lobectomy
5. oximetry
6. pleurocentesis
7. bradypnea
8. pyothorax
9. spirometer
10. tracheotomy

Matching

1. p
2. k
3. w
4. t
5. r
6. o
7. u
8. q
9. x
10. s
11. y
12. n
13. v
14. l
15. b
16. e
17. d
18. h
19. g
20. j
21. i
22. f
23. a
24. m
25. c

Chapter 11
Gastroenterology: Digestive System

Learning Objectives

After completing this chapter, students will be able to:

1. Understand the functions of the digestive system.
2. Describe the medical specialty of gastroenterology.
3. Define gastroenterology-related combining forms, prefixes, and suffixes.
4. Identify the organs treated in gastroenterology.
5. Build gastroenterology medical terms from word parts.
6. Explain gastroenterology medical terms.
7. Use gastroenterology abbreviations.

Use this word list to focus your studying for the chapter test.

Anal	Esophagitis	Rectocele
Appendicitis	Gastralgia	Sigmoidoscopy
Appendectomy	Gastrectomy	
Cholelithiasis	Gastric	**Abbreviations**
Cholecystectomy	Gastritis	
Cholecystitis	Gastroenteritis	Ba
Colitis	Gastroenterologist	BE
Colonoscopy	Gastroscopy	BM
Colorectal	Hematemesis	BS
Colostomy	Hepatic	EGD
Diverticulitis	Hepatitis	GB
Diverticulosis	Hyperemesis	GERD
Duodenal	Ileostomy	GI
Duodenostomy	Jejunal	IBD
Dyspepsia	Laparotomy	N&V
Dysphagia	Laparoscopy	TPN
Enteric	Pancreatic	UGI
Esophageal	Polyphagia	

Worksheet 11A
New Word Parts

Directions: Write out the meaning for each combining form, prefix, and suffix. Then locate a new term from the chapter that uses the word part.

Combining Forms	Meaning	Chapter Term	Meaning
1. an/o	_____	_____	_____
2. appendic/o	_____	_____	_____
3. append/o	_____	_____	_____
4. chol/e	_____	_____	_____
5. cholangi/o	_____	_____	_____
6. cholecyst/o	_____	_____	_____
7. choledoch/o	_____	_____	_____
8. col/o	_____	_____	_____
9. colon/o	_____	_____	_____
10. diverticul/o	_____	_____	_____
11. duoden/o	_____	_____	_____
12. enter/o	_____	_____	_____
13. esophag/o	_____	_____	_____
14. gastr/o	_____	_____	_____
15. hepat/o	_____	_____	_____
16. ile/o	_____	_____	_____
17. jejun/o	_____	_____	_____
18. lapar/o	_____	_____	_____
19. lith/o	_____	_____	_____
20. pancreat/o	_____	_____	_____
21. polyp/o	_____	_____	_____

(*Continued*)

Combining Forms	Meaning	Chapter Term	Meaning
22. proct/o	_____	_____	_____
23. rect/o	_____	_____	_____
24. sigmoid/o	_____	_____	_____

Suffixes

	Meaning	Chapter Term	Meaning
25. -cele	_____	_____	_____
26. -emesis	_____	_____	_____
27. -ostomy	_____	_____	_____
28. -pepsia	_____	_____	_____
29. -phagia	_____	_____	_____
30. -ptosis	_____	_____	_____
31. -tripsy	_____	_____	_____

Worksheet 11B
Word Part Review

Directions: Write out the meaning for each combining form, prefix, and suffix.

Combining Form   **Meaning**

1. hemat/o   _____

Suffixes

2. -algia   _____

3. -dynia   _____

4. -ectomy   _____

5. -gram   _____

6. -graphy   _____

7. -iasis   _____

8. -itis   _____

9. -logist   _____

10. -logy   _____

11. -oma   _____

12. -osis   _____

13. -otomy   _____

14. -plasty   _____

15. -scope   _____

16. -scopy   _____

Prefixes

17. a-   _____

18. brady-   _____

19. dys-   _____

20. hyper-   _____

21. poly-   _____

Worksheet 11C
Word Surgery

Directions: Below are terms built from word parts. Analyze each term by listing and defining the word parts used to build it.

Medical Term   Word Part Meanings

1. anal   _____

   _____

2. appendicitis   _____

   _____

3. cholelithiasis   _____

   _____

4. cholangiogram   _____

   _____

5. cholecystectomy   _____

   _____

6. choledocholithotripsy _____

   _____

7. colorectal   _____

   _____

8. colonoscopy   _____

   _____

9. diverticulosis   _____

   _____

10. duodenal   _____

    _____

11. hematemesis   _____

    _____

(*Continued*)

Medical Term	Word Part Meanings
12. enteric	
13. esophagitis	
14. esophagoplasty	
15. gastroenteritis	
16. gastralgia	
17. hepatoma	
18. pancreatic	
19. dysphagia	
20. laparotomy	
21. polyposis	
22. rectocele	
23. sigmoidoscope	
24. proctoptosis	
25. bradypepsia	

Worksheet 11D
Word Search

Directions: Find and circle the answer for each fill-in-the-blank question in the word search puzzle.

1. _____ refers to chronic liver disease.

2. Esophageal _____ is the congenital lack of a connection between esophagus and stomach.

3. _____ means varicose veins in the rectum.

4. _____ occurs when one section of intestine telescopes into another section.

5. The term _____ describes very dark, tarry stools due to presence of blood.

6. _____ is feeling the urge to vomit.

7. _____ occurs when a length of bowel becomes twisted around itself.

8. _____ is a term describing the accumulation of fluid in the abdominal cavity.

9. _____ refers to the yellow skin color associated with liver disease.

10. Esophageal _____ are varicose veins in the esophagus.

```
I  M  R  P  V  N  D  N  T  C  M  L  Z  F  S
T  N  D  H  E  M  O  R  R  H  O  I  D  S  I
M  Q  T  H  V  Z  R  R  Y  L  G  F  L  M  S
E  M  L  U  X  M  Q  S  A  F  R  Z  M  C  O
C  E  R  T  S  N  T  I  E  R  N  Q  M  N  H
I  L  Y  L  D  S  S  N  L  T  S  T  A  V  R
D  E  R  M  M  E  U  J  T  E  I  U  K  V  R
N  N  P  K  R  P  Z  S  C  M  S  C  J  M  I
U  A  F  T  T  H  N  I  C  E  N  V  S  P  C
A  Y  A  L  H  D  R  G  A  E  T  F  N  A  M
J  B  W  F  N  A  N  M  N  W  P  T  C  M  M
M  T  L  X  V  F  W  K  K  Y  C  T  L  K  H
G  Q  X  S  U  L  U  V  L  O  V  C  I  G  F
V  F  K  G  L  Y  M  T  C  L  C  L  K  O  M
L  K  R  R  D  D  D  C  W  Y  P  C  N  H  N
```

Worksheet 11E
Unscramble

Directions: Unscramble each medical term below. A definition for the term is given below each scrambled term.

1. g o o l m g c n h a a i r _____

    an x-ray film of a common bile duct

2. o p p o y c l e y m t _____

    surgical excision of polyps

3. c p t o o o s r g l t i _____

    medical specialist in the study of the rectum and anus

4. h r i c r o i s s _____

    chronic liver disease

5. o m r s h i r h d e o _____

    varicose veins in the rectum

6. n t s e d y e y r _____

    condition with pain, diarrhea, and blood and mucus in the stool

7. s a t g o n e r r e i t i s t _____

    inflammation of stomach and small intestines

8. m s e a h m e s e t i _____

    vomiting blood

9. a i n e d j c u _____

    yellow skin color associated with liver disease

10. m i r i t c v u l u e d _____

    small abnormal pouch that forms off intestinal or colon wall

Worksheet 11F
Abbreviations

Directions: Write the full term that each abbreviation stands for.

1. Ba _____
2. BE _____
3. BM _____
4. BS _____
5. CBD _____
6. CUC _____
7. EGD _____
8. ERCP _____
9. GB _____
10. GERD _____
11. GI _____
12. IBD _____
13. IBS _____
14. N & V _____
15. O & P _____
16. PUD _____
17. TPN _____
18. UGI _____

Worksheet 11G
Case Study

Directions: Below is a case study presentation of a patient with a condition covered in this chapter. Read the case study and answer the questions below. Some questions will ask for information not included within this chapter. Use your text, a medical dictionary, or any other reference material you choose to answer these questions.

A 70-year-old female has come into the office complaining about "difficult digestion, acid backing up into the esophagus, difficulty swallowing, and vomiting blood." Over the past 10 years, she reports that an x-ray of her bowels, that required an enema containing barium be given to her by the x-ray technician, revealed some small mushroom-shaped tumors in her colon, and a gallstone condition requiring surgical removal of her gallbladder. The physician ordered several diagnostic procedures with the following results: an FOBT confirmed melena, *H. pylori* antibody test was positive for presence of bacteria, and gastroscopy did reveal an active PUD.

1. What pathological condition does this patient currently have? Look this condition up in a reference source and include a short description of it.

   _____

   _____

2. What is the medical term for each of this patient's complaints?

   _____

   _____

3. What is the medical term for each of the procedures or conditions she has had over the past 10 years?

   _____

   _____

4. Describe the diagnostic procedures performed at this time in your own words.

   _____

   _____

5. Describe the results of each test.

   _____

   _____

6. What is the location of this patient's peptic ulcer? What are other common locations for digestive system ulcers?

   _____

   _____

Worksheet 11H
Web Destinations

Peptic Ulcer Disease

Recent research has shown that the majority of peptic ulcers appear to be caused by a bacterium, *Helicobacter pylori*. Visit the following National Institute of Diabetes, Digestive, and Kidney Diseases peptic ulcer website at http://www.niddk.nih.gov. Type "h pylori and peptic ulcer" into the search box and select the article titled "H. pylori and Peptic Ulcer." Write a summary of the information, including, what *Helicobacter pylori* is and how it causes an ulcer, the signs and symptoms of an ulcer, and how ulcers are diagnosed and treated.

Gallstones

According to the National Institute of Diabetes and Digestive and Kidney Diseases website, several populations of people have been identified as having a higher risk of developing gallstones. These groups include:

- Women
- Persons over age 60
- American Indians
- Mexican Americans
- Overweight men and women
- People who gain or lose a lot of weight quickly
- People with a family history of gallstones
- Diabetics
- People who take cholesterol-lowering drugs

Visit this organizations website at http://www2.niddk.nih.gov. Type "Gallstones" into the search box and select the articled titled "Gallstones." From the information presented on this page, write a summary including what gallstones are and how they form, the signs and symptoms of gallstone disease, and the diagnosis and treatment of gallstones.

Worksheet 11I
Professional Profile and Journal

Professional Profile

Dietetics

Registered dietitians are specialists in food and nutrition. Their duties include using diet to prevent and treat diseases, educating the public regarding good nutrition, and advancing the science of how diet and nutrition affect our bodies. Dietitians are found in many settings. Clinical dietitians work in hospitals and nursing homes, evaluating and adjusting patients' diets to treat illness. Consultant dietitians work with individual clients or facilities. Educator dietitians teach the science of nutrition to healthcare workers and dietitian students. Research dietitians engage in nutritional research for the food industry, government, and pharmaceutical companies. Business and management dietitians work in the food industry ensuring the nutritional quality of food served to the public. See Medical Terminology Interactive for a video on Registered Dietitians.

Registered Dietitian (RD)

- Promotes health and prevents or treats illnesses through diet modification and nutritional education
- Graduates from a 4-year baccalaureate degree program accredited by the American Dietetic Association
- Completes a 6- to 12-month internship
- Passes a certification exam

Dietetic Technician, Registered (DTR)

- Assists registered dietitian
- Graduates from an accredited 2-year associate's degree program
- Completes period of supervised practical experience
- Passes registration exam

Dietetic Assistant

- Assists registered dietitian
- Completes on-the-job training program

For more information regarding these health careers, visit the following websites:

- American Dietetic Association at www.eatright.org
- Society for Nutrition Education at www.sne.org

Professional Journal

In this exercise you will now have an opportunity to put the words you have learned into practice. Imagine yourself in the role of a dietitian. If you refer back to the Professional Profile, you will see that this healthcare professional uses diet to prevent and treat diseases, educates the public regarding good nutrition, and advances the science of how diet and nutrition affect our bodies. Use the 10 words listed below, or any other new terms from this or previous chapters, to write sentences to describe the patients you saw today.

An example of a sentence is: *The patient was newly diagnosed with* **hypertension** *and required instruction in a low-salt diet.*

1. peptic ulcer disease _____

2. dysentery _____

3. gastroesophageal reflux disease _____

4. total parenteral nutrition _____

5. iron-deficiency anemia _____

6. gastroenteritis _____

7. diverticulosis _____

8. dyspepsia _____

9. cholecystitis _____

10. aphagia _____

Name _____ Date _____ Score _____

Chapter 11 Word Parts Quiz

Directions: Define the combining form, prefix, or suffix in the spaces provided.

1. duoden/o _____
2. col/o _____
3. gastr/o _____
4. appendic/o _____
5. diverticul/o _____
6. cholecyst/o _____
7. jejun/o _____
8. sigmoid/o _____
9. chol/e _____
10. proct/o _____
11. ile/o _____
12. enter/o _____
13. polyp/o _____
14. esophag/o _____
15. pancreat/o _____
16. an/o _____
17. lapar/o _____
18. choledoch/o _____
19. -emesis _____
20. -pepsia _____
21. -phagia _____
22. -ptosis _____

(Continued)

23. poly- _____

24. dys- _____

25. brady- _____

Name _____ Date _____ Score _____

Chapter 11 Spelling Quiz

Directions: Write each term as your instructor pronounces it.

1. _____
2. _____
3. _____
4. _____
5. _____
6. _____
7. _____
8. _____
9. _____
10. _____
11. _____
12. _____
13. _____
14. _____
15. _____
16. _____
17. _____
18. _____
19. _____
20. _____

Name _____ Date _____ Score _____

Chapter 11 Labeling Quiz

Directions: Label the organs of the digestive system.

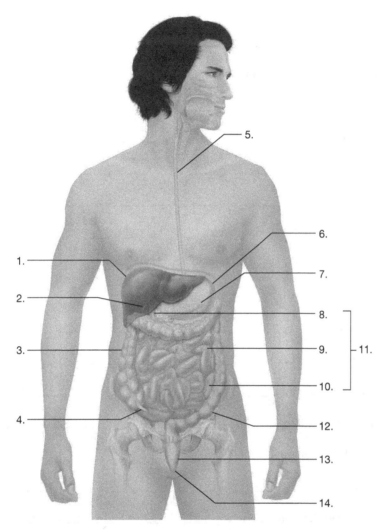

1. _____   8. _____
2. _____   9. _____
3. _____   10. _____
4. _____   11. _____
5. _____   12. _____
6. _____   13. _____
7. _____   14. _____

Name _____ Date _____ Score _____

Chapter 11 Word Building Quiz

Directions: Build a single medical term for each phrase below.

1. study of rectum and anus _____
2. excessive eating _____
3. surgical removal of polyp _____
4. surgically create a new opening in jejunum _____
5. liver tumor _____
6. surgical removal of appendix _____
7. without digestion _____
8. drooping rectum and anus _____
9. abnormal condition of having diverticula _____
10. process of visually examining sigmoid colon _____
11. pertaining to the duodenum _____
12. pertaining to anus _____
13. study of stomach and small intestine _____
14. record of common bile duct _____
15. pertaining to the esophagus _____
16. condition of having gallstones _____
17. protrusion of rectum _____
18. instrument to visually examine colon _____
19. process of recording gallbladder _____
20. pancreas inflammation _____
21. vomiting blood _____
22. surgical crushing of stone in common bile duct _____
23. instrument to visually examine abdomen _____
24. colon inflammation _____
25. stomach pain _____

Name _____   Date _____   Score _____

Chapter 11 Quiz

Fill-in-the-Blank

1. Another name for the digestive system is the _____ system.
2. The _____ is a small pouch attached to the cecum.
3. Bile aids in _____ digestion.
4. The _____ stores bile that is made by the liver.
5. The three sections of the small intestines are the _____, _____, and _____.
6. A medical term meaning excessive vomiting is _____.
7. An instrument used to visually examine the stomach is called a(n) _____.
8. The _____ produces digestive enzymes for food digestion.
9. A _____ is a small mushroom-shaped tumor growing in the colon.
10. The accessory organs for digestion are the _____, _____, and _____.

Word Building
Build a term that means:

1. difficult digestion   _____
2. pertaining to the colon   _____
3. create new opening in ileum   _____
4. surgical repair of esophagus   _____
5. gallbladder inflammation   _____
6. surgical removal of stomach   _____
7. abnormal condition of diverticula   _____
8. cutting into the abdomen   _____
9. pancreas inflammation   _____
10. gallbladder record   _____

Matching

____ 1. ascites
____ 2. esophageal atresia
____ 3. gastric bypass
____ 4. *H. pylori*
____ 5. melena
____ 6. O&P
____ 7. GERD
____ 8. IBS
____ 9. volvulus
____ 10. barium enema
____ 11. jaundice
____ 12. hemorrhoids
____ 13. esophageal varices
____ 14. FOBT
____ 15. nausea
____ 16. intussusception
____ 17. cirrhosis
____ 18. bradypepsia
____ 19. barium swallow
____ 20. dysentery
____ 21. diverticulum
____ 22. total parenteral nutrition
____ 23. Crohn disease
____ 24. ileus
____ 25. cecum

a. varicose veins in esophagus
b. nutrient solution given directly into bloodstream
c. slow digestion
d. lower GI series
e. abnormal pouch forms off intestinal wall
f. inflammatory bowel disease, mainly in ileum
g. varicose veins in rectum
h. section of large intestine
i. chronic liver disease
j. upper GI series
k. dark, tarry stools
l. obstructed intestines
m. spastic colon
n. pain, diarrhea, and bloody mucus in stool
o. may cause peptic ulcers
p. test for parasites and their eggs in stool
q. fluid accumulating in abdominal cavity
r. intestine telescopes into itself
s. stomach stapling
t. twisted intestines
u. no connection between stomach and esophagus
v. yellow skin color from liver disease
w. stomach acid backs up into esophagus
x. urge to vomit
y. test for blood in stool

Chapter 11 Answer Keys

Worksheet 11A Answer Key

1. anus
2. appendix
3. appendix
4. bile
5. bile duct
6. gallbladder
7. common bile duct
8. colon
9. colon
10. diverticulum
11. duodenum
12. intestine
13. esophagus
14. stomach
15. liver
16. ileum
17. jejunum
18. abdomen
19. stone
20. pancreas
21. polyps
22. rectum and anus
23. rectum
24. sigmoid colon
25. protrusion
26. vomit
27. surgically create an opening
28. digestion
29. eat, swallow
30. dropping
31. surgical crushing

Worksheet 11B Answer Key

1. blood
2. pain
3. pain
4. surgical removal
5. record
6. process of recording
7. abnormal condition
8. inflammation
9. one who studies
10. study of
11. tumor
12. abnormal condition
13. cutting into
14. surgical repair
15. instrument for viewing
16. process of viewing
17. without
18. slow
19. painful, difficult
20. excessive
21. many

Worksheet 11C Answer Key

1. an/o = anus; -al = pertaining to
2. appendic/o = appendix; -itis = inflammation
3. chol/e = bile; lith/o = stone; -iasis = condition
4. cholangi/o = bile ducts; -gram = record
5. cholecyst/o = gallbladder; -ectomy = surgical removal
6. choledoch/o = common bile duct; lith/o = stone; -tripsy = surgical crushing
7. col/o = colon; rect/o = rectum; -al = pertaining to
8. colon/o = colon; -scopy = process of visually examining
9. diverticu/o = diverticulum; -osis = abnormal condition
10. duoden/o = duodenum; -al = pertaining to
11. hemat/o = blood; -emesis = vomiting
12. enter/o = small intestine; -ic = pertaining to
13. esophag/o = esophagus; -itis = inflammation
14. esophag/o = esophagus; -plasty = surgical repair
15. gastr/o = stomach; enter/o = small intestine; -itis = inflammation
16. gastr/o = stomach; -algia = pain
17. hepat/o = liver; -oma = tumor
18. pancreat/o = pancreas; -ic = pertaining to
19. dys- = difficult; -phagia = swallowing
20. lapar/o = abdomen; -otomy = cutting into
21. polyp/o = polyp; -osis = abnormal condition
22. rect/o = rectum; -cele = protrusion
23. sigmoid/o = sigmoid colon; -scope = instrument for viewing
24. proct/o = rectum and anus; -ptosis = dropping
25. brady- = slow; -pepsia = digestion

Worksheet 11D Answer Key

1. cirrhosis
2. atresia
3. hemorrhoids
4. intussusception
5. melena
6. nausea
7. volvulus
8. ascites
9. jaundice
10. varices

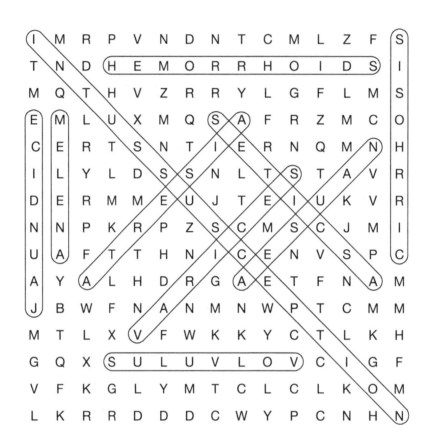

Worksheet 11E Answer Key

1. cholangiogram
2. polypectomy
3. proctologist
4. cirrhosis
5. hemorrhoids
6. dysentery
7. gastroenteritis
8. hematemesis
9. jaundice
10. diverticulum

Worksheet 11F Answer Key

1. barium
2. barium enema
3. bowel movement
4. bowel sounds
5. common bile duct
6. chronic ulcerative colitis
7. esophagogastroduodenoscopy
8. endoscopic retrograde cholangiopancreatography
9. gallbladder
10. gastroesophageal reflux disease

11. gastrointestinal
12. inflammatory bowel disease
13. irritable bowel syndrome
14. nausea and vomiting
15. ova and parasites
16. peptic ulcer disease
17. total parenteral nutrition
18. upper gastrointestinal series

Worksheet 11G Answer Key

1. Peptic ulcer disease
2. Difficult digestion—dyspepsia; acid backing up into esophagus—gastroesophageal reflux disease; difficulty swallowing—dysphagia; vomiting blood—hematemesis
3. X-ray of bowel after a enema—barium enema; small mushroom shaped tumors—polyposis; gallstone condition—cholelithiasis; surgical removal of gallbladder—cholecystectomy
4. FOBT (fecal occult blood test)—determines if a microscopic amount of blood is in the stool; *H. pylori* antibody test—blood test for presence of the bacteria that may cause peptic ulcers; gastroscopy—visually examine the inside of the stomach
5. FOBT revealed melena (blood in the stools), *H. pylori* antibody test indicated exposure to the bacteria that causes ulcers; gastroscopy revealed an ulcer in the stomach
6. In her stomach; duodenum (small intestine) and esophagus

Worksheet 11H Answer Key

Essay activity, student answers will vary.

Worksheet 11I Answer Key

Student answers will vary.

Chapter 11 Word Parts Quiz Answer Key

1. duodenum
2. colon
3. stomach
4. appendix
5. diverticulum
6. gallbladder
7. jejunum
8. sigmoid colon
9. bile
10. rectum and anus
11. ileum
12. intestine
13. polyps
14. esophagus
15. pancreas
16. anus
17. abdomen
18. common bile duct
19. vomit
20. digestion
21. eat, swallow
22. drooping
23. many
24. painful, difficult
25. slow

Chapter 11 Spelling Quiz Answer Key

1. gastrointestinal
2. diverticulosis
3. dysentery
4. intussusception
5. volvulus
6. polyposis
7. cholelithiasis
8. cholangiography
9. choledocholithotripsy
10. gallbladder
11. gastroenterologist
12. ascites

13. cirrhosis
14. atresia
15. varices
16. hemorrhoids
17. jaundice
18. sigmoidoscopy
19. jejunostomy
20. proctoptosis

Chapter 11 Labeling Quiz Answer Key

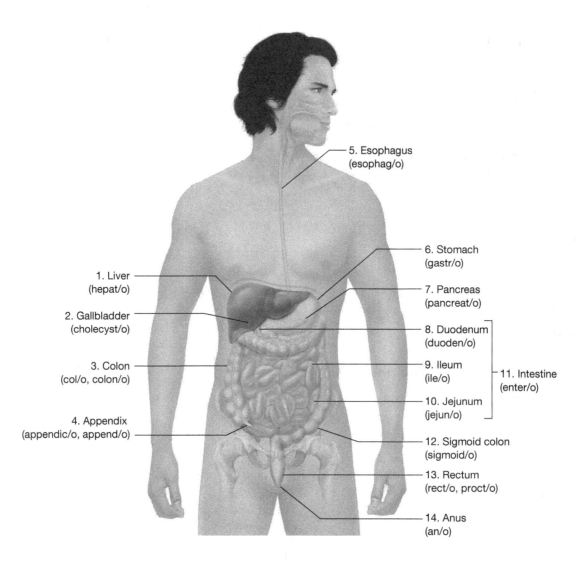

Chapter 11 Word Building Quiz Answer Key

1. proctology
2. polyphagia
3. polypectomy
4. jejunostomy
5. hepatoma
6. appendectomy
7. apepsia
8. proctoptosis
9. diverticulosis
10. sigmoidoscopy
11. duodenal
12. anal
13. gastroenterology
14. cholangiogram
15. esophageal
16. cholelithiasis
17. rectocele
18. colonoscope

19. cholecystography
20. pancreatitis
21. hematemesis
22. choledocholithotripsy
23. laparoscope
24. colitis
25. gastralgia or gastrodynia

Chapter 11 Quiz Answer Key

Fill-in-the-Blank

1. gastrointestinal
2. appendix
3. fat
4. gallbladder
5. duodenum, jejunum, ileum
6. hyperemesis
7. gastroscope
8. pancreas
9. polyp
10. liver, gallbladder, pancreas

Word Building

1. dyspepsia
2. colonic
3. ileostomy
4. esophagoplasty
5. cholecystitis
6. gastrectomy
7. diverticulosis
8. laparotomy
9. pancreatitis
10. cholecystogram

Matching

1. q
2. u
3. s
4. o
5. k
6. p
7. w
8. m
9. t
10. d
11. v
12. g
13. a
14. y
15. x
16. r
17. i
18. c
19. j
20. n
21. e
22. b
23. f
24. l
25. h

Chapter 12
Urology and Nephrology: Urinary System and Male Reproductive System

Learning Objectives

After completing this chapter, students will be able to:

1. Understand the functions of the urinary and male reproductive systems.
2. Describe the medical specialties of urology and nephrology.
3. Define urology- and nephrology-related combining forms, prefixes, and suffixes.
4. Identify the organs treated in urology and nephrology.
5. Build urology and nephrology medical terms from word parts.
6. Explain urology and nephrology medical terms.
7. Use urology and nephrology abbreviations.

Use this word list to focus your studying for the chapter test.

Albuminuria	Hydrocele	Prostatitis	**Abbreviations**
Anuria	Lithotripsy	Pyelonephritis	
Aspermia	Nephrolithiasis	Renal	BPH
Calculus	Nephrologist	Seminal	BUN
Chlamydia	Nephrology	Spermatogenesis	CC
Circumcision	Nephromegaly	Spermatolysis	Cysto
Cystitis	Nephroptosis	Syphilis	ESWL
Cystocele	Nephropexy	Testicular	GU
Cystoscopy	Nocturia	Uremia	HPV
Dysuria	Oligospermia	Urinalysis	I & O
Epididymitis	Oliguria	Urinary	IVP
Enuresis	Orchidectomy	Urologist	KUB
Frequency	Orchialgia	Urology	PSA
Genital Herpes	Orchitis	Ureteral	STD
Glycosuria	Cryptorchism	Urethritis	TURP
Gonorrhea	(cryptorchidism)	Vasectomy	UA
Hematuria	Polyuria	Vasorrhaphy	UTI
Hesitancy			

Worksheet 12A
New Word Parts

Directions: Write out the meaning for each combining form, prefix, and suffix. Then locate a new term from the chapter that uses the word part.

Combining Forms	Meaning	Chapter Term	Meaning
1. balan/o			
2. cyst/o			
3. epididym/o			
4. glomerul/o			
5. lith/o			
6. nephr/o			
7. orchid/o			
8. orchi/o			
9. orch/o			
10. prostat/o			
11. pyel/o			
12. ren/o			
13. semin/i			
14. spermat/o			
15. sperm/o			
16. testicul/o			
17. ur/o			
18. ureter/o			
19. urethr/o			
20. urin/o			
21. vas/o			
22. vesicul/o			

(*Continued*)

Prefixes	Meaning	Chapter Term	Meaning
23. extra-	_____	_____	_____
24. poly-	_____	_____	_____
25. trans-	_____	_____	_____

Suffixes

	Meaning	Chapter Term	Meaning
26. -cele	_____	_____	_____
27. -lith	_____	_____	_____
28. -ptosis	_____	_____	_____
29. -tripsy	_____	_____	_____
30. -uria	_____	_____	_____

Worksheet 12B
Word Part Review

Directions: Write out the meaning for each combining form, prefix, and suffix.

Combining Forms   Meaning

1. azot/o _____
2. bacteri/o _____
3. corpor/o _____
4. crypt/o _____
5. genit/o _____
6. glycos/o _____
7. hemat/o _____
8. hem/o _____
9. hydr/o _____
10. noct/i _____
11. olig/o _____
12. py/o _____
13. rect/o _____
14. ven/o _____

Prefixes

15. a- _____
16. an- _____
17. dys- _____
18. hyper- _____
19. intra- _____

Suffixes

20. -algia _____
21. -cyte _____

(Continued)

Suffixes	Meaning
22. -ectomy	
23. -emia	
24. -genesis	
25. -gram	
26. -graphy	
27. -itis	
28. -logist	
29. -logy	
30. -lysis	
31. -megaly	
32. -meter	
33. -oma	
34. -ostomy	
35. -otomy	
36. -pathy	
37. -pexy	
38. -plasty	
39. -rrhaphy	
40. -rrhea	
41. -sclerosis	
42. -scope	
43. -scopy	
44. -stenosis	
45. -trophy	

Worksheet 12C
Word Surgery

Directions: Below are terms built from word parts. Analyze each term by listing and defining the word parts used to build it.

Medical Term   Word Part Meanings

1. balanorrhea   _____
                           _____

2. cystocele   _____
                           _____

3. cystalgia   _____
                           _____

4. epididymal   _____
                           _____

5. lithotripsy   _____
                           _____

6. nephromegaly   _____
                           _____

7. nephrosis   _____
                           _____

8. orchidectomy   _____
                           _____

9. orchiopexy   _____
                           _____

10. cryptorchism   _____
                            _____

11. vasovasostomy   _____
                            _____

(*Continued*)

Medical Term	Word Part Meanings
12. prostatitis	_____
13. pyelonephritis	_____
14. renography	_____
15. spermatolysis	_____
16. aspermia	_____
17. testicular	_____
18. ureterostenosis	_____
19. urethroplasty	_____
20. dysuria	_____
21. oliguria	_____
22. urinometer	_____
23. uremia	_____
24. vasorrhaphy	_____
25. vesiculectomy	_____

Worksheet 12D
Word Search

Directions: Find and circle the answer for each fill-in-the-blank question in the word search puzzle.

1. Another term for a stone is _____.
2. _____ is the removal of the prepuce.
3. Feeling the urge to urinate more often than normal is called _____.
4. Difficulty initiating the flow of urine is called _____.
5. _____ is the accumulation of fluid within the scrotum.
6. A narrowing of the prepuce of the glans penis is called _____.
7. A semen analysis evaluates the semen for _____.
8. _____ is the inability to produce children.
9. _____ cancer is commonly seen in young men or boys.
10. _____ is feeling the need to urinate immediately.

```
H  R  H  K  Y  R  J  H  X  F  G  N  V
Y  F  R  E  Q  U  E  N  C  Y  O  R  T
D  R  C  H  S  C  R  H  B  I  T  A  P
R  Y  N  C  P  I  V  X  S  S  Q  L  Y
O  Q  C  F  C  K  T  I  N  U  B  U  T
C  X  C  N  Z  Y  C  A  P  L  W  C  I
E  L  Q  W  E  M  K  H  N  U  K  I  L
L  N  Z  B  U  G  I  Q  Y  C  M  T  I
E  B  M  C  T  M  R  K  K  L  Y  S  R
T  K  R  F  O  X  T  U  W  A  N  E  E
R  I  L  S  M  K  P  J  M  C  Y  T  T
C  N  I  T  Q  V  N  B  K  V  P  R  S
L  S  K  Y  T  I  L  I  T  R  E  F  T
```

Worksheet 12E
Unscramble

Directions: Unscramble each medical term below. A definition for the term is given below each scrambled term.

1. m s r e t g a i o s e n e p s _____

    sperm producing

2. n i r u y i s a l s _____

    physical, chemical, and microscopic examination of urine

3. a y l m a h d i c _____

    bacterial sexually transmitted disease

4. l e y d o i s h m a s i _____

    using artificial kidney machine to filter waste from blood

5. c a i r o v e c l e _____

    varicose veins in scrotum

6. t a h c t e i r e a t i z n o _____

    inserting flexible tube into bladder

7. n h r i c t o o m i a i s s _____

    protozoan sexually transmitted disease

8. l a a h b o r n e a r _____

    discharge from glans penis

9. r u i a p y _____

    pus in the urine

10. c a e m v t o s y _____

    surgical removal of vas deferens

Worksheet 12F
Abbreviations

Directions: Write the full term that each abbreviation stands for.

1. ARF _____
2. BPH _____
3. BUN _____
4. cath _____
5. CC _____
6. CRF _____
7. C & S _____
8. cysto _____
9. DRE _____
10. ESRD _____
11. ESWL _____
12. GU _____
13. HD _____
14. HPV _____
15. I & O _____
16. IVP _____
17. KUB _____
18. PKD _____
19. PSA _____
20. RP _____
21. STD _____
22. TUR _____
23. TURP _____
24. U/A, UA _____

(Continued)

25. UC _____

26. UTI _____

27. VUCG _____

Worksheet 12G
Case Study

Directions: Below is a case study presentation of a patient with a condition covered in this chapter. Read the case study and answer the questions below. Some questions will ask for information not included within this chapter. Use your text, a medical dictionary, or any other reference material you choose to answer these questions.

A 32-year-old female is seen in the urologist's office because of a fever, chills, and generalized fatigue. She also reported urgency, frequency, dysuria, and hematuria. In addition, she noticed that her urine was cloudy with a fishy odor. The physician ordered the following tests: a clean catch specimen for a U/A, a urine C&S, and a KUB. The U/A revealed pyuria and bacteriuria. A common type of bacteria was grown in the culture. X-rays reveal acute pyelonephritis resulting from cystitis which has spread up to the kidney from the bladder. The patient was placed on an antibiotic and encouraged to "push fluids" by drinking 2L of water a day.

1. This patient has two urinary system infections in different locations; name them. Which one caused the other and how? Look these conditions up in a reference source and include a short description of each.

   _____
   _____

2. List and define each of the patient's presenting symptoms that are medical terms in your own words.

   _____
   _____

3. What diagnostic tests did the urologist order? Describe them in your own words.

   _____
   _____

4. Explain the results of each diagnostic test in your own words.

   _____
   _____

5. What were the physician's treatment instructions for this patient? Explain the purpose of each treatment.

   _____
   _____

6. Go to www.mayoclinic.com and type "urinalysis results" in the search box. Select the results entitled Urinalysis. Then list the things a dipstick tests for.

   _____
   _____

Worksheet 12H
Web Destinations

Kidney Stones

The National Kidney and Urologic Diseases Information Clearinghouse found at http://www.niddk.nih.gov gives the following overview of kidney stones:

> Kidney stones, one of the most painful of the urologic disorders, are not a product of modern life. Scientists have found evidence of kidney stones in a 7,000-year-old Egyptian mummy. Unfortunately, kidney stones are among the most common disorders of the urinary tract; more than 1 million cases were diagnosed in 1996. An estimated 10 percent of people in the United States will have a kidney stone at some point in their lives. Men tend to be affected more frequently than women.

Most kidney stones pass out of the body without any intervention by a physician. Stones that cause lasting symptoms or other complications may be treated by various techniques, most of which do not involve major surgery. Also, research advances have led to a better understanding of the many factors that promote stone formation.

Go to this website. Type "Kidney stones in adults" in the search box and select the article with the same title. Use the information on this webpage to write a summary of the following topics:

- What is a kidney stone?
- What causes kidney stones?
- What are the symptoms?
- How are kidney stones diagnosed?
- How are kidney stones treated?
- Surgical treatment

Kidney Transplant

Some day you may be in a position to help someone make a decision regarding whether or not to donate a kidney. Visit the National Kidney Foundation's website at http://www.kidney.org. Type "25 facts about organ donation and transplantation" and select the Fact Sheet with the same title. Use the information presented on the webpage to write an argument in favor of organ donation.

Worksheet 12I
Professional Profile and Journal

Professional Profile

Health Information Management

Health information management professionals maintain accurate, orderly, and permanent records of each patient's condition and treatment. They also prepare patient information for release as appropriate to health personnel, insurance companies, researchers, lawyers, and the courts. They work in acute and long-term care facilities, health maintenance organizations, clinics, physicians' offices, public health departments, and insurance companies. See Medical Terminology Interactive for a video on Medical Transcriptionists.

Registered Health Information Administrator (RHIA)

- Directs the functioning of a health information department
- Graduates from an accredited 4-year bachelor's degree program in health information administration
- Passes national certification examination

Registered Health Information Technician (RHIT)

- Makes certain that medical records are complete and accurate
- Graduates from an accredited 2-year associate's degree program in health information technology
- Passes national certification examination

Certified Coding Specialist (CCS)

- Classifies medical information using an established coding system for billing and insurance purposes
- Graduates from an accredited 2-year associate's degree program in health information technology
- Passes national certification examination

Medical Transcriptionist

- Transcribes dictated medical notes
- Completes a vocational education program or receives on-the-job training
- May opt to take an examination to become a certified medical transcriptionist (CMT)

For more information regarding these health careers, visit the following websites:

- Association for Healthcare Documentation Integrity at www.ahdionline.org
- American Health Information Management Association at www.ahima.org

Professional Journal

In this exercise you will now have an opportunity to put the words you have learned into practice. Imagine yourself in the role of a registered health information technician. If you refer back to the Professional Profile, you will see that this healthcare professional is responsible for checking that healthcare records are accurate and complete. Double check the 10 sentences below to find terms that are either misspelled or used incorrectly and correct them. Terms may have come from this chapter or any previous chapter.

Example: A gastroscopy was inserted into the patient's stomach to look for an ulcer.

The suffix *-scopy* means *a procedure of visually examining inside an organ*, while the suffix *-scope* refers to the *instrument used to examine inside an organ*. This sentence is referring to the instrument being inserted into the stomach, so the correct sentence is *A gastroscope was inserted into the patient's stomach to look for an ulcer.*

1. The patient was diagnosed with a stomach tumor that required a gastrektomy.

2. The child was suspected of having a bladder infection and was referred to a nephrologist.

3. A urethrectomy was performed for sterilization purposes.

4. Listening to the patient's chest revealed wheezing within her lungs, leading to the diagnosis of an interpulmonary infection.

5. The patient complained of urgency because he had to urinate more often than normal.

6. The doctor carefully explained to the patient that hemodialysis removed waste by placing a chemically balanced solution into the peritoneal cavity.

7. Vasorrhea was performed to sew up the tear in the vas deferens.

8. A BUN was performed to test for prostatic cancer.

9. The patient had bradycardia and required medicine to slow down his heart rate.

10. Circumcision was necessary to treat the patient's hydrocele.

Name _____ Date _____ Score _____

Chapter 12 Word Parts Quiz

Directions: Define the combining form, prefix, or suffix in the spaces provided.

1. epididym/o _____
2. pyel/o _____
3. glomerul/o _____
4. nephr/o _____
5. ur/o _____
6. spermat/o _____
7. testicul/o _____
8. prostat/o _____
9. orchid/o _____
10. urethr/o _____
11. ren/o _____
12. semin/i _____
13. cyst/o _____
14. ureter/o _____
15. orch/o _____
16. balan/o _____
17. py/o _____
18. olig/o _____
19. glycos/o _____
20. crypt/o _____
21. -uria _____
22. -tripsy _____
23. -lith _____
24. trans- _____
25. extra- _____

Name _____   Date _____   Score _____

Chapter 12 Spelling Quiz

Directions: Write each term as your instructor pronounces it.

1. _____
2. _____
3. _____
4. _____
5. _____
6. _____
7. _____
8. _____
9. _____
10. _____
11. _____
12. _____
13. _____
14. _____
15. _____
16. _____
17. _____
18. _____
19. _____
20. _____

Name _____ Date _____ Score _____

Chapter 12 Labeling Quiz 1

Directions: Label the organs of the urinary system.

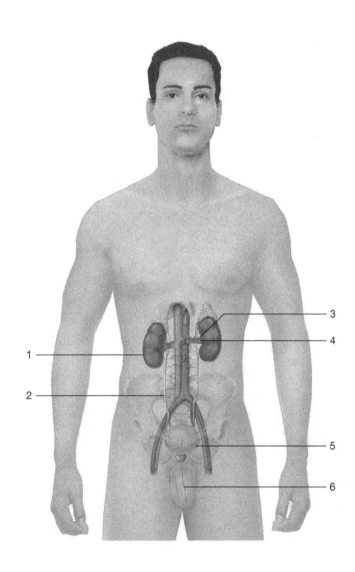

1. _____   4. _____
2. _____   5. _____
3. _____   6. _____

Name _____ Date _____ Score _____

Chapter 12 Labeling Quiz 2

Directions: Label the organs of the male reproductive system.

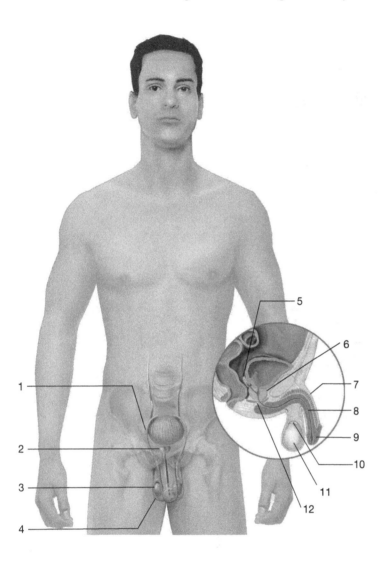

1. _____
2. _____
3. _____
4. _____
5. _____
6. _____
7. _____
8. _____
9. _____
10. _____
11. _____
12. _____

Name _____   Date _____   Score _____

Chapter 12 Word Building Quiz

Directions: Build a single medical term for each phrase below.

1. surgical removal of testes _____
2. inflammation of glans penis _____
3. create a new opening into urethra _____
4. pertaining to the kidney _____
5. condition of semen in the urine _____
6. instrument to visually examine bladder _____
7. generates sperm _____
8. drooping kidney _____
9. state of hidden testes _____
10. inflammation of renal pelvis and kidney _____
11. state of without sperm _____
12. sugar urine condition _____
13. bladder stone _____
14. one who studies urine _____
15. surgical fixation of testes _____
16. bacteria urine condition _____
17. inflammation of epididymis _____
18. pertaining to the prostate gland _____
19. suture the vas deferens _____
20. urethra pain _____
21. abnormal condition of stone in ureter _____
22. narrowing of the ureter _____
23. kidney tumor _____
24. night urine condition _____
25. surgical removal of seminal vesicle _____

Name _____ Date _____ Score _____

Chapter 12 Quiz

Fill-in-the-Blank

1. The urinary system is responsible for maintaining _____, a stable internal environment.

2. When urine is released from the bladder it flows out through the _____.

3. The urinary system and male reproductive system may be referred to together as the _____ system.

4. Nephrology is different from urology because it specializes in treating diseases affecting the _____.

5. The _____ stores sperm made by the _____.

6. Each kidney consists of thousands of _____.

7. Each testes secretes the male hormone, _____.

8. A new opening created on the surface of the body is called a(n) _____.

9. The kidneys are connected to the bladder by the _____.

10. Albuminuria means there is _____ in the urine.

Word Building

Build a term that means:

1. epididymis inflammation   _____

2. surgical fixation of testes   _____

3. discharge from glans penis   _____

4. condition of scanty sperm   _____

5. surgical repair of urethra   _____

6. instrument to measure urine   _____

7. enlarged kidney   _____

8. surgical crushing of a stone   _____

9. process of recording the bladder   _____

10. surgical removal of prostate gland   _____

Matching

_____ 1. BUN
_____ 2. hesitancy
_____ 3. calculus
_____ 4. urinary incontinence
_____ 5. prepuce
_____ 6. polycystic kidney disease
_____ 7. hydrocele
_____ 8. ESWL
_____ 9. phimosis
_____ 10. BPH
_____ 11. varicocele
_____ 12. urgency
_____ 13. nocturia
_____ 14. hemodialysis
_____ 15. erectile dysfunction
_____ 16. IVP
_____ 17. PSA
_____ 18. bladder
_____ 19. transurethral resection
_____ 20. chlamydia
_____ 21. sterility
_____ 22. frequency
_____ 23. circumcision
_____ 24. renal failure
_____ 25. digital rectal exam

a. non-cancerous enlargement of prostate gland
b. inability to produce children
c. also called impotence
d. kidney x-ray
e. surgical removal of prepuce
f. urge to urinate more often than normal
g. exam for presence of enlarged prostate gland
h. inability of kidneys to filter wastes
i. stores urine
j. difficulty initiating flow of urine
k. an STD
l. blood test for prostate gland cancer
m. uses machine to filter impurities from blood
n. accumulation of fluid in scrotum
o. foreskin
p. surgical treatment for BPH
q. narrowing of the prepuce
r. urination at night
s. blood test of kidney function
t. stone
u. involuntary urination
v. inherited kidney disease
w. treatment for urinary system stones
x. varicose veins in scrotum
y. feeling need to urinate immediately

Chapter 12 Answer Keys

Worksheet 12A Answer Key

1. glans penis
2. bladder
3. epididymis
4. glomerulus
5. stone
6. kidney
7. testes
8. testes
9. testes
10. prostate gland
11. renal pelvis
12. kidney
13. semen
14. sperm
15. sperm
16. testicle
17. urine
18. ureter
19. urethra
20. urine
21. vas deferens
22. seminal vesicle
23. outside of
24. many
25. across
26. hernia, protrusion
27. stone
28. drooping
29. crushing
30. urine condition

Worksheet 12B Answer Key

1. nitrogen waste
2. bacteria
3. body
4. hidden
5. genitals
6. sugar, glucose
7. blood
8. blood
9. water
10. night
11. scanty
12. pus
13. rectum
14. vein
15. without
16. without
17. abnormal
18. excessive
19. within
20. pain
21. cell
22. surgical removal
23. blood condition
24. produces, generates
25. record, picture
26. process of recording
27. inflammation
28. one who studies
29. study
30. destruction
31. enlargement
32. instrument for measuring
33. tumor, mass
34. surgically create an opening
35. cutting into
36. disease
37. surgical fixation
38. surgical repair
39. suture
40. discharge, flow
41. hardened condition
42. instrument for viewing
43. process of visually examining
44. narrowing
45. development

Worksheet 12C Answer Key

1. balan/o = glans penis; -rrhea = discharge, flow
2. cyst/o = bladder; -cele = protrusion
3. cyst/o = bladder; -algia = pain
4. epididym/o = epididymis; -al = pertaining to
5. lith/o = stone; -tripsy = surgical crushing
6. nephr/o = kidney; -megaly = enlarged
7. nephr/o = kidney; -osis = abnormal condition
8. orchid/o = testes; -ectomy = surgical removal
9. orchi/o = testes; -pexy = surgical fixation
10. crypt/o = hidden; orch/o = testes; -ism = state of
11. vas/o = vas deferens; vas/o = vas deferens; -ostomy = create a new opening
12. prostat/o = prostate gland; -itis = inflammation
13. pyel/o = renal pelvis; nephr/o = kidney; -itis = inflammation
14. ren/o = kidney; -graphy = process of recording

15. spermat/o = sperm; -lysis = destruction
16. a- = without; sperm/o = sperm; -ia = state
17. testicul/o = testicle; -ar = pertaining to
18. ureter/o = ureter; -stenosis = narrowing
19. urethr/o = urethra; -plasty = surgical repair
20. dys- = difficult/painful; -uria = urine condition
21. olig/o = scanty; -uria = urine condition
22. urin/o = urine; -meter = instrument to measure
23. ur/o = urine; -emia = blood condition
24. vas/o = vas deferens; -rrhaphy = suture
25. vesicul/o = seminal vesicle; -ectomy = surgical removal

Worksheet 12D Answer Key

1. calculus
2. circumcision
3. frequency
4. hesitancy
5. hydrocele
6. phimosis
7. fertility
8. sterility
9. testicular
10. urgency

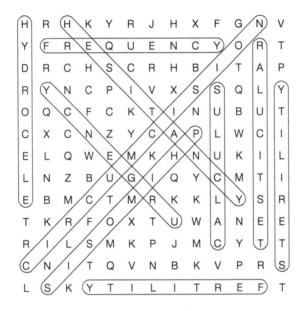

Worksheet 12E Answer Key

1. spermatogenesis
2. urinalysis
3. chlamydia
4. hemodialysis
5. varicocele
6. catheterization
7. trichomoniasis
8. balanorrhea
9. pyuria
10. vasectomy

Worksheet 12F Answer Key

1. acute renal failure
2. benign prostatic hypertrophy
3. blood urea nitrogen
4. catheterization
5. clean-catch urine specimen
6. chronic renal failure
7. culture and sensitivity test
8. cystoscopy
9. digital rectal exam
10. end stage renal disease
11. extracorporeal shock-wave lithotripsy
12. genitourinary
13. hemodialysis
14. human papilloma virus
15. intake and output
16. intravenous pyelogram
17. kidney, ureter, bladder
18. polycystic kidney disease
19. prostate-specific antigen
20. retrograde pyelogram
21. sexually transmitted disease
22. transurethral resection
23. transurethral resection and prostatectomy
24. urinalysis
25. urine culture
26. urinary tract infection
27. voiding urethrocystography

Worksheet 12G Answer Key

1. Cystitis and pyelonephritis
2. Fever; chills; fatigue; urgency—feeling the need to urinate immediately; frequency—urge to urinate more often than normal; dysuria—difficult or painful urination; hematuria—blood in the urine; urine that was not clear and smelled bad
3. Clean catch specimen—collecting an uncontaminated urine sample; U/A (urinalysis) – a physical, chemical, and microscopic examination of the urine; urine C&S (culture & sensitivity)—test for the presence and identification of bacteria in the urine; KUB (kidney, ureters, and bladder)—an x-ray of the urinary organs
4. Pyuria—pus in the urine; bacteriuria—bacteria in the urine; culture and sensitivity revealed a common type of bacteria; KUB—pyelonephritis
5. Antibiotic—to kill the bacteria; push fluids—to flush out the bladder
6. acidity, concentration, protein, sugar, ketones, bilirubin, evidence of infection, blood

Worksheet 12H Answer Key

Essay activity, student answers will vary.

Worksheet 12I Answer Key

1. The patient was diagnosed with a stomach ulcer that required a *gastrectomy*.
2. The child was suspected of having a bladder infection and was referred to a *urologist*.
3. A *vasectomy* was performed for sterilization purposes.
4. Listening to the patient's chest revealed wheezing within her lungs, leading to the diagnosis of an *intrapulmonary* infection.
5. The patient complained of *frequency* because he had to urinate more often than normal.
6. The doctor carefully explained to the patient that *peritoneal dialysis* removed waste by placing a chemically balanced solution into the peritoneal cavity.
7. *Vasorrhaphy* was performed to sew up the tear in the vas deferens.
8. A *PSA* was performed to test for prostatic cancer.
9. The patient had bradycardia and required medicine to *speed up* his heart rate.
10. Circumcision was necessary to treat the patient's *phimosis*.

Chapter 12 Word Parts Quiz Answer Key

1. epididymis
2. renal pelvis
3. glomerulus
4. kidney
5. urine
6. sperm
7. testicle
8. prostate gland
9. testes
10. urethra
11. kidney
12. semen
13. bladder
14. ureter
15. testes
16. glans penis
17. pus
18. scanty
19. sugar
20. hidden
21. urine condition
22. crushing
23. stone
24. across
25. outside of

Chapter 12 Spelling Quiz Answer Key

1. bacteriuria
2. calculus
3. catheterization
4. cystalgia
5. genitourinary
6. glomerulus
7. pyelonephritis
8. lithotripsy
9. nephrolithiasis
10. circumcision
11. trichomoniasis
12. gonorrhea
13. cryptorchism
14. testicular
15. orchidectomy
16. epididymis
17. prepuce
18. balanorrhea
19. hemodialysis
20. transurethral

Chapter 12 Labeling Quiz 1 Answer Key

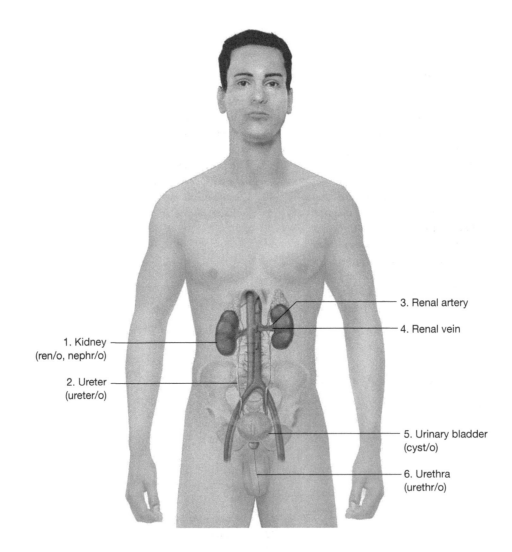

1. Kidney (ren/o, nephr/o)
2. Ureter (ureter/o)
3. Renal artery
4. Renal vein
5. Urinary bladder (cyst/o)
6. Urethra (urethr/o)

Chapter 12 Labeling Quiz 2 Answer Key

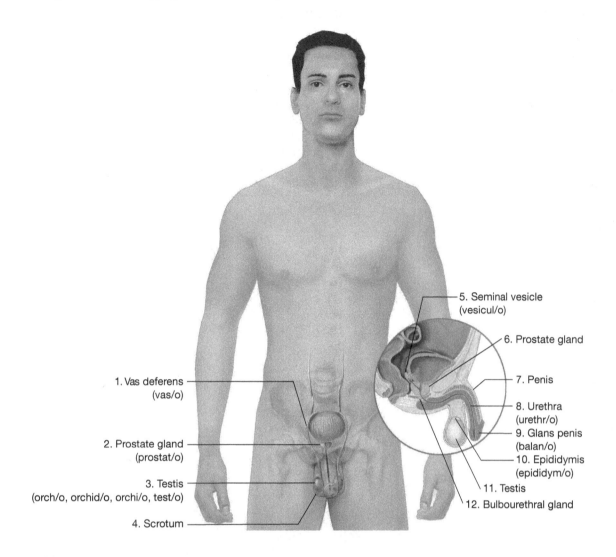

1. Vas deferens (vas/o)
2. Prostate gland (prostat/o)
3. Testis (orch/o, orchid/o, orchi/o, test/o)
4. Scrotum
5. Seminal vesicle (vesicul/o)
6. Prostate gland
7. Penis
8. Urethra (urethr/o)
9. Glans penis (balan/o)
10. Epididymis (epididym/o)
11. Testis
12. Bulbourethral gland

Chapter 12 Word Building Quiz Answer Key

1. orchidectomy
2. balanitis
3. urethrostomy
4. renal
5. seminuria
6. cystoscope
7. spermatogenesis
8. nephroptosis
9. cryptorchism
10. pyelonephritis
11. aspermia
12. glycosuria
13. cystolith
14. urologist
15. orchiopexy
16. bacteriuria
17. epididymitis
18. prostatic
19. vasorrhaphy
20. urethralgia
21. ureterolithiasis
22. ureterostenosis
23. nephroma
24. nocturia
25. vesiculectomy

Chapter 12 Quiz Answer Key

Fill-in-the-Blank

1. homeostasis
2. urethra
3. genitourinary
4. kidneys
5. epididymis; testes
6. nephrons
7. testosterone
8. stoma
9. ureters
10. protein

Word Building

1. epididymitis
2. orchiopexy
3. balanorrhea
4. oligospermia
5. urethroplasty
6. urinometer
7. nephromegaly
8. lithotripsy
9. cystography
10. prostatectomy

Matching

1. s
2. j
3. t
4. u
5. o
6. v
7. n
8. w
9. q
10. a
11. x
12. y
13. r
14. m
15. c
16. d
17. l
18. i
19. p
20. k
21. b
22. f
23. e
24. h
25. g

CHAPTER 13
OBSTETRICS AND GYNECOLOGY: FEMALE REPRODUCTIVE SYSTEM

LEARNING OBJECTIVES

After completing this chapter, students will be able to:

1. Understand the function of the female reproductive system.
2. Describe the medical specialties of obstetrics and gynecology.
3. Define obstetrics- and gynecology-related combining forms, prefixes, and suffixes.
4. Identify the organs treated in obstetrics and gynecology.
5. Build obstetrics and gynecology medical terms from word parts.
6. Explain obstetrics and gynecology medical terms.
7. Use obstetrics and gynecology abbreviations.

Use this word list to focus your studying for the chapter test.

Amenorrhea	Infertility	Oogenesis	**Abbreviations**
Amniocentesis	Intrauterine	Oophorectomy	
Amniorrhexis	Laparoscope	Ovarian	C-section
Antepartum	Mammogram	Placenta	D&C
Cervical	Mammography	Postpartum	FHR
Cervicitis	Mammoplasty	Primigravida	GI, GII, etc., grav I,
Colposcopy	Mastectomy	Primipara	grav II etc.
Cystocele	Mastitis	Rectocele	GYN
Dysmenorrhea	Menorrhagia	Salpingectomy	HPV
Ectopic pregnancy	Metrorrhagia	Salpingitis	HRT
Embryonic	Metrorrhea	Stillbirth	IUD
Endometriosis	Multigravida	Transvaginal	LMP
Episiotomy	Multipara	Tubal ligation	OB
Fetal	Neonatal	Uterine	PAP
Fistula	Neonatologist	Vaginitis	PI, PII, etc., para I,
Gynecologist	Nulligravida		para II etc.
Gynecology	Nullipara		PID
Hysterectomy	Obstetrics		PMS

Worksheet 13A
New Word Parts

Directions: Write out the meaning for each combining form, prefix, and suffix. Then locate a new term from the chapter that uses the word part.

Combining Forms	Meaning	Chapter Term	Meaning
1. amni/o	_____	_____	_____
2. cervic/o	_____	_____	_____
3. chori/o	_____	_____	_____
4. colp/o	_____	_____	_____
5. embry/o	_____	_____	_____
6. episi/o	_____	_____	_____
7. fet/o	_____	_____	_____
8. gynec/o	_____	_____	_____
9. hyster/o	_____	_____	_____
10. lapar/o	_____	_____	_____
11. mamm/o	_____	_____	_____
12. mast/o	_____	_____	_____
13. men/o	_____	_____	_____
14. metr/o	_____	_____	_____
15. nat/o	_____	_____	_____
16. o/o	_____	_____	_____
17. oophor/o	_____	_____	_____
18. ovari/o	_____	_____	_____
19. salping/o	_____	_____	_____
20. uter/o	_____	_____	_____
21. vagin/o	_____	_____	_____

(Continued)

Prefixes	Meaning	Chapter Term	Meaning
22. endo-	_____	_____	_____
23. nulli-	_____	_____	_____
24. multi-	_____	_____	_____
25. neo-	_____	_____	_____
26. post-	_____	_____	_____
27. pre-	_____	_____	_____
28. primi-	_____	_____	_____

Suffixes

29. -cyesis	_____	_____	_____
30. -gravida	_____	_____	_____
31. -para	_____	_____	_____
32. -partum	_____	_____	_____

Worksheet 13B
Word Part Review

Directions: Write out the meaning for each combining form, prefix, and suffix.

Combining Forms   Meaning

1. carcin/o   _____

2. cyst/o   _____

3. fibr/o   _____

4. hem/o   _____

5. olig/o   _____

6. pelv/o   _____

7. rect/o   _____

Prefixes

8. a-   _____

9. ante-   _____

10. dys-   _____

11. intra-   _____

12. trans-   _____

Suffixes

13. -algia   _____

14. -cele   _____

15. -centesis   _____

16. -cyte   _____

17. -ectomy   _____

18. -genesis   _____

19. -genic   _____

20. -gram   _____

21. -graphy   _____

(*Continued*)

Suffixes	Meaning
22. -itis	
23. -logist	
24. -logy	
25. -lytic	
26. -metry	
27. -oma	
28. -otomy	
29. -pexy	
30. -plasty	
31. -rrhagia	
32. -rrhaphy	
33. -rrhea	
34. -rrhexis	
35. -scope	
36. -scopy	

Worksheet 13C
Word Surgery

Directions: Below are terms built from word parts. Analyze each term by listing and defining the word parts used to build it.

Medical Term	Word Part Meanings
1. amniotic	_____
2. endocervicitis	_____
3. choriocarcinoma	_____
4. colposcopy	_____
5. embryonic	_____
6. episiotomy	_____
7. fetometry	_____
8. primigravida	_____
9. gynecology	_____
10. hysteropexy	_____
11. laparoscope	_____

(*Continued*)

Medical Term	Word Part Meanings
12. mammogram	_____
13. mastalgia	_____
14. dysmenorrhea	_____
15. metrorrhagia	_____
16. neonatologist	_____
17. oogenesis	_____
18. oophorectomy	_____
19. ovariosalpingitis	_____
20. salpingocyesis	_____
21. intrauterine	_____
22. nullipara	_____
23. postpartum	_____
24. transvaginal	_____
25. hysterogram	_____

Worksheet 13D
Word Search

Directions: Find and circle the answer for each fill-in-the-blank question in the word search puzzle.

1. _____ is the lack of a normal body opening.

2. A(n) _____ pregnancy occurs outside the uterus.

3. A(n) _____ uterus is a fallen uterus that can cause the cervix to protrude through the vaginal opening.

4. A(n) _____ is the death of a viable-aged fetus.

5. _____ typically occurs in the fallopian tube.

6. _____ occurs when endometrial tissue appears throughout the pelvic or abdominal cavity.

7. _____ are physicians specialized in pregnancy and childbirth.

8. An abnormal passage that develops between two structures is called a(n) _____.

9. The fetus floats in _____ fluid.

10. A protrusion of the rectum into the vagina is called a(n) _____.

```
N O B S T E T R I C I A N S
F S P C I T O I N M A D E N
E H I N S Y N J T R R A L R
R N M S F T L Y V L D I E R
T C Z Q O M I F P H Q S C H
I T R B H I I L C V N E O L
L M L X N S R I L L M R T Z
I W X R T F P T L B H T C Z
Z B Z U M O X T E M I A E V
A P L L T R W F F M X R R B
T A H C B V R L F Z O C T L
I L E C T Z F Y M C G D Q H
O J Z M C C N W P Z Q N N P
N P R O L A P S E D V G Z E
```

272   Chapter 13/OBSTETRICS AND GYNECOLOGY: FEMALE REPRODUCTIVE SYSTEM   © 2012 Pearson Education, Inc.

Worksheet 13E
Unscramble

Directions: Unscramble each medical term below. A definition for the term is given below each scrambled term.

1. b t r a o n i o _____

   loss of embryo before about 20th week of gestation

2. o c i n n a i t o z _____

   removal of core of cervical tissue for biopsy

3. t i e r l a f i z t n i o _____

   joining of ova and sperm

4. y g e o c n g l o y _____

   study of the female

5. r h c o o n i _____

   outer sac protecting fetus

6. g a n i a v _____

   birth canal

7. l e s o t c c y e _____

   protrusion of bladder into vagina

8. g a s l a t i a m _____

   breast pain

9. u v a l t o o n i _____

   release of ovum from ovary

10. d u m o e r t i m e n _____

    inner layer of the uterus

Worksheet 13F
Abbreviations

Directions: Write the full term that each abbreviation stands for.

1. AB _____
2. BSE _____
3. CS, C-section _____
4. CVS _____
5. Cx _____
6. D&C _____
7. EMB _____
8. ERT _____
9. FHR _____
10. FHT _____
11. FTND _____
12. GI, grav I _____
13. GYN, gyn _____
14. HDN _____
15. HPV _____
16. HRT _____
17. HSG _____
18. IUD _____
19. IVF _____
20. LMP _____
21. NB _____
22. OB _____
23. OCPs _____
24. PAP _____

(*Continued*)

Directions: Write the full term that each abbreviation stands for.

25. PI, para I _____

26. PID _____

27. PMS _____

28. SB _____

29. TAH-BSO _____

Worksheet 13G
Case Study

Directions: Below is a case study presentation of a patient with a condition covered in this chapter. Read the case study and answer the questions below. Some questions will ask for information not included within this chapter. Use your text, a medical dictionary, or any other reference material you choose to answer these questions.

Patient is seen by obstetrician today for moderate vaginal bleeding without any cramping or pelvic pain. Patient is 23 years old. She is currently estimated to be at 175 days of gestation. Amniocentesis at 20 weeks indicated male fetus with no evidence of genetic or developmental disorders. This patient is multigravida but nullipara with three early spontaneous abortions without obvious causes. She was diagnosed with cancer of the left ovary 4 years ago. It was treated with a left oophorectomy and chemotherapy. She continues to undergo full-body CT scan every six months, and there has been no evidence of cancer since that time. Pelvic ultrasound indicates placenta previa with placenta almost completely overlying cervix. However, there is no evidence of abruptio placentae at this time. Fetal size estimate is consistent with 25 weeks of gestation. Fetal monitoring revealed that the FHR is strong with a rate of 130 beats/minute. The placenta appears to be well attached on ultrasound, but the bleeding is cause for concern. With the extremely low position of the placenta, this patient is at very high risk for developing abruptio placentae. She may require early delivery by cesarean section if bleeding increases. She will definitely require C-section at onset of labor.

1. Describe in your own words the treatment this patient received for her ovarian cancer. What procedure does she continue to have every six months?

2. This patient had an amniocentesis at 20 weeks of gestation. Describe this procedure and why it is performed.

3. What occurred during this patient's first three pregnancies? Describe what terminated the pregnancies.

4. Describe what fetal monitoring is. What is FHR?

5. This patient has placenta previa. What procedure discovered this condition? The physician, however, is much more concerned about abruptio placentae. Explain why.

6. How will this infant need to be delivered? Describe this procedure.

Worksheet 13H
Web Destinations

Infertility

Below are "Quick Facts About Fertility" presented by the American Reproductive Medicine Society.

- Infertility is NOT an inconvenience; it is a disease of the reproductive system that impairs the body's ability to perform the basic function of reproduction.
- Infertility affects about 6.1 million people in the United States; about ten percent of the reproductive-age population.
- Infertility affects men and women equally.
- Most infertility cases, 85% to 90%, are treated with conventional medical therapies such as medication or surgery.
- While vital for some patients, in vitro fertilization and similar treatments account for less than 5% of infertility services and only three hundredths of one percent (.003%) of U.S. health care costs.

Visit the U.S. Department of Health & Human Services womenshealth.gov website at www.womenshealth.gov and type "frequently asked questions about infertility" in the search box. Select the article by the same name and write a report on what infertility is, the causes, diagnosis, and treatment of infertility, and in vitro fertilization.

Endometriosis

The following statement is from The National Institute of Child Health and Human Development website at www.nichd.nih.gov: "Endometriosis is a common yet poorly understood disease."

Visit this website and type "Endometriosis" into the search box. Select the article titled "Endometriosis—Here's what we do know about Endometriosis" and write a summary on what endometriosis is, the causes, diagnosis, and treatment.

Worksheet 13I
Professional Profile and Journal

Professional Profile

Emergency Medical Service

Emergency medical services provide basic and advanced prehospital emergency care for traumatic or medical emergencies. They evaluate the patient's condition, initiate medical care according to a set of protocols, and stabilize and transport the patient to a hospital. Emergency medical services may work out of rescue, police, and fire departments; hospital emergency rooms; free-standing governmental emergency medical services; and private ambulance services. See Medical Terminology Interactive for a video on Emergency Medical Technicians.

Emergency Medical Technician–Paramedic (EMT-P)

- Performs advanced life support procedures, administers drugs, interprets electrocardiograms, intubates patients, and utilizes the most complex monitoring equipment
- Completes the longest and most rigorous training program, 750 to 2,000 hours of training above the basic emergency medical technician level
- Completes an approved paramedic program in advanced emergency medical techniques
- Completes clinical training period

Emergency Medical Technician–Intermediate (EMT-I)

- Performs certain advanced life support procedures, completes patient assessments, administers intravenous fluids, and uses a defibrillator
- Completes an approved emergency medical technician intermediate program
- Completes additional hours of training above the basic emergency medical technician level

Emergency Medical Technician–Basic (EMT-B)

- Performs basic life support procedures such as establishing open airways, treating shock, assisting in childbirth, controlling bleeding, bandaging wounds, immobilizing fractures, and transporting patients
- Completes 140 hours of classroom instruction and a 10-hour internship in a hospital emergency room
- Completes an approved emergency medical technician basic program

For more information regarding these health careers, visit the following websites:

- National Association of Emergency Medical Technicians at www.naemt.org
- National Registry of Emergency Medical Technicians at www.nremt.org

Professional Journal

In this exercise you will now have an opportunity to put the words you have learned into practice. Imagine yourself in the role of a paramedic. If you refer back to the Professional Profile, you will see that this healthcare professional performs advanced life support procedures. Use the 10 words listed below, or any other new terms from this chapter or previous chapters, to write sentences to describe the patients you saw today.

An example of a sentence is: *A diagnosis of* **hysterorrhexis** *was suspected because the woman in labor was experiencing severe bleeding.*

1. abruptio placentae _____

2. ectopic pregnancy _____

3. C-section _____

4. fetal monitoring _____

5. pulmonary embolism _____

6. multipara _____

7. myocardial infarction _____

8. amniotic fluid _____

9. greenstick fracture _____

10. spontaneous abortion _____

Chapter 13 Word Parts Quiz

Directions: Define the combining form, prefix, or suffix in the spaces provided.

1. amni/o _____
2. cervic/o _____
3. chori/o _____
4. colp/o _____
5. embry/o _____
6. episi/o _____
7. fet/o _____
8. fibr/o _____
9. gynec/o _____
10. hyster/o _____
11. mamm/o _____
12. mast/o _____
13. men/o _____
14. metr/o _____
15. nat/o _____
16. o/o _____
17. oophor/o _____
18. salping/o _____
19. vagin/o _____
20. -cyesis _____
21. -gravida _____
22. -para _____
23. -partum _____
24. nulli- _____
25. neo- _____

Name _____ Date _____ Score _____

Chapter 13 Spelling Quiz

Directions: Write each term as your instructor pronounces it.

1. _____
2. _____
3. _____
4. _____
5. _____
6. _____
7. _____
8. _____
9. _____
10. _____
11. _____
12. _____
13. _____
14. _____
15. _____
16. _____
17. _____
18. _____
19. _____
20. _____

Name _____ Date _____ Score _____

Chapter 13 Labeling Quiz 1

Directions: Label the organs of the female reproductive system.

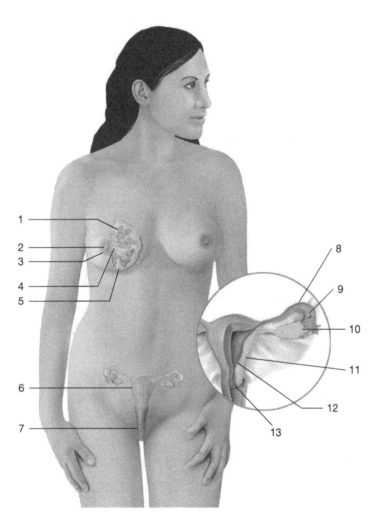

1. _____
2. _____
3. _____
4. _____
5. _____
6. _____
7. _____
8. _____
9. _____
10. _____
11. _____
12. _____
13. _____

Name _____ Date _____ Score _____

Chapter 13 Labeling Quiz 2

Directions: Label the female reproductive organs and fetal structures.

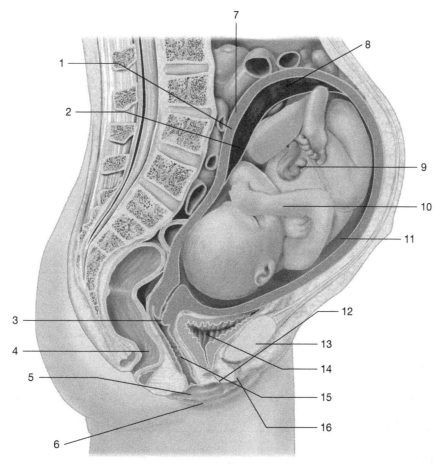

1. _____
2. _____
3. _____
4. _____
5. _____
6. _____
7. _____
8. _____
9. _____
10. _____
11. _____
12. _____
13. _____
14. _____
15. _____
16. _____

Name _____ Date _____ Score _____

Chapter 13 Word Building Quiz

Directions: Build a single medical term for each phrase below.

1. flow from amnion _____
2. suture the vulva _____
3. pertaining to the fetus _____
4. cancerous tumor of chorion _____
5. surgical removal of uterus _____
6. many pregnancies _____
7. cutting into the abdomen _____
8. pertaining to the newborn _____
9. instrument for viewing vagina _____
10. egg cell _____
11. record of the fallopian tube _____
12. pertaining to across the vagina _____
13. surgical fixation of ovary _____
14. before childbirth _____
15. surgical repair of cervix _____
16. first birth _____
17. ruptured uterus _____
18. surgical repair of the breast _____
19. inflammation of inner uterus _____
20. pertaining to the embryo _____
21. pertaining to the ovary _____
22. process of viewing uterus _____
23. without menstrual flow _____
24. one who studies the female _____
25. breast inflammation _____

Name _____ Date _____ Score _____

Chapter 13 Quiz

Fill-in-the-Blank

1. Ova are produced by the _____.

2. Another name for the fallopian tubes is _____ tubes.

3. _____ specialize in female health while _____ specifically specialize in pregnancy and childbirth.

4. The inner sac surrounding the fetus is called the _____.

5. Ovaries secrete two sex hormones, _____ and _____.

6. The cervix, or neck of the uterus, opens into the _____.

7. The labia major, labia minora, and clitoris are all part of the _____.

8. During the early stage of development (before the 3rd month) the baby is referred to as a(n) _____ and during the later stages of pregnancy is called a(n) _____.

9. The term _____ refers to a woman who has had no pregnancies.

10. The inner lining of the uterus is called the _____.

Word Building
Build a term that means:

1. surgical removal of cervix   _____

2. instrument to view abdomen   _____

3. record of breast   _____

4. first birth   _____

5. scanty menstrual flow   _____

6. cutting into the vulva   _____

7. pertaining to newborn   _____

8. puncture amnion to remove fluid   _____

9. ruptured uterus   _____

10. fallopian tube pregnancy   _____

Matching

____ 1. vagina
____ 2. abruptio placentae
____ 3. HPV
____ 4. ectopic pregnancy
____ 5. D&C
____ 6. fetal monitoring
____ 7. infertility
____ 8. cervix
____ 9. HDN
____ 10. fistula
____ 11. atresia
____ 12. fibrocystic breast disease
____ 13. Pap smear
____ 14. CVS
____ 15. stillbirth
____ 16. ova
____ 17. tubal ligation
____ 18. spontaneous abortion
____ 19. prematurity
____ 20. conization
____ 21. IVF
____ 22. antepartum
____ 23. pelvic inflammatory disease
____ 24. C-section
____ 25. fibroid

a. time before childbirth
b. fiber-like tumor
c. benign
d. narrow neck of the uterus
e. erythroblastosis fetalis
f. delivers baby through abdominal incision
g. test tube baby
h. occurs outside of uterus
i. cell that carries half mother's chromosomes
j. tying fallopian tubes to prevent pregnancy
k. removes piece of chorion for genetic testing
l. born before 37 weeks of gestation
m. placenta separates from uterine wall
n. removes core of cervix tissue for testing
o. birth canal
p. may produce scarring leading to infertility
q. may cause cervical cancer
r. test for early detection of cervical cancer
s. checks FHR and FHT
t. lack of normal body opening
u. death of viable-aged fetus
v. abnormal passageway
w. inability to produce children
x. miscarriage
y. widens cervix to scrape out endometrium

Chapter 13 Answer Keys

Worksheet 13A Answer Key

1. amnion
2. neck, cervix
3. chorion
4. vagina
5. embryo
6. vulva
7. fetus
8. woman, female
9. uterus
10. abdomen
11. breast
12. breast
13. menses, menstruation
14. uterus
15. birth
16. egg
17. ovary
18. ovary
19. fallopian tubes, uterine tubes
20. uterus
21. vagina
22. inner
23. none
24. many
25. new
26. after
27. before
28. first
29. pregnancy
30. pregnancy
31. to bear (offspring)
32. childbirth

Worksheet 13B Answer Key

1. cancer
2. bladder
3. fibrous
4. blood
5. scanty
6. pelvis
7. rectum
8. without
9. before
10. painful
11. inside
12. across
13. pain
14. protrusion
15. puncture to withdraw fluid
16. cell
17. surgical removal
18. generates
19. producing
20. record
21. process of recording
22. inflammation
23. one who studies
24. study of
25. destruction
26. process of measuring
27. tumor
28. cutting into
29. surgical fixation
30. surgical repair
31. bursting forth
32. suture
33. flow
34. rupture
35. instrument for viewing
36. process of viewing

Worksheet 13C Answer Key

1. amni/o = amnion; -tic = pertaining to
2. endo- = within; cervic/o = cervix; -itis = inflammation
3. chori/o = chorion; carcin/o = cancer; -oma = tumor
4. colp/o = vagina; -scopy = process of viewing
5. embry/o = embryo; -nic = pertaining to
6. episi/o = vulva; -otomy = cutting into
7. fet/o = fetus; -metry = process of measuring
8. primi- = first; -gravida = pregnancy
9. gynec/o = female; -logy = study of
10. hyster/o = uterus; -pexy = surgical fixation
11. lapar/o = abdomen; -scope = instrument for viewing
12. mamm/o = breast; -gram = record
13. mast/o = breast; -algia = pain
14. dys- = painful; men/o = menstrual; -rrhea = flow
15. metr/o = uterus; -rrhagia = bursting forth

16. neo- = new; nat/o = birth; -logist = one who studies
17. o/o = egg; -genesis = produces
18. oophor/o = ovary; -ectomy = surgical removal
19. ovari/o = ovary; salping/o = fallopian tube; -itis = inflammation
20. salping/o = fallopian tube; -cyesis = pregnancy
21. intra- = inside; uter/o = uterus; -ine = pertaining to
22. nulli-none; -para = birth
23. post- = after; -partum = childbirth
24. trans- = across; vagin/o = vagina; -al = pertaining to
25. hyster/o = uterus; -gram = record

Worksheet 13D Answer Key

1. atresia
2. ectopic
3. prolapsed
4. stillbirth
5. fertilization
6. endometriosis
7. obstetricians
8. fistula
9. amniotic
10. rectocele

```
N O B S T E T R I C I A N S
F S P C I T O I N M A D E N
E H I N S Y N J T R R A L R
R N M S F T L Y V L D I E R
T C Z Q O M I F P H Q S C H
I T R B H I L C V N E O L
L M L X N S R I L L M R T Z
I W X R T F P T L B H T C Z
Z B Z U M O X T E M I A E V
A P L L T R W F F M X R B
T A H C B V R L F Z O C T L
I L E C T Z F Y M C G D Q H
O J Z M C C N W P Z Q N N P
N P R O L A P S E D V G Z E
```

Worksheet 13E Answer Key

1. abortion
2. conization
3. fertilization
4. gynecology
5. chorion
6. vagina
7. cystocele
8. mastalgia
9. ovulation
10. endometrium

Worksheet 13F Answer Key

1. abortion
2. breast self-examination
3. cesarean section
4. chorionic villus sampling
5. cervix
6. dilation and curettage
7. endometrial biopsy
8. estrogen replacement therapy
9. fetal heart rate
10. fetal heart tone
11. full-term normal delivery
12. first pregnancy
13. gynecology
14. hemolytic disease of the newborn
15. human papilloma virus
16. hormone replacement therapy
17. hysterosalpingography
18. intrauterine device
19. *in vitro* fertilization
20. last menstrual period
21. newborn
22. obstetrics
23. oral contraceptive pills
24. Papanicolaou test
25. first delivery
26. pelvic inflammatory disease
27. premenstrual syndrome
28. stillbirth
29. total abdominal hysterectomy–bilateral salpingo-oophorectomy

Worksheet 13G Answer Key

1. Oophorectomy— ovary removed; chemotherapy—using chemicals to treat and kill cancer cells; CT scan
2. Needle is inserted into amniotic sac to withdraw fluid which contains fetal cells; cells are tested for genetic problems
3. Spontaneous abortion or miscarriage; the cause for the miscarriages is unknown
4. Use of electronic equipment placed on mother's abdomen to check fetal heart rate and fetal heart tone; FHR is fetal heart rate
5. Placenta previa—placenta overlies opening of the cervix, blocking it from the baby; pelvic ultrasonography; abruptio placentae—placenta prematurely detaches from uterine wall, require immediate C-section to deliver the baby because it is no longer receiving oxygen from the mother
6. Cesarean delivery—baby is delivered through an abdominal incision

Worksheet 13H Answer Key

Essay activity, student answers will vary.

Worksheet 13I Answer Key

Student answers will vary.

Chapter 13 Word Parts Quiz Answer Key

1. amnion
2. neck, cervix
3. chorion
4. vagina
5. embryo
6. vulva
7. fetus
8. fibrous
9. woman, female
10. uterus
11. breast
12. breast
13. menses, menstruation
14. uterus
15. birth
16. egg
17. ovary
18. fallopian tubes, uterine tubes
19. vagina
20. pregnancy
21. pregnancy
22. to bear (offspring)
23. childbirth
24. none
25. new

Chapter 13 Spelling Quiz Answer Key

1. amniocentesis
2. menstruation
3. hysterorrhexis
4. episiorrhaphy
5. intrauterine
6. dysmenorrhea
7. endometriosis
8. cesarean
9. chorionic
10. colposcope
11. curettage
12. cystocele
13. atresia
14. conization
15. fibrocystic
16. fistula
17. gynecologist
18. oophorectomy
19. salpingocyesis
20. cervicitis

Chapter 13 Labeling Quiz 1 Answer Key

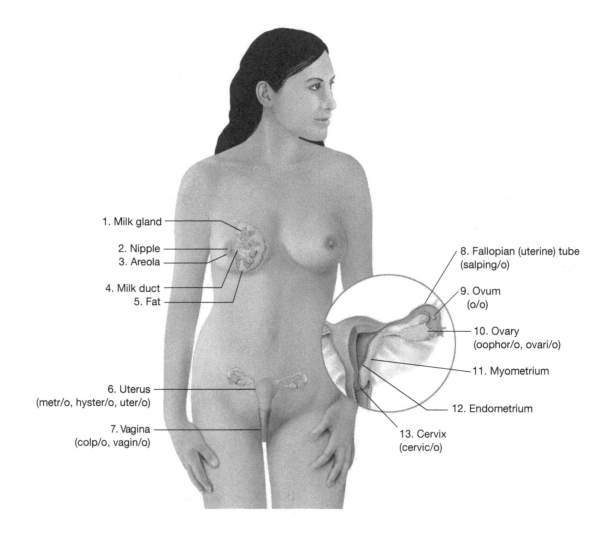

1. Milk gland
2. Nipple
3. Areola
4. Milk duct
5. Fat
6. Uterus (metr/o, hyster/o, uter/o)
7. Vagina (colp/o, vagin/o)
8. Fallopian (uterine) tube (salping/o)
9. Ovum (o/o)
10. Ovary (oophor/o, ovari/o)
11. Myometrium
12. Endometrium
13. Cervix (cervic/o)

Chapter 13 Labeling Quiz 2 Answer Key

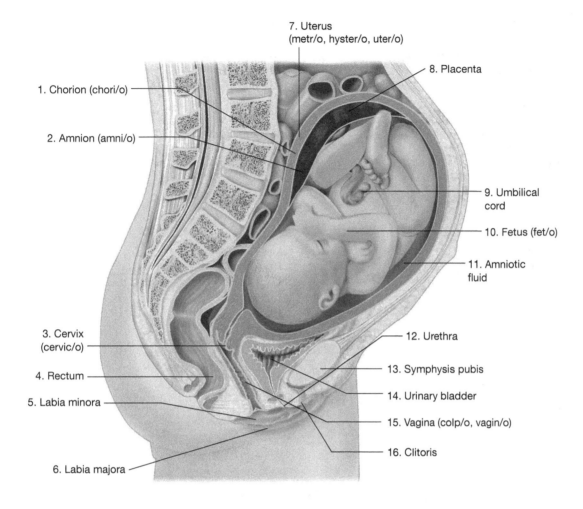

Chapter 13 Word Building Quiz Answer Key

1. amniorrhea
2. episiorrhaphy
3. fetal
4. choriocarcinoma
5. hysterectomy
6. multigravida
7. laparotomy
8. neonatal
9. colposcope
10. oocyte
11. salpingogram
12. transvaginal
13. oophoropexy
14. antepartum
15. cervicoplasty
16. primipara
17. hysterorrhexis
18. mammoplasty
19. endometritis
20. embryonic
21. ovarian
22. uteroscopy
23. amenorrhea
24. gynecologist
25. mastitis

Chapter 13 Quiz Answer Key

Fill-in-the-Blank

1. ovary or ovaries
2. uterine
3. gynecologists; obstetricians
4. amnion
5. estrogen, progesterone
6. vagina
7. vulva
8. embryo; fetus
9. nulligravida
10. endometrium

Word Building

1. cervicectomy
2. laparoscope
3. mammogram
4. primipara
5. oligomenorrhea
6. episiotomy
7. neonatal
8. amniocentesis
9. hysterorrhexis
10. salpingocyesis

Matching

1. o
2. m
3. q
4. h
5. y
6. s
7. w
8. d
9. e
10. v
11. t
12. c
13. r
14. k
15. u
16. i
17. j
18. x
19. l
20. n
21. g
22. a
23. p
24. f
25. b

Chapter 14
Neurology: Nervous System

Learning Objectives

After completing this chapter, students will be able to:

1. Understand the function of the nervous system.
2. Describe the medical specialty of neurology.
3. Define neurology-related combining forms, prefixes, and suffixes.
4. Identify the organs treated in neurology.
5. Build neurology medical terms from word parts.
6. Explain neurology medical terms.
7. Use neurology abbreviations.

Use this word list to focus your studying for the chapter test.

Anticonvulsant	Meningitis	**Abbreviations**
Anesthesia	Migraine	
Aphasia	Myelogram	CNS
Cerebral	Myelitis	CP
Cerebrovascular	Neural	CSF
Concussion	Neuralgia	CVA
Dementia	Neurologist	EEG
Dysphasia	Neurology	ICP
Electroencephalogram	Neuropathy	LP
Encephalalgia	Neuroplasty	MS
Encephalitis	Polyneuritis	PET
Epilepsy	Quadriplegia	TIA
Hemiplegia	Seizure	
Hydrocephalus	Subdural hematoma	
Hyperesthesia	Syncope	
Meningocele		

Worksheet 14A
New Word Parts

Directions: Write out the meaning for each combining form, prefix, and suffix. Then locate a new term from the chapter that uses the word part.

Combining Forms	Meaning	Chapter Term	Meaning
1. cerebell/o	_____	_____	_____
2. cerebr/o	_____	_____	_____
3. encephal/o	_____	_____	_____
4. medull/o	_____	_____	_____
5. mening/o	_____	_____	_____
6. myel/o	_____	_____	_____
7. neur/o	_____	_____	_____
8. pont/o	_____	_____	_____
9. thalam/o	_____	_____	_____

Prefixes

10. di-	_____	_____	_____
11. hemi-	_____	_____	_____
12. mono-	_____	_____	_____
13. poly-	_____	_____	_____
14. quadri-	_____	_____	_____

Suffixes

15. -asthenia	_____	_____	_____
16. -esthesia	_____	_____	_____
17. -phasia	_____	_____	_____
18. -plegia	_____	_____	_____
19. -trophic	_____	_____	_____

Worksheet 14B
Word Part Review

Directions: Write out the meaning for each combining form, prefix, and suffix.

Combining Forms	Meaning
1. cephal/o	
2. electr/o	
3. hemat/o	
4. hydr/o	
5. lumb/o	
6. my/o	
7. scler/o	
8. spin/o	
9. vascul/o	

Prefixes

10. a-	
11. an-	
12. anti-	
13. dys-	
14. hyper-	
15. sub-	

Suffixes

16. -algia	
17. -cele	
18. -eal	
19. -ectomy	
20. -gram	

(Continued)

Suffixes	Meaning
21. -graphy	_____
22. -itis	_____
23. -logist	_____
24. -logy	_____
25. -malacia	_____
26. -oma	_____
27. -otomy	_____
28. -pathy	_____
29. -plasty	_____
30. -rrhaphy	_____
31. -sclerosis	_____

Worksheet 14C
Word Surgery

Directions: Below are terms built from word parts. Analyze each term by listing and defining the word parts used to build it.

Medical Term	Word Part Meanings
1. cerebellar	_____
2. meningomyelocele	_____
3. cerebrospinal	_____
4. cerebrovascular	_____
5. encephalitis	_____
6. electroencephalogram	_____
7. encephalomalacia	_____
8. anesthesia	_____
9. medullary	_____
10. meningeal	_____
11. meningomyelitis	_____

(*Continued*)

Medical Term	Word Part Meanings
12. myelography	
13. myelopathy	
14. neuralgia	
15. polyneuritis	
16. neurorrhaphy	
17. dysphasia	
18. quadriplegia	
19. neuroplegia	
20. pontocerebellar	
21. thalamotomy	
22. neurectomy	
23. myelosclerosis	
24. encephalalgia	
25. cerebrotomy	

Worksheet 14D
Word Search

Directions: Find and circle the answer for each fill-in-the-blank question in the word search puzzle.

1. _____ disease is a chronic condition with progressive disorientation and loss of memory.

2. _____ medication reduces excitability of neurons to prevent uncontrolled neuron activity.

3. Cerebral _____ is the bruising of the brain from impact, with symptoms lasting longer than 24 hours.

4. _____ is brain damage resulting from defect in fetal development or oxygen deprivation at time of birth.

5. The state of profound unconsciousness is called _____.

6. Progressive impairment of intellectual function interfering with performing daily activities is called _____.

7. _____ results from the build up of cerebrospinal fluid.

8. Multiple _____ is an autoimmune disease affecting the central nervous system.

9. _____ is the loss of muscle function and movement.

10. The medical term for fainting is _____.

```
C G R Z C N T L G Z D K Y T
R E K T C O N T U S I O N R
R H R N K R G M V D W A Z E
F S B E C Z H V E T S Z D M
S P I J B K V P N L Z E J I
I B P S Z R O Y U T M F C E
S T T N O C A V Y E L W O H
Y D V L N R N L N T T L M Z
L P G Y J O E T P V L K A L
A M S M C C I L L A K W K A
R D G I X A V K C C L C F B
A Z T V R N V R L S D S W M
P N D J Z P F R N J J G Y X
A S U L A H P E C O R D Y H
```

© 2012 Pearson Education, Inc.   Chapter 14/NEUROLOGY: NERVOUS SYSTEM   299

Worksheet 14E
Unscramble

Directions: Unscramble each medical term below. A definition for the term is given below each scrambled term.

1. s e i p l e p y _____

   seizures and loss of consciousness due to uncontrolled neuron electrical activity

2. s n o n u c c s o i _____

   brain injury due to brain shaken inside skull, symptoms last 24 hrs or less

3. i n t c n v u a l o n a t s _____

   medication to control seizures

4. n e i l n m o e c g e _____

   protrusion of the meninges

5. h g n i l e s s _____

   eruption of painful blisters along nerve path

6. n e e c l o h a l a c p a m i a _____

   softening of the brain

7. o l p e y n i u r i s t _____

   inflammation of many nerves

8. a r p y s a l s i _____

   temporary or permanent loss of muscle function and movement

9. e h p m i g l i e a _____

   paralysis of half the body

10. h a p i a s a _____

    unable to speak

Worksheet 14F
Abbreviations

Directions: Write the full term that each abbreviation stands for.

1. ALS _____
2. ANS _____
3. CNS _____
4. CP _____
5. CSF _____
6. CVA _____
7. CVD _____
8. EEG _____
9. HA _____
10. ICP _____
11. LP _____
12. MS _____
13. PET _____
14. PNS _____
15. SCI _____
16. TIA _____

Worksheet 14G
Case Study

Directions: Below is a case study presentation of a patient with a condition covered in this chapter. Read the case study and answer the questions below. Some questions will ask for information not included within this chapter. Use your text, a medical dictionary, or any other reference material you choose to answer these questions.

Anna Moore, an 83-year-old female, is admitted to the ER with aphasia, hemiplegia on her left side, and syncope. Her daughter called the ambulance after discovering her mother in this condition at home. Mrs. Moore has a history of hypertension, atherosclerosis, and diabetes mellitus. She was admitted to the hospital after a CT scan revealed an infarct in the right cerebral hemisphere leading to a diagnosis of CVA of the middle cerebral artery.

1. What pathological condition does Mrs. Moore have? Look this condition up in a reference source and include a short description of it.

   _____
   _____

2. List and define each of the patient's presenting symptoms in the ER.

   _____
   _____

3. The patient has a history of three significant conditions. Describe each in your own words.

   _____
   _____

4. What diagnostic test confirmed the diagnosis?

   _____
   _____

5. What did the diagnostic test reveal?

   _____
   _____

6. List and describe the four common causes of a CVA.

   _____
   _____

Worksheet 14H
Web Destinations

Alzheimer Disease

Alzheimer disease is the most common form of dementia in older people. The Alzheimer's Disease Education and Referral (ADEAR) Center's website, www.nia.nih.gov/alzheimers, contains information regarding this disease. Type "Fact Sheet" in the search box and select the article titled "Alzheimer's Disease Fact Sheet." Use the information presented on this site to write a description of Alzheimer's disease, its symptoms, diagnosis, treatment, and the direction of current research.

Cerebrovascular Accident

Below are the five warning signs of a stroke according to the American Heart Association website.

- Sudden numbness or weakness of the face, arm, or leg, especially on one side of the body
- Sudden confusion, trouble speaking or understanding
- Sudden trouble seeing in one or both eyes
- Sudden trouble walking, dizziness, loss of balance or coordination
- Sudden, severe headache with no known cause

Follow this link, www.americanheart.org, to the American Heart Association's home page. Left click on Heart and Stroke Encyclopedia. Scroll down to the S entries and left click on Stroke. From the information on this page, identify and describe the three types of strokes in your own words. Scroll to the bottom of this webpage and left click on Stroke Tests and describe the imaging, electrical activity, and blood flow test that may be used to diagnose a stroke. Finally, scroll to the bottom of that webpage and left click on Stroke Treatment and describe what tissue plasminogen activator is and how it is used in the treatment of stroke.

Worksheet 14I
Professional Profile and Journal

Professional Profile

Electroneurodiagnostics

Electroneurodiagnostics (END) is the science that studies and records electrical activity of the brain and nervous system, with tests performed by END technologists who conduct diagnostic tests using electronic equipment and machines. Potential areas of specialization include electroencephalography (recording the electrical activity of the brain), electromyography (recording the electrical activity of muscles), polysomnography (recording brain activity, respiratory rate, and heart rate during stages of sleep), evoked potential tests (recording the brain's response to different types of sensory stimuli), and nerve conduction tests (recording how fast electrical messages travel along a nerve). These tests are useful in diagnosing brain, spinal cord, and nerve diseases and conditions such as strokes, tumors, and pinched nerves. The majority of electroneurodiagnostic technologists work in hospitals, but they are also found in clinics and physicians' offices.

Electroneurodiagnostic Technologist

- Performs diagnostic tests as ordered by a physician
- Graduates from a 2-year associate's degree or certification program
- May choose to become a Registered Electroencephalography Technologist (R. EEG T.), a Registered Evoked Potential Technologist (R. EP T.), a Registered Polysomnographic Technologist (RPSGT), or earn a Certification in Neurophysiologic Intraoperative Monitoring (CNIM), if qualification criteria are met
- Some facilities provide on-the-job training sufficient for persons to qualify for some of these positions, especially if the person has training or experience in other healthcare fields

For more information regarding these health careers, visit the following websites:

- American Society of Electroneurodiagnostic Technologists at www.aset.org
- Association of Polysomnographic Technologists at www.aptweb.org

Professional Journal

In this exercise you will now have an opportunity to put the words you have learned into practice. Imagine yourself in the role of an electroneurodiagnostic technologist. If you refer back to the Professional Profile, you will see that this healthcare professional conducts diagnostic tests that record the electrical activity of the brain and nervous system. Use the 10 words listed below, or any other new terms from this chapter, to write sentences to describe the patients you saw today.

An example of a sentence is: *Dr. Jones ordered an* **EEG** *after her patient came to the emergency room having* **convulsions.**

1. brain tumor _____

2. syncope _____

3. cerebrovascular accident _____

4. coma _____

5. encephalitis _____

6. epilepsy _____

7. hyperesthesia _____

8. electroencephalography _____

9. cerebral contusion _____

10. neuralgia _____

Name _____ Date _____ Score _____

Chapter 14 Word Parts Quiz

Directions: Define the combining form, prefix, or suffix in the spaces provided.

1. cephal/o _____
2. cerebell/o _____
3. cerebr/o _____
4. electr/o _____
5. encephal/o _____
6. hydr/o _____
7. medull/o _____
8. mening/o _____
9. myel/o _____
10. neur/o _____
11. pont/o _____
12. spin/o _____
13. thalam/o _____
14. vascul/o _____
15. -asthenia _____
16. -esthesia _____
17. -malacia _____
18. -phasia _____
19. -plegia _____
20. -sclerosis _____
21. -trophic _____
22. di- _____
23. hemi- _____
24. mono- _____
25. quadri- _____

Name _____ Date _____ Score _____

Chapter 14 Spelling Quiz

Directions: Write each term as your instructor pronounces it.

1. _____
2. _____
3. _____
4. _____
5. _____
6. _____
7. _____
8. _____
9. _____
10. _____
11. _____
12. _____
13. _____
14. _____
15. _____
16. _____
17. _____
18. _____
19. _____
20. _____

Name _____ Date _____ Score _____

Chapter 14 Labeling Quiz 1

Directions: Label the organs of the nervous system.

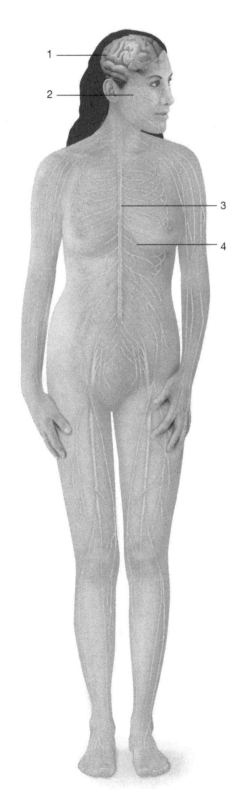

1. _____
2. _____
3. _____
4. _____

308 Chapter 14/NEUROLOGY: NERVOUS SYSTEM   © 2012 Pearson Education, Inc.

Name _____ Date _____ Score _____

Chapter 14 Labeling Quiz 2

Directions: Label the regions of the brain.

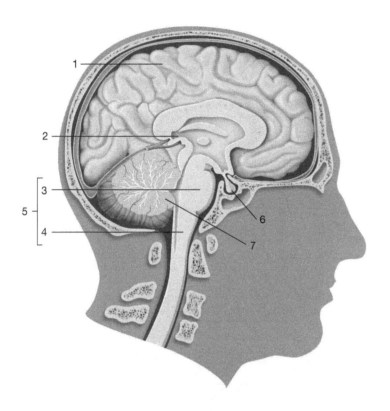

1. _____   5. _____
2. _____   6. _____
3. _____   7. _____
4. _____

Name _____   Date _____   Score _____

Chapter 14 Word Building Quiz

Directions: Build a single medical term for each phrase below.

1. inflammation of cerebellum _____
2. protrusion of meninges _____
3. cutting into cerebrum _____
4. pertaining to cerebrum and blood vessels _____
5. brain pain _____
6. brain tumor _____
7. brain softening _____
8. excessive feeling _____
9. pertaining to medulla oblongata _____
10. meninges inflammation _____
11. record of the spinal cord _____
12. spinal cord and nerve inflammation _____
13. cutting into spinal cord _____
14. inflammation of many nerves _____
15. one who studies nerves _____
16. surgical repair of nerve _____
17. without speech _____
18. suture a nerve _____
19. paralysis of one (limb) _____
20. paralysis of half _____
21. pertaining to pons and cerebellum _____
22. pertaining to the thalamus _____
23. hardening of cerebrum _____
24. process of recording brain electricity _____
25. spinal cord disease _____

Name _____ Date _____ Score _____

Chapter 14 Quiz

Fill-in-the-Blank

1. The central nervous system consists of the _____ and _____.

2. The structures of the nervous system are composed of _____.

3. The largest region of the brain is the _____.

4. In a _____, a portion of the meninges protrudes through the spinal canal wall.

5. The pons and medulla oblongata make up the _____.

6. The inner layer of the meninges is the _____.

7. _____ nerves carry information to the CNS and _____ nerves carry messages from CNS to muscles and organs.

8. Many neurons are covered by _____, an insulating substance.

9. The cerebrum is composed of four lobes, the _____, _____, _____, and _____.

10. A person with paralysis of half the body has _____.

Word Building

Build a term that means:

1. pertaining to cerebrum and blood vessels   _____

2. brain inflammation   _____

3. difficult speech   _____

4. nerve disease   _____

5. pertaining to pons and cerebellum   _____

6. pertaining to meninges   _____

7. without feeling   _____

8. hardening of spinal cord   _____

9. record of brain electricity   _____

10. softening of cerebrum   _____

Matching

_____ 1. TIA
_____ 2. shingles
_____ 3. absence seizure
_____ 4. PET scan
_____ 5. syncope
_____ 6. Parkinson disease
_____ 7. multiple sclerosis
_____ 8. lumbar puncture
_____ 9. spina bifida
_____ 10. hydrocephalus
_____ 11. epilepsy
_____ 12. tonic-clonic
_____ 13. concussion
_____ 14. migraine
_____ 15. subdural hematoma
_____ 16. CVA
_____ 17. dementia
_____ 18. brain tumor
_____ 19. paralysis
_____ 20. coma
_____ 21. anticonvulsant
_____ 22. SCI
_____ 23. cerebral contusion
_____ 24. myasthenia gravis
_____ 25. CP

a. loss of muscle function and movement
b. spinal tap
c. blood pooling underneath dura mater
d. autoimmune disease affecting synapse
e. result of uncontrolled neuron electrical activity
f. damage to the spinal cord
g. profound unconsciousness
h. impairment of intellectual function
i. temporary reduction of blood supply to brain
j. intracranial mass
k. immune system damages myelin
l. indicates metabolic activity
m. reduces excitability of neurons
n. caused by *Herpes zoster* virus
o. bruising of the brain
p. brain injury lasting 24 hours or less
q. petit mal
r. severe pain, light sensitivity, dizziness, nausea
s. may be caused by oxygen deprivation at birth
t. congenital defect in walls of spinal canal
u. a stroke
v. fainting
w. buildup of cerebrospinal fluid in brain
x. tremors, muscular weakness, and rigidity
y. grand mal seizure

Chapter 14 Answer Keys

Worksheet 14A Answer Key

1. cerebellum
2. cerebrum
3. brain
4. medulla oblongata
5. meninges
6. spinal cord
7. nerve
8. pons
9. thalamus
10. two
11. half
12. one
13. many
14. four
15. weakness
16. feeling, sensation
17. speech
18. paralysis
19. development

Worksheet 14B Answer Key

1. head
2. electricity
3. blood
4. water
5. low back
6. muscle
7. hardening
8. spine
9. blood vessels
10. without
11. without
12. against
13. painful, difficult
14. excessive
15. under
16. pain
17. hernia, protrusion
18. pertaining to
19. surgical removal
20. record
21. process of recording
22. inflammation
23. one who studies
24. study of
25. softening
26. tumor
27. cutting into
28. disease
29. surgical repair
30. suture
31. hardening

Worksheet 14C Answer Key

1. cerebell/o = cerebellum; -ar = pertaining to
2. mening/o = meninges; myel/o = spinal cord; -cele = protrusion
3. cerebr/o = cerebrum; spin/o = spine; -al = pertaining to
4. cerebr/o = cerebrum; vascul/o = blood vessels; -ar = pertaining to
5. encephal/o = brain; -itis = inflammation
6. electr/o = electricity; encephal/o = brain; -gram = record
7. encephal/o = brain; -malacia = softening
8. an- = without; -esthesia = feeling
9. medull/o = medulla oblongata; -ary = pertaining to
10. mening/o = meninges; -eal = pertaining to
11. mening/o = meninges; myel/o = spinal cord; -itis = inflammation
12. myel/o = spinal cord; -graphy = process of recording
13. myel/o = spinal cord; -pathy = disease
14. neur/o = nerve; -algia = pain
15. poly- = many; neur/o = nerve; -itis = inflammation
16. neur/o = nerve; -rrhaphy = suture
17. dys- = abnormal; -phasia = speech
18. quadri- = four; -plegia = paralysis
19. neur/o = nerve; -plegia = paralysis
20. pont/o = pons; cerebell/o = cerebellum; -ar = pertaining to
21. thalam/o = thalamus; -otomy = cutting into
22. neur/o = nerve; -ectomy = surgical removal
23. myel/o = spinal cord; -sclerosis = hardening
24. encephal/o = brain; -algia = pain
25. cerebr/o = cerebrum; -otomy = cutting into

Worksheet 14D Answer Key

1. Alzheimer
2. anticonvulsant
3. contusion
4. cerebral palsy
5. coma
6. dementia
7. hydrocephalus
8. sclerosis
9. paralysis
10. syncope

```
C G R Z C N T L G Z D K Y T
R E K T C O N T U S I O N R
R H R N K R G M V D W A Z E
F S B E C Z H V E T S Z D M
S P I J B K V P N L Z E J I
I B P S Z R O Y U T M F C E
S T T N O C A V Y E L W O H
Y D V L N R N L N T T L M Z
L P G Y J O E T P V L K A L
A M S M C C I L L A K W K A
R D G I X A V K C C L C F B
A Z T V R N V R L S D S W M
P N D J Z P F R N J J G Y X
A S U L A H P E C O R D Y H
```

Worksheet 14E Answer Key

1. epilepsy
2. concussion
3. anticonvulsant
4. meningocele
5. shingles
6. encephalomalacia
7. polyneuritis
8. paralysis
9. hemiplegia
10. aphasia

Worksheet 14F Answer Key

1. amyotrophic lateral sclerosis
2. autonomic nervous system
3. central nervous system
4. cerebral palsy
5. cerebrospinal fluid
6. cerebrovascular accident
7. cerebrovascular disease
8. electroencephalography or electroencephalogram
9. headache
10. intracranial pressure
11. lumbar puncture
12. multiple sclerosis
13. positron emission tomography
14. peripheral nervous system
15. spinal cord injury
16. transient ischemic attack

Worksheet 14G Answer Key

1. Cerebrovascular accident (CVA or stroke)
2. Aphasia—inability to speak; hemiparesis—weakness on one side of the body; syncope—fainting; delirium—abnormal mental state with confusion, disorientation, and agitation
3. Hypertension—high blood pressure; atherosclerosis—hardening of arteries due to build up of yellow fatty substances; diabetes mellitus—inability to make or use insulin properly to control blood sugar levels
4. CT scan
5. infarct—dead area of necrosis due to ischemia, loss of blood supply
6. Hemorrhage—ruptured blood vessel; thrombus—stationary clot; embolus—floating clot; compression—pinching off a blood vessel

Worksheet 14H Answer Key

Essay activity, student answers will vary.

Worksheet 14I Answer Key

Student answers will vary.

Chapter 14 Word Parts Quiz Answer Key

1. head
2. cerebellum
3. cerebrum
4. electricity
5. brain
6. water
7. medulla oblongata
8. meninges
9. spinal cord
10. nerve
11. pons
12. spine
13. thalamus
14. blood vessels
15. weakness
16. feeling, sensation
17. softening
18. speech
19. paralysis
20. hardening
21. development
22. two
23. half
24. one
25. four

Chapter 14 Spelling Quiz Answer Key

1. synapse
2. meninges
3. hydrocephalus
4. syncope
5. unconscious
6. Alzheimer
7. cerebrovascular
8. amyotrophic
9. myasthenia
10. ischemic
11. seizure
12. migraine
13. epilepsy
14. concussion
15. anticonvulsant
16. electroencephalography
17. meningomyelitis
18. quadriplegia
19. pontomedullary
20. meningomyelocele

Chapter 14 Labeling Quiz 1 Answer Key

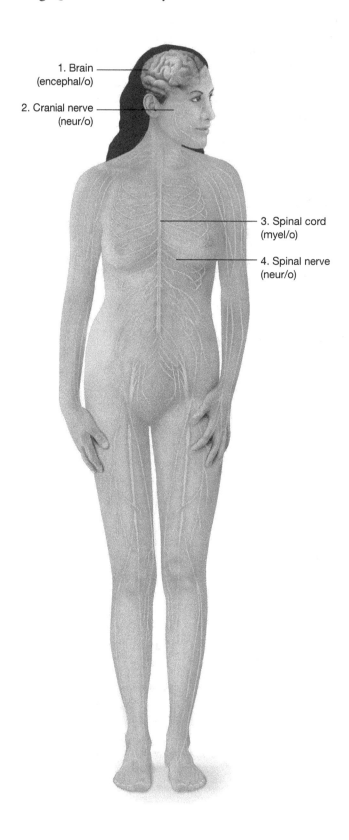

316 Chapter 14/NEUROLOGY: NERVOUS SYSTEM

Chapter 14 Labeling Quiz 2 Answer Key

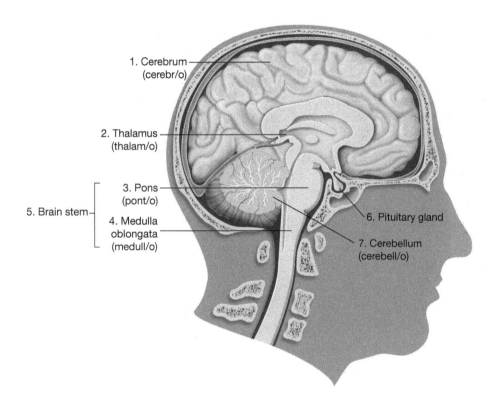

Chapter 14 Word Building Quiz Answer Key

1. cerebellitis
2. meningocele
3. cerebrotomy
4. cerebrovascular
5. encephalalgia
6. encephaloma
7. encephalomalacia
8. hyperesthesia
9. medullary
10. meningitis
11. myelogram
12. myeloneuritis
13. myelotomy
14. polyneuritis
15. neurologist
16. neuroplasty
17. aphasia
18. neurorrhaphy
19. monoplegia
20. hemiplegia
21. pontocerebellar
22. thalamic
23. cerebrosclerosis
24. electroencephalography
25. myelopathy

Chapter 14 Quiz Answer Key

Fill-in-the-Blank

1. brain; spinal cord
2. neurons
3. cerebrum
4. meningocele
5. brainstem
6. pia mater
7. sensory; motor
8. myelin
9. frontal; parietal; temporal; occipital
10. hemiplegia

Word Building

1. cerebrovascular
2. encephalitis
3. dysphagia
4. neuropathy
5. pontocerebellar
6. meningeal
7. anesthesia
8. myelosclerosis
9. electroencephalogram
10. cerebromalacia

Matching

1. i
2. n
3. q
4. l
5. v
6. x
7. k
8. b
9. t
10. w
11. e
12. y
13. p
14. r
15. c
16. u
17. h
18. j
19. a
20. g
21. m
22. f
23. o
24. d
25. s

Chapter 15
Endocrinology: Endocrine System

Learning Objectives

After completing this chapter, students will be able to:

1. Understand the function of the endocrine system.
2. Describe the medical specialty of endocrinology.
3. Define endocrinology-related combining forms, prefixes, and suffixes.
4. Identify the organs treated in endocrinology.
5. Build endocrinology medical terms from word parts.
6. Explain endocrinology medical terms.
7. Use endocrinology abbreviations.

Worksheet 15A
New Word Parts

Directions: Write out the meaning for each combining form, prefix, and suffix. Then locate a new term from the chapter that uses the word part.

Combining Forms	Meaning	Chapter Term	Meaning
1. aden/o			
2. adren/o			
3. adrenal/o			
4. crin/o			
5. glyc/o			
6. glycos/o			
7. oophor/o			
8. orchi/o			
9. ovari/o			
10. pancreat/o			
11. parathyroid/o			
12. pineal/o			
13. pituitar/o			
14. testicul/o			
15. thym/o			
16. thyr/o			
17. thyroid/o			

Prefixes

	Meaning	Chapter Term	Meaning
18. endo-			
19. ex-			

Suffix

	Meaning	Chapter Term	Meaning
20. -dipsia			

Worksheet 15B
Word Part Review

Directions: Write out the meaning for each combining form, prefix, and suffix.

Combining Forms — Meaning

1. acr/o _____
2. carcin/o _____
3. cyt/o _____
4. ophthalm/o _____
5. toxic/o _____

Prefixes

6. hyper- _____
7. hypo- _____
8. poly- _____

Suffixes

9. -centesis _____
10. -cyte _____
11. -ectomy _____
12. -edema _____
13. -emia _____
14. -itis _____
15. -logist _____
16. -logy _____
17. -malacia _____
18. -megaly _____
19. -oid _____
20. -oma _____
21. -otomy _____

(Continued)

Suffixes	Meaning
22. -pathy	_____
23. -pexy	_____
24. -plasty	_____
25. -rrhexis	_____
26. -uria	_____

Worksheet 15C
Word Surgery

Directions: Below are terms built from word parts. Analyze each term by listing and defining the word parts used to build it.

Medical Term   Word Part Meanings

1. adenocarcinoma   _____

   _____

2. adenomalacia   _____

   _____

3. adrenomegaly   _____

   _____

4. adrenalitis   _____

   _____

5. endocrinology   _____

   _____

6. hyperglycemia   _____

   _____

7. glycosuria   _____

   _____

8. oophoroplasty   _____

   _____

9. oophorotomy   _____

   _____

10. orchiopexy   _____

    _____

11. orchiectomy   _____

    _____

(*Continued*)

Medical Term	Word Part Meanings
12. ovarian	_____
13. ovariorrhexis	_____
14. pancreatic	_____
15. pancreatotomy	_____
16. parathyroidal	_____
17. hypoparathyroidism	_____
18. pinealectomy	_____
19. hyperpituitarism	_____
20. polydipsia	_____
21. testicular	_____
22. thymoma	_____
23. thyromegaly	_____
24. thyroidal	_____
25. hypothyroidism	_____

Worksheet 15D
Word Search

Directions: Find and circle the answer for each fill-in-the-blank question in the word search puzzle.

1. _____ results in the enlargement of bones of head and extremities.

2. Adrenal _____ is the appearance of male secondary sexual characteristics in a female.

3. _____ are hormones with a strong anti-inflammatory action.

4. The congenital lack of thyroid hormones results in the development of _____.

5. Diabetes _____ is caused by insufficient antidiuretic hormone while diabetes _____ is a disorder of sugar metabolism.

6. Hypersecretion of growth hormone in a child or teenager results in _____.

7. A(n) _____ is an enlarged thyroid gland.

8. _____ is nerve irritability and painful muscle cramps from hypocalcemia.

9. _____ is usually a benign tumor of the adrenal medulla.

10. _____ is a term meaning excessive thirst.

```
A M O T Y C O M O R H C O E H P
C O R T I C O S T E R O I D S J
M V Q Q Z L K L W C R C L L T V
Y C V I N Y N M S I T N A G I G
L K Y N W A P R P V K T V W A R
A M H S D L I V E R H X H M I M
G T L I K C R S Q T T K G W M X
E F C P T K R L P L I F Y S Y T
M N J I L T R E G I M O I G N K
O N K D L Q J T T E D L G H A Z
R V L U T B L R L I I Y N N T R
C Q T S D K L L G R N F L C E K
A Z W D B Z I H I T X I Z O T B
R V C B M T D V L T Z K S N P T
N F B T U M T K X P X X L M Y Z
T L D S L H Q X L X Q Q K D H L
```

Worksheet 15E
Unscramble

Directions: Unscramble each medical term below. A definition for the term is given below each scrambled term.

1. e n a t t y _____

   nerve irritability and muscle cramps from hypocalcemia

2. a m i d r i o m o a n s a u s y _____

   measures levels of hormones in blood plasma

3. y m d e a m x e _____

   results from hyposecretion of thyroid hormones in an adult

4. a h m s t i h o o disease _____

   autoimmune form of thyroiditis

5. r e i g t o _____

   enlarged thyroid gland

6. h p x h o t a e l o s m _____

   protruding eyeballs

7. w i r f a s m d _____

   being excessively short in height

8. i h g u n c s syndrome _____

   results from hypersecretion of adrenal cortex hormones

9. adrenal z i f n e i a m i t n o _____

   female secondary sexual characteristics in a male

10. y c r l o i s g u a _____

    sugar in the urine

Worksheet 15F
Abbreviations

Directions: Write the full term that each abbreviation stands for.

1. ACTH _____
2. ADH _____
3. DI _____
4. DM _____
5. FBS _____
6. FSH _____
7. GH _____
8. GTT _____
9. IDDM _____
10. K^+ _____
11. LH _____
12. MSH _____
13. Na^+ _____
14. NIDDM _____
15. NPH _____
16. PRL _____
17. PTH _____
18. RAI _____
19. RIA _____
20. T_3 _____
21. T_4 _____

Worksheet 15G
Case Study

Directions: Below is a case study presentation of a patient with a condition covered in this chapter. Read the case study and answer the questions below. Some questions will ask for information not included within this chapter. Use your text, a medical dictionary, or any other reference material you choose to answer these questions.

A 22-year-old college student was admitted to the emergency room after his friends called an ambulance when he passed out in a bar. He had become confused, developed slurred speech, and had difficulty walking after having only one beer to drink. In the ER he was noted to have cephalalgia, vomiting, dyspnea, and was disoriented. Upon examination, needle marks were found on his arms and stomach. The physician ordered a blood sugar test that revealed hyperglycemia. Unknown to his friends, this young man has had diabetes mellitus since early childhood. The patient quickly recovered following an insulin injection.

1. What pathological condition has this patient had since childhood? Look this condition up in a reference source and include a short description of it.

2. List and define each symptom noted in the ER in your own words.

3. What diagnostic test was performed? Describe it in your own words.

4. Explain the results of the test.

5. What specific type of diabetes mellitus does this young man probably have? Justify your answer.

6. Describe the other form of diabetes mellitus.

Worksheet 15H
Web Destinations

Hypopituitarism

The Pituitary Network Association (PNA) provides information and support to persons with pituitary gland tumors, their healthcare providers, and their families. Hypopituitarism is used to describe conditions in which there is undersecretion of one or more of the pituitary hormones. We have studied six hormones secreted by the anterior pituitary: adrenocorticotropin, thyroid stimulating hormone, follicle stimulating hormone, luteinizing hormone, growth hormone, and antidiuretic hormone. Visit the PNA's website at www.pituitary.org. Roll the cursor over the "Knowledge Base" tab and select "Disorders." Then left click on the Hypopituitarism link. Use the information it presents to describe what happens when these hormones are undersecreted.

Diabetes Mellitus

American Diabetes Association (ADA) is an excellent information source for persons with diabetes mellitus. Diabetes mellitus appears in two forms, Type 1 or Type 2. Both forms result in hyperglycemia, but they have different causes and different treatments. Go to the following ADA website at www.diabetes.org. Select the "Diabetes Basics" link from the navigation bar. Read this general information, then more specific information on Type 1 and Type 2 Diabetes. Use this information to compare and contrast the two forms of diabetes mellitus.

Worksheet 15I
Professional Profile and Journal

Professional Profile

Pharmacy

Pharmacists prepare and dispense drugs. The pharmacist receives drug requests made by physicians and also gathers pertinent information that would affect the dispensing of certain drugs, such as allergies, previous drug interactions, and patient history. They also review patients' medications for drug interactions, provide healthcare workers with information regarding drugs, and educate the public concerning their drugs. Pharmacy workers are found in acute and long-term care facilities, clinics, community-based pharmacies, health departments, and pharmaceutical companies. See Medical Terminology Interactive for a video on Pharmacy Technicans.

Pharmacist (RPh or PharmD)

- Fills prescriptions as written by physicians, dentists, and other doctors
- Graduates from an accredited 5-year baccalaureate or 6-year graduate pharmacy program
- Completes an internship
- Passes an examination

Pharmacy Technician

- Works under the supervision of a pharmacist
- Performs computer order entry, generates prescription labels, and keeps electronic patient profiles
- Completes a 1- to 2-year associate's degree program
- Some states offer certification

For more information regarding these health careers, visit the following websites:

- American Association of Colleges of Pharmacy at www.aacp.org
- American Association of Pharmacy Technicians at www.pharmacytechnician.com
- American Pharmacists Association at www.pharmacist.com

Professional Journal

In this exercise you will now have an opportunity to put the words you have learned into practice. Imagine yourself in the role of a pharmacist. If you refer back to the Professional Profile, you will see that this healthcare professional is responsible for receiving drug requests, gathering pertinent patient information, reviewing patient medications, dispensing medications, and educating the public. Use the 10 words listed below, or any other new terms from this chapter, to write sentences to describe the patients you saw today.

An example of a sentence is: *The patient's puffy and dry skin from* **myxedema** *improved dramatically after receiving replacement thyroid hormones.*

1. adrenal feminization _____

2. corticosteroids _____

3. cretinism _____

4. diabetes insipidus _____

5. dwarfism _____

6. Hashimoto's disease _____

7. diabetes mellitus _____

8. hormone replacement therapy _____

9. goiter _____

10. fasting blood sugar _____

Name _____ Date _____ Score _____

Chapter 15 Word Parts Quiz

Directions: Define the combining form, prefix, or suffix in the spaces provided.

1. acr/o _____
2. aden/o _____
3. adren/o _____
4. crin/o _____
5. glyc/o _____
6. oophor/o _____
7. orchi/o _____
8. pancreat/o _____
9. parathyroid/o _____
10. pineal/o _____
11. pituitar/o _____
12. thym/o _____
13. thyr/o _____
14. toxic/o _____
15. endo- _____
16. hypo- _____
17. -centesis _____
18. -dipsia _____
19. -edema _____
20. -malacia _____
21. -megaly _____
22. -oid _____
23. -pathy _____
24. -pexy _____
25. -rrhexis _____

Name _____ Date _____ Score _____

Chapter 15 Spelling Quiz

Directions: Write each term as your instructor pronounces it.

1. _____
2. _____
3. _____
4. _____
5. _____
6. _____
7. _____
8. _____
9. _____
10. _____
11. _____
12. _____
13. _____
14. _____
15. _____
16. _____
17. _____
18. _____
19. _____
20. _____

Name _____ Date _____ Score _____

Chapter 15 Labeling Quiz

Directions: Label the organs of the endocrine system.

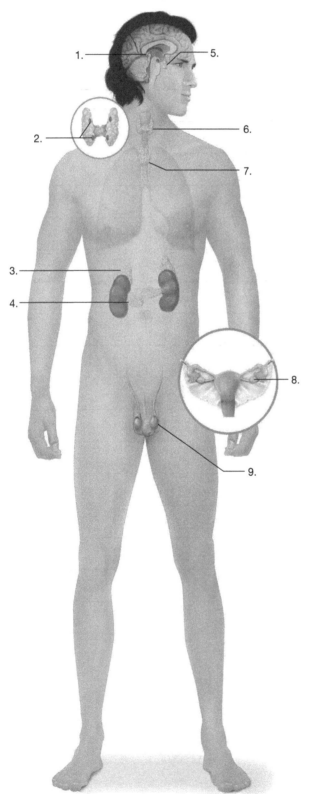

1. _____
2. _____
3. _____
4. _____
5. _____
6. _____
7. _____
8. _____
9. _____

Name _____ Date _____ Score _____

Chapter 15 Word Building Quiz

Directions: Build a single medical term for each phrase below.

1. surgical removal of pineal gland _____
2. pertaining to the testes _____
3. gland cell _____
4. adrenal gland disease _____
5. excessive sugar blood condition _____
6. surgical repair of ovary _____
7. surgical fixation of testes _____
8. one who studies (the glands that) secrete within _____
9. pertaining to the pancreas _____
10. condition of insufficient parathyroid gland _____
11. inflammation of ovary _____
12. abnormal condition of thyroid gland poison _____
13. too much thirst _____
14. resembling a gland _____
15. pertaining to the ovary _____
16. enlarged thyroid gland _____
17. a tumor that secretes within _____
18. pertaining to the thymus gland _____
19. puncture to withdraw fluid from ovary _____
20. enlarged adrenal gland _____
21. inflammation of thyroid gland _____
22. condition of insufficient pituitary gland _____
23. inflammation of adrenal gland _____
24. ruptured ovary _____
25. sugar urine condition _____

Name _____ Date _____ Score _____

Chapter 15 Quiz

Fill-in-the-Blank

1. The endocrine system plays a vital role in maintaining _____, a stable internal body environment.

2. Hormones enter the bloodstream and travel to _____.

3. The adrenal gland is subdivided into the _____ and _____.

4. The two main sex hormones are _____ and _____.

5. _____ is the primary sugar used by the body for energy production.

6. Hypersecretion means that the gland is secreting too much _____.

7. Insulin and glucagon are secreted by the _____.

8. Parathyroid hormone raises the level of _____ in the blood.

9. The _____ is often referred to as the master gland.

10. Thymosin is important for the development of the _____ system.

Word Building

Build a term that means:

1. gland softening   _____

2. excessive sugar blood condition   _____

3. enlarged thyroid gland   _____

4. thymus gland tumor   _____

5. condition of insufficient pituitary gland   _____

6. surgical removal of pineal gland   _____

7. too much urine condition   _____

8. inflammation of pancreas   _____

9. ruptured ovary   _____

10. surgical fixation of testes   _____

Matching

____ 1. blood serum test
____ 2. exophthalmos
____ 3. goiter
____ 4. Hashimoto disease
____ 5. melatonin
____ 6. IDDM
____ 7. myxedema
____ 8. HRT
____ 9. adrenal virilism
____ 10. GTT
____ 11. dwarfism
____ 12. diabetes mellitus
____ 13. cretinism
____ 14. tetany
____ 15. corticosteroids
____ 16. thyrotoxicosis
____ 17. gigantism
____ 18. Na⁺
____ 19. Cushing syndrome
____ 20. NIDDM
____ 21. adenocarcinoma
____ 22. diabetes insipidus
____ 23. polydipsia
____ 24. RAIU
____ 25. acromegaly

a. results from hypersecretion of adrenal cortex
b. regulates circadian rhythm
c. may result from lack of growth hormone
d. poor mental and physical development
e. have strong anti-inflammatory action
f. glandular cancer
g. type 2 diabetes mellitus
h. results from low antidiuretic hormone
i. extreme hypersecretion of thyroid hormones
j. test of thyroid function
k. enlarged bones of head and extremities
l. sodium
m. autoimmune form of thyroiditis
n. bulging eyeballs
o. may come in pill, injection, or skin patch form
p. excessive thirst
q. test to diagnose diabetes mellitus
r. irritable nerves and painful muscle cramps
s. excessive testosterone in a female
t. patient must take insulin injections
u. enlarged thyroid gland
v. used to study function of endocrine glands
w. patients have puffy face and dry, puffy skin
x. excessive growth in height
y. comes in two distinctly different forms

Chapter 15 Answer Keys

Worksheet 15A Answer Key

1. gland
2. adrenal glands
3. adrenal glands
4. secrete
5. sugar
6. sugar
7. ovary
8. testes
9. ovary
10. pancreas
11. parathyroid gland
12. pineal gland
13. pituitary gland
14. testes
15. thymus gland
16. thyroid gland
17. thyroid gland
18. within
19. outward
20. thirst

Worksheet 15B Answer Key

1. extremities
2. cancer
3. cell
4. eye
5. poison
6. excessive
7. insufficient
8. many, much
9. puncture to withdraw fluid
10. cell
11. surgical removal
12. swelling
13. blood condition
14. inflammation
15. one who studies
16. study of
17. softening
18. enlarged
19. resembling
20. tumor
21. cutting into
22. disease
23. surgical fixation
24. surgical repair
25. rupture
26. urine condition

Worksheet 15C Answer Key

1. aden/o = gland; carcin/o = cancer; -oma = tumor
2. aden/o = gland; -malacia = softening
3. adren/o = adrenal gland; -megaly = enlarged
4. adrenal/o = adrenal gland; -itis = inflammation
5. endo- = within; crin/o = to secrete; -logy = study of
6. hyper- = excessive; glyc/o = sugar; -emia = blood condition
7. glycos/o = sugar; -uria = urine condition
8. oophor/o = ovary; -plasty = surgical repair
9. oophor/o = ovary; -otomy = cutting into
10. orchi/o = testes; -pexy = surgical fixation
11. orchi/o = testes; -ectomy = surgical removal
12. ovari/o = ovary; -ian = pertaining to
13. ovari/o = ovary; -rrhexis = ruptured
14. pancreat/o = pancreas; -ic = pertaining to
15. pancreat/o = pancreas; -otomy = cutting into
16. parathyroid/o = parathyroid gland; -al = pertaining to
17. hypo- = insufficient; parathyroid/o = parathyroid gland; -ism = condition
18. pineal/o = pineal gland; -ectomy = surgical removal
19. hyper- = excessive; pituitar/o = pituitary gland; -ism = condition
20. poly- = too much; -dipsia = thirst
21. testicul/o = testes; -ar = pertaining to
22. thym/o = thymus gland; -oma = tumor
23. thyr/o = thyroid gland; -megaly = enlarged
24. thyroid/o = thyroid gland; -al = pertaining to
25. hypo- = insufficient; thyroid/o = thyroid gland; -ism = condition

Worksheet 15D Answer Key

1. acromegaly
2. virilism
3. corticosteroids
4. cretinism
5. insipidus; mellitus
6. gigantism
7. goiter
8. tetany
9. pheochromocytoma
10. polydipsia

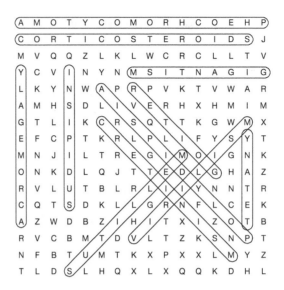

Worksheet 15E Answer Key

1. tetany
2. radioimmunoassay
3. myxedema
4. Hashimoto disease
5. goiter
6. exophthalmos
7. dwarfism
8. Cushing syndrome
9. adrenal feminization
10. glycosuria

Worksheet 15F Answer Key

1. adrenocorticotropic hormone
2. antidiuretic hormone
3. diabetes insipidus
4. diabetes mellitus
5. fasting blood sugar
6. follicle-stimulating hormone
7. growth hormone
8. glucose tolerance test
9. insulin-dependent diabetes mellitus
10. potassium
11. luteinizing hormone
12. melanocyte-stimulating hormone
13. sodium
14. non–insulin-dependent diabetes mellitus
15. neutral protamine Hagedorn (insulin)
16. prolactin
17. parathyroid hormone
18. radioactive iodine
19. radioimmunoassay
20. triiodothyronine
21. thyroxine

Worksheet 15G Answer Key

1. Diabetes mellitus
2. cephalalgia—head ache; vomiting—expelling food from stomach; dyspnea—difficulty breathing; disorientation—confused about his surroundings
3. blood sugar test—to measure the level of sugar present in the blood
4. Hyperglycemia—blood level of glucose is too high
5. Type 1, insulin-dependent diabetes mellitus because he has had it since childhood and he is taking insulin shots
6. Type 2 or non-insulin dependent diabetes mellitus; develops later in life, patients typically take medication to improve insulin function rather than insulin itself

Worksheet 15H Answer Key

Essay activity, student answers will vary.

Worksheet 15I Answer Key

Student answers will vary.

Chapter 15 Word Parts Quiz Answer Key

1. extremities
2. gland
3. adrenal glands
4. secrete
5. sugar
6. ovary
7. testes
8. pancreas
9. parathyroid gland
10. pineal gland
11. pituitary gland
12. thymus gland
13. thyroid gland
14. poison
15. within
16. insufficient
17. puncture to withdraw fluid
18. thirst
19. swelling
20. softening
21. enlarged
22. resembling
23. disease
24. surgical fixation
25. rupture

Chapter 15 Spelling Quiz Answer Key

1. homeostasis
2. circadian
3. adrenocorticotropin
4. testosterone
5. triiodothyronine
6. exophthalmos
7. pheochromocytoma
8. cretinism
9. thyrotoxicosis
10. radioimmunoassay
11. acromegaly
12. virilism
13. corticosteroids
14. Hashimoto
15. goiter
16. myxedema
17. ovariocentesis
18. glycosuria
19. hyperparathyroidism
20. endocrinoma

Chapter 15 Labeling Quiz Answer Key

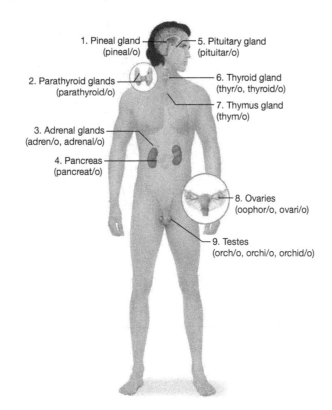

Chapter 15 Word Building Quiz Answer Key

1. pinealectomy
2. testicular
3. adenocyte
4. adrenalopathy
5. hyperglycemia
6. oophoroplasty
7. orchiopexy
8. endocrinologist
9. pancreatic
10. hypoparathyroidism
11. oophoritis
12. thyrotoxicosis
13. polydipsia
14. adenoid
15. ovarian
16. thyromegaly
17. endocrinoma
18. thymic
19. ovariocentesis
20. adrenomegaly
21. thyroiditis
22. hypopituitarism
23. adrenalitis
24. ovariorrhexis
25. glycosuria

Chapter 15 Quiz Answer Key

Fill-in-the-Blank

1. homeostasis
2. target organs
3. adrenal cortex; adrenal medulla
4. estrogen; testosterone
5. glucose
6. hormone
7. pancreas
8. calcium
9. pituitary gland
10. immune

Word Building

1. adenomalacia
2. hyperglycemia
3. thyromegaly
4. thymoma
5. hypopituitarism
6. pinealectomy
7. polyuria
8. pancreatitis
9. ovariorrhexis
10. orchiopexy

Matching

1. v
2. n
3. u
4. m
5. b
6. t
7. w
8. o
9. s
10. q
11. c
12. y
13. d
14. r
15. e
16. i
17. x
18. l
19. a
20. g
21. f
22. h
23. p
24. j
25. k

Chapter 16
Ophthalmology: The Eye

Learning Objectives

After completing this chapter, students will be able to:

1. Understand the function of the eye.
2. Describe the medical specialty of ophthalmology.
3. Define ophthalmology-related combining forms, prefixes, and suffixes.
4. Identify the structures treated in ophthalmology.
5. Build ophthalmology medical terms from word parts.
6. Explain ophthalmology medical terms.
7. Use ophthalmology abbreviations.

Use this word list to focus your studying for the chapter test.

Blepharoptosis
Blepharoplasty
Conjunctivitis
Coreometry
Corneal abrasion
Diabetic retinopathy
Diplopia
Hyperopia
Intraocular
Iritis
Myopia
Nasolacrimal
Nyctalopia
Ophthalmologist
Ophthalmology
Ophthalmoscope
Optometry
Pupillary
Radial keratotomy
Retinal detachment
Scleral
Tonometer

Abbreviations

IOL
OD
OS
OU
PERRLA

Worksheet 16A
New Word Parts

Directions: Write out the meaning for each combining form, prefix, and suffix. Then locate a new term from the chapter that uses the word part.

Combining Forms	Meaning	Chapter Term	Meaning
1. aque/o	_____	_____	_____
2. blephar/o	_____	_____	_____
3. choroid/o	_____	_____	_____
4. conjunctiv/o	_____	_____	_____
5. core/o	_____	_____	_____
6. corne/o	_____	_____	_____
7. cycl/o	_____	_____	_____
8. dacry/o	_____	_____	_____
9. ir/o	_____	_____	_____
10. irid/o	_____	_____	_____
11. kerat/o	_____	_____	_____
12. lacrim/o	_____	_____	_____
13. ocul/o	_____	_____	_____
14. ophthalm/o	_____	_____	_____
15. opt/o	_____	_____	_____
16. phac/o	_____	_____	_____
17. pupill/o	_____	_____	_____
18. retin/o	_____	_____	_____
19. scler/o	_____	_____	_____
20. ton/o	_____	_____	_____
21. vitre/o	_____	_____	_____

(Continued)

Prefixes	Meaning	Chapter Term	Meaning
22. hemi-	_____	_____	_____
23. micro-	_____	_____	_____

Suffixes

24. -ician	_____	_____	_____
25. -opia	_____	_____	_____
26. -phobia	_____	_____	_____

Worksheet 16B
Word Part Review

Directions: Write out the meaning for each combining form, prefix, and suffix.

Combining Forms Meaning

1. aden/o _____
2. ambly/o _____
3. angi/o _____
4. chrom/o _____
5. cry/o _____
6. cyst/o _____
7. dipl/o _____
8. myc/o _____
9. nas/o _____
10. phot/o _____
11. xer/o _____

Prefixes

12. a- _____
13. an- _____
14. hyper- _____
15. intra- _____

Suffixes

16. -ectomy _____
17. -graphy _____
18. -itis _____
19. -lith _____
20. -logist _____

(Continued)

Suffixes	Meaning
21. -logy	_____
22. -lysis	_____
23. -malacia	_____
24. -meter	_____
25. -metry	_____
26. -otomy	_____
27. -pathy	_____
28. -pexy	_____
29. -plasty	_____
30. -plegia	_____
31. -ptosis	_____
32. -rrhea	_____
33. -sclerosis	_____
34. -scope	_____
35. -scopy	_____

Worksheet 16C
Word Surgery

Directions: Below are terms built from word parts. Analyze each term by listing and defining the word parts used to build it.

Medical Term	Word Part Meanings
1. blepharoptosis	_____
2. choroiditis	_____
3. iridoplegia	_____
4. nasolacrimal	_____
5. intraocular	_____
6. keratectomy	_____
7. ophthalmoscope	_____
8. phacosclerosis	_____
9. hemianopia	_____
10. conjunctivitis	_____
11. retinopathy	_____

(*Continued*)

Medical Term	Word Part Meanings
12. optometry	_____
13. dacryocystitis	_____
14. phacolysis	_____
15. ophthalmologist	_____
16. scleromalacia	_____
17. coreometer	_____
18. tonometry	_____
19. keratoplasty	_____
20. dacryorrhea	_____
21. oculomycosis	_____
22. cryoretinopexy	_____
23. cyclotomy	_____
24. diplopia	_____
25. xerophthalmia	_____

Worksheet 16D
Word Search

Directions: Find and circle the answer for each fill-in-the-blank question in the word search puzzle.

1. The ability of the eye to adjust to various distances is called _____.

2. _____ is a bright green dye used to highlight corneal abrasions.

3. _____ uses sound waves to break up a cataract.

4. A(n) _____ causes the lens to become opaque or cloudy.

5. Jerky involuntary eye movements are called _____.

6. _____ causes vision to be fuzzy due to irregular curvature of the cornea.

7. _____ actually means an excessive sensitivity to light.

8. An increase in intraocular pressure may cause _____.

9. A(n) _____ chart is used to test visual acuity.

10. Farsightedness is also called _____.

```
P H A C O E M U L S I F I C A T I O N
X Z K T B N L H V R A N C F V J C V Z
B D N M K J C L M S I V W L L Q G W H
H G W T M T H H T E N A M P M D F W N
T C T Y T R F I C Z O V M V W K J Z L
N K A N F N G S X B I L F O Z F N R G
P M L T R M E W A K T P Q H C Y G L F
T B T P A R M I L V A N B W N U D G Z
C T Z T O R P P C D D N C Y R W A C T
R R I U Y O A R G L O M G L X L D L M
J S L M R Q Q C R G M Y D N M V M R G
M F Q E Q R R Y T J M T J Y X Z F W L
C C P J L K W B K V O T B S W B N X P
K Y X T M K F T N M C K V T Z M E Y V
H T G P K R N J H N C R T A Z K L Z F
Q L Z B J K Y N M L A H H G X L L R J
J A I B O H P O T O H P H M Y H E Y L
F B G M W B Z Y B L M J C U D N N R X
M K Q H L K K R Q W R H T S L T S R Z
```

350 Chapter 16/OPHTHALMOLOGY: THE EYE © 2012 Pearson Education, Inc.

Worksheet 16E
Unscramble

Directions: Unscramble each medical term below. A definition for the term is given below each scrambled term.

1. a a i o b l m p y _____

   loss of vision not due to any disease

2. a a a a i o c c h l m p _____

   lens softening

3. a e i o l n p r t s t y _____

   surgical repair of the retina

4. p o y a m i _____

   near-sighted

5. a a a i o c h m p r s t o _____

   profound inability to see color

6. a e u u o s q _____

   pertaining to water

7. y r o c t r e c t i x n o a _____

   removing lens using a cold probe

8. p o n c i i t a _____

   healthcare professional trained to make corrective lenses

9. a t s r s i b s u m _____

   weakness of external eye muscles

10. l u c o c o m i o s s y _____

    fungus infection of the eye

Worksheet 16F
Abbreviations

Directions: Write the full term that each abbreviation stands for.

1. Acc _____

2. Astigm _____

3. c.gl. _____

4. cyl _____

5. D _____

6. ECCE _____

7. ICCE _____

8. IOL _____

9. IOP _____

10. LASIK _____

11. MY _____

12. OD _____

13. Ophth _____

14. OS _____

15. OU _____

16. PERRLA _____

17. PRK _____

18. REM _____

19. RK _____

20. s.gl. _____

21. VA _____

22. VF _____

Worksheet 16G
Case Study

Directions: Below is a case study presentation of a patient with a condition covered in this chapter. Read the case study and answer the questions below. Some questions will ask for information not included within this chapter. Use your text, a medical dictionary, or any other reference material you choose to answer these questions.

Patient is a 79-year-old female who has noted gradual deterioration of vision and increasing photophobia during the past year, particularly in the right eye. She states that it feels like there is a film over her right eye. She denies any change in vision in her left eye. Patient has used corrective lenses her entire adult life to correct hyperopia. Visual acuity test showed no change in this patient's long-standing hyperopia. The eye muscles function properly and there is no evidence of conjunctivitis or nystagmus. The pupils react properly to light. Intraocular pressure is normal. Ophthalmoscopy revealed presence of large opaque cataract in lens of right eye. There is a very small cataract forming in the left eye. Patient was scheduled for phacoemulsification of cataract and IOL implant.

1. The results of the physical exam state that the patient's pupils react properly to light. How do pupils react in bright and dim light? Why is this important?

   _____
   _____

2. Carefully read the results of the physical examination and list all tests that were normal.

   _____
   _____

3. Intraocular pressure is normal. What pathology is caused by increased intraocular pressure?

   _____
   _____

4. This patient wears corrective lenses for what condition? What is the common name for this condition?

   _____
   _____

5. Her cataract was removed by phacoemulsification. Describe this procedure. What does IOL mean?

   _____
   _____

6. Using your text as a reference, describe another procedure that could have been used to remove the cataract.

   _____
   _____

Worksheet 16H
Web Destinations

Strabismus

Prevent Blindness America is the nation's leading volunteer eye health and safety organization dedicated to fighting blindness and saving sight. Visit its website at www.preventblindness.org. Left click on the Your Child's Sight link. Scroll towards the bottom of this page and click on the Strabismus link. Write a description of this condition with the goal of informing new parents what is wrong with their baby's eyes. Use the Back Button to return to the previous webpage. Left click the Amblyopia link and conclude your essay by explaining what would happen to their child if the strabismus developed into amblyopia.

Common Vision Problems

According to the National Eye Institute, the most common vision problems are refractive errors, more commonly known as nearsightedness, farsightedness, and astigmatism. Visit the National Eye Institute's Health Vision site at www.nei.nih.gov/healthyeyes and click on the Common vision problems link. Navigate through these pages to learn about vision problems and describe: refraction, myopia, hyperopia, and astigmatism.

Worksheet 16I
Professional Profile and Journal

Professional Profile

Optometry

Optometry is the professional practice that provides care for the eyes including examining the eyes for diseases, assessing visual acuity, prescribing corrective lenses and eye treatments, and educating patients. Optometry services are found in private offices, acute care facilities, and clinics. See Medical Terminology Interactive for a video on Opticians.

Doctor of Optometry (OD)

- Also referred to as an optometrist
- Graduates from an accredited 4-year college of optometry after attending at least 3 years of undergraduate college
- May take additional training in pediatric optometry, geriatric optometry, vision therapy, ocular disease, low-vision rehabilitation, or family practice optometry
- Passes written and clinical examinations by the state of employment

Optician

- Grinds and fits prescription lenses and contacts as prescribed by a physician or optometrist
- Completes a 2- to 4-year apprenticeship
- Licensure required by some states

For more information regarding these health careers, visit the following websites:

- American Optometric Association at www.aoanet.org
- National Optometric Association at www.natoptassoc.org
- Prevent Blindness America at www.preventblindness.org

Professional Journal

In this exercise you will now have an opportunity to put the words you have learned into practice. Imagine yourself in the role of an optometrist. If you refer back to the Professional Profile, you will see that this healthcare professional is responsible for examining eyes for diseases, assessing visual acuity, prescribing corrective lenses and eye treatments, and educating patients. Use the 10 words listed below, or any other new terms from this chapter, to write sentences to describe the patients you saw today.

An example of a sentence is: *The patient's increased* **intraocular** *pressure and* **glaucoma** *eventually resulted in her blindness.*

1. blepharoptosis _____

2. cataract _____

3. conjunctivitis _____

4. myopia _____

5. fluorescein angiography _____

6. macular degeneration _____

7. achromatopsia _____

8. radial keratotomy _____

9. cornea _____

10. photophobia _____

Name _____   Date _____   Score _____

Chapter 16 Word Parts Quiz

Directions: Define the combining form, prefix, or suffix in the spaces provided.

1. ambly/o _____
2. blephar/o _____
3. choroid/o _____
4. chrom/o _____
5. conjunctiv/o _____
6. core/o _____
7. corne/o _____
8. cry/o _____
9. cycl/o _____
10. dipl/o _____
11. irid/o _____
12. lacrim/o _____
13. myc/o _____
14. ocul/o _____
15. ophthalm/o _____
16. phac/o _____
17. phot/o _____
18. retin/o _____
19. scler/o _____
20. xer/o _____
21. hemi- _____
22. micro- _____
23. -phobia _____
24. -ician _____
25. -opia _____

Name _____ Date _____ Score _____

Chapter 16 Spelling Quiz

Directions: Write each term as your instructor pronounces it.

1. _____
2. _____
3. _____
4. _____
5. _____
6. _____
7. _____
8. _____
9. _____
10. _____
11. _____
12. _____
13. _____
14. _____
15. _____
16. _____
17. _____
18. _____
19. _____
20. _____

Name _____ Date _____ Score _____

Chapter 16 Labeling Quiz 1

Directions: Label the parts of the eye.

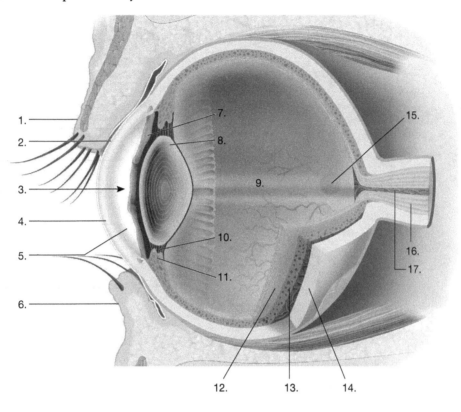

1. _____
2. _____
3. _____
4. _____
5. _____
6. _____
7. _____
8. _____
9. _____
10. _____
11. _____
12. _____
13. _____
14. _____
15. _____
16. _____
17. _____

Name _____ Date _____ Score _____

Chapter 16 Labeling Quiz 2

Directions: Label the accessory structures to the eye.

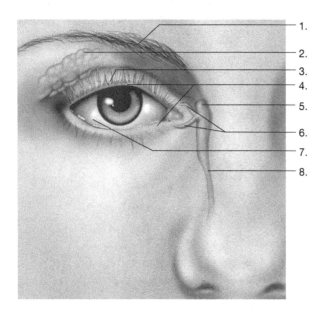

1. _____
2. _____
3. _____
4. _____
5. _____
6. _____
7. _____
8. _____

Name _____ Date _____ Score _____

Chapter 16 Word Building Quiz

Directions: Build a single medical term for each phrase below.

1. pertaining to glassy _____
2. surgical repair of cornea _____
3. inflammation of choroid layer _____
4. abnormal condition of eye fungus _____
5. inflammation of iris _____
6. tear flow _____
7. process of measuring pupil _____
8. instrument to measure pressure _____
9. destruction of the lens _____
10. cutting into ciliary body _____
11. drooping eyelid _____
12. pertaining to the sclera _____
13. state of dry eyes _____
14. surgical fixation of retina with cold _____
15. pertaining to the conjunctiva _____
16. without half vision _____
17. inflammation of tear sac _____
18. instrument to measure vision _____
19. softening of the sclera _____
20. paralysis of ciliary body _____
21. pertaining to the pupil _____
22. cutting into the iris _____
23. hardening of the lens _____
24. tear stone _____
25. pertaining to the nose and tears _____

Name _____ Date _____ Score _____

Chapter 16 Quiz

Fill-in-the-Blank

1. Images are carried to the brain via the _____.

2. The accessory organs to the eye include the _____,
   _____, and _____.

3. An OD is called a(n) _____ while an MD or DO specializing in eye care
   is called a(n) _____.

4. The _____ is a mucous membrane protecting the anterior surface of the eyeball.

5. The opening in the center of the iris is called the _____.

6. The _____ is a ring of muscle around the outer edge of the lens.

7. The three layers of the eyeball are the _____,
   _____, and _____.

8. The _____ is a region of the retina that contains only cones and is the point of clearest vision.

9. The _____ is a gel-like substance filling the large open cavity inside the eyeball between the lens and retina.

10. Light receptors are called _____ and _____.

Word Building

Build a term that means:

1. instrument to measure pupil   _____
2. tear gland inflammation   _____
3. pertaining to within the eye   _____
4. surgical repair of eyelid   _____
5. double vision   _____

(Continued)

Build a term that means:

6. retina disease _____

7. softening of sclera _____

8. paralysis of ciliary body _____

9. cutting into the cornea _____

10. pertaining to water _____

Matching

1. cilia
2. astigmatism
3. glaucoma
4. LASIK
5. accommodation
6. macular degeneration
7. diabetic retinopathy
8. nyctalopia
9. cataract
10. myopia
11. optician
12. IOL
13. photophobia
14. amblyopia
15. Snellen chart
16. fluorescein
17. OD
18. hyperopia
19. strabismus
20. cryoextraction
21. RK
22. laser retinal photocoagulation
23. phacoemulsification
24. achromatopsia
25. nystagmus

a. farsightedness
b. opaque or cloudy lens
c. artificial lens
d. loss of vision in center of visual field
e. using cold to remove cataract
f. stabilizes detached retina
g. bright green dye
h. also called lazy eye
i. jerky involuntary eye movements
j. removes cataract using sound waves
k. color blindness
l. nearsightedness
m. right eye
n. caused by irregular curvature of cornea
o. spoke-like incisions in cornea; corrects myopia
p. small hemorrhages and edema in retina
q. corrects myopia using lasers
r. used to test visual acuity
s. eyelashes
t. excessive sensitivity to light
u. caused by increased intraocular pressure
v. trained to make corrective lenses
w. ability of eye to adjust to various distances
x. weakness of external eye muscles
y. night blindness

Chapter 16 Answer Keys

Worksheet 16A Answer Key

1. water
2. eyelid
3. choroid layer
4. conjunctiva
5. pupil
6. cornea
7. ciliary body
8. tears
9. iris
10. iris
11. cornea
12. tears
13. eye
14. eye
15. eye, vision
16. lens
17. pupil
18. retina
19. sclera
20. tension, pressure
21. glassy
22. half
23. small
24. specialist
25. vision
26. fear

Worksheet 16B Answer Key

1. gland
2. dull or dim
3. vessel
4. color
5. cold
6. sac
7. double
8. fungus
9. nose
10. light
11. dry
12. without
13. without
14. excessive
15. within
16. surgical removal
17. process of recording
18. inflammation
19. stone
20. one who studies
21. study of
22. destruction
23. softening
24. instrument to measure
25. process of measuring
26. cutting into
27. disease
28. surgical fixation
29. surgical repair
30. paralysis
31. drooping
32. flow
33. hardening
34. instrument to view
35. process of viewing

Worksheet 16C Answer Key

1. blephar/o = eyelid; -ptosis = drooping
2. choroid/o = choroid layer; -itis = inflammation
3. irid/o = iris; -plegia = paralysis
4. nas/o = nose; lacrim/o = tears; -al = pertaining to
5. intra- = within; ocul/o = eye; -ar = pertaining to
6. kerat/ = cornea; -ectomy = surgical removal
7. ophthalm/o = eye; -scope = instrument to view
8. phac/o = lens; -sclerosis = hardening
9. hemi- = half; an- = without; -opia = vision
10. conjunctiv/o = conjunctiva; -itis = inflammation
11. retin/o = retina; -pathy = disease
12. opt/o = vision; -metry = process of measuring
13. dacry/o = tears; cyst/o = sac; -itis = inflammation
14. phac/o = lens; -lysis = destruction
15. ophthalm/o = eye; -logist = one who studies
16. scler/o = sclera; -malacia = softening
17. core/o = pupil; -meter = instrument to measure
18. ton/o = pressure; -metry = process of measuring
19. kerat/o = cornea; -plasty = surgical repair
20. dacry/o = tears; -rrhea = flow
21. ocul/o = eye; myc/o = fungus; -osis = abnormal condition
22. cry/o = cold; retin/o = retina; -pexy = surgical fixation
23. cycl/o = ciliary body; -otomy = cutting into
24. dipl/o = doub;e; -opia = vision
25. xer/o = dry; ophthalm/o = eye; -ia = state/condition

Worksheet 16D Answer Key

1. accommodation
2. fluorescein
3. phacoemulsification
4. cataract
5. nystagmus
6. astigmatism
7. photophobia
8. glaucoma
9. Snellen
10. hyperopia

```
P H A C O E M U L S I F I C A T I O N
X Z K T B N L H V R A N C F V J C V Z
B D N M K J C L M S I V W L L Q G W H
H G W T M T H H T E N A M P M D F W N
T C T Y T R F I C Z O V M V W K J Z L
N K A N F N G S X B I L F O Z F N R G
P M L T R M E W A K T P Q H C Y G L F
T B T P A R M I L V A N B W N U D G Z
C T Z T O R P P C D D N C Y R W A C T
R R I U Y O A R G L O M G L X L D L M
J S L M R Q Q C R G M Y D N M V M R G
M F Q E Q R R Y T J M T J Y X Z F W L
C C P J L K W B K V O T B S W B N X P
K Y X T M K F T N M C K V T Z M E Y V
H T G P K R N J H N C R T A Z K L Z F
Q L Z B J K Y N M L A H H G X L L R J
J A I B O H P O T O H P H M Y H E Y L
F B G M W B Z Y B L M J C U D N N R X
M K Q H L K K R Q W R H T S L T S R Z
```

Worksheet 16E Answer Key

1. amblyopia
2. phacomalacia
3. retinoplasty
4. myopia
5. achromatopsia
6. aqueous
7. cryoextraction
8. optician
9. strabismus
10. oculomycosis

Worksheet 16F Answer Key

1. accommodation
2. astigmatism
3. correction with glasses
4. cylindrical lens
5. diopter (lens strength)
6. extracapsular cataract extraction
7. intracapsular cataract cryoextraction
8. intraocular lens
9. intraocular pressure
10. laser-assisted in-situ keratomileusis
11. myopia
12. right eye (oculus dexter), doctor of optometry
13. ophthalmology
14. left eye (oculus sinister)
15. both eyes (oculus uterque)
16. pupils equal, round, react to light and accommodation
17. photo-refractive keratectomy
18. rapid eye movement
19. radial keratotomy
20. without correction or glasses
21. visual acuity
22. visual field

Worksheet 16G Answer Key

1. Pupils contract in bright light and dilate in dim light to make sure the proper amount of light gets into the eyeball.
2. eye muscles function properly, no evidence of conjunctivitis or nystagmus, pupils react properly to light, intraocular pressure is normal
3. glaucoma
4. hyperopia; farsightedness
5. phacoemulsification—high frequency sound waves used to beak up cataract which is then removed by suction with a needle; IOL—intraocular lens implant
6. cryoextraction—removes cataract from lens with extremely cold probe

Worksheet 16H Answer Key

Essay activity, student answers will vary.

Worksheet 16I Answer Key

Student answers will vary.

Chapter 16 Word Parts Quiz Answer Key

1. dull or dim
2. eyelid
3. choroid layer
4. color
5. conjunctiva
6. pupil
7. cornea
8. cold
9. ciliary body
10. double
11. iris
12. tears
13. fungus
14. eye
15. eye
16. lens
17. light
18. retina
19. sclera
20. dry
21. half
22. small
23. fear
24. specialist
25. vision

Chapter 16 Spelling Quiz Answer Key

1. sclera
2. aqueous
3. nasolacrimal
4. blepharoptosis
5. dacryocystitis
6. xerophthalmia
7. achromatopsia
8. astigmatism
9. amblyopia
10. glaucoma
11. ophthalmoscope
12. accommodation
13. cryoextraction
14. fluorescein
15. intraocular
16. photocoagulation
17. nyctalopia
18. nystagmus
19. phacoemulsification
20. strabismus

Chapter 16 Labeling Quiz 1 Answer Key

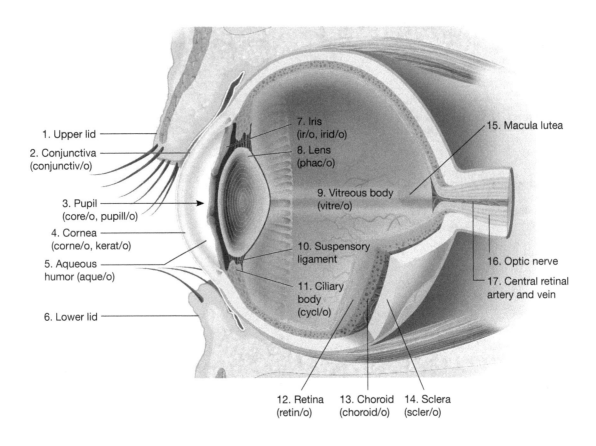

1. Upper lid
2. Conjunctiva (conjunctiv/o)
3. Pupil (core/o, pupill/o)
4. Cornea (corne/o, kerat/o)
5. Aqueous humor (aque/o)
6. Lower lid
7. Iris (ir/o, irid/o)
8. Lens (phac/o)
9. Vitreous body (vitre/o)
10. Suspensory ligament
11. Ciliary body (cycl/o)
12. Retina (retin/o)
13. Choroid (choroid/o)
14. Sclera (scler/o)
15. Macula lutea
16. Optic nerve
17. Central retinal artery and vein

Chapter 16 Labeling Quiz 2 Answer Key

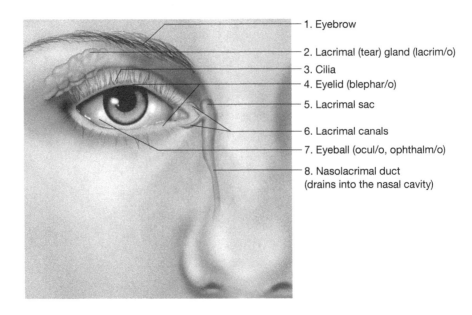

1. Eyebrow
2. Lacrimal (tear) gland (lacrim/o)
3. Cilia
4. Eyelid (blephar/o)
5. Lacrimal sac
6. Lacrimal canals
7. Eyeball (ocul/o, ophthalm/o)
8. Nasolacrimal duct (drains into the nasal cavity)

Chapter 16 Word Building Quiz Answer Key

1. vitreous
2. keratoplasty
3. choroiditis
4. oculomycosis
5. iritis
6. dacryorrhea
7. coreometry
8. tonometer
9. phacolysis
10. cyclotomy
11. blepharoptosis
12. scleral
13. xerophthalmia
14. cryoretinopexy
15. conjunctival
16. hemianopia
17. dacryocystitis
18. optometer
19. scleromalacia
20. cycloplegia
21. pupillary
22. iridotomy
23. phacosclerosis
24. dacryolith
25. nasolacrimal

Chapter 16 Quiz Answer Key

Fill-in-the-Blank

1. optic nerve
2. conjunctiva, eyelids, lacrimal glands
3. optometrist; ophthalmologist
4. conjunctiva
5. pupil
6. ciliary body
7. sclera, choroid, retina
8. fovea centralis
9. vitreous humor
10. rods; cones

Word Building

1. pupillometer
2. dacryoadenitis
3. intraocular
4. blepharoplasty
5. diplopia
6. retinopathy
7. scleromalacia
8. cycloplegia
9. keratotomy
10. aqueous

Matching

1. s
2. n
3. u
4. q
5. w
6. d
7. p
8. y
9. b
10. l
11. v
12. c
13. t
14. h
15. r
16. g
17. m
18. a
19. x
20. e
21. o
22. f
23. j
24. k
25. i

Chapter 17
Otorhinolaryngology: The Ear, Nose, and Throat

Learning Objectives

After completing this chapter, students will be able to:

1. Understand the function of the ear, nose, and throat.
2. Describe the medical specialty of otorhinolaryngology.
3. Define otorhinolaryngology-related combining forms, prefixes, and suffixes.
4. Identify the organs treated in otorhinolaryngology.
5. Build otorhinolaryngology medical terms from word parts.
6. Explain otorhinolaryngology medical terms.
7. Use otorhinolaryngology abbreviations.

Use this word list to focus your studying for the chapter test.

Adenoidectomy	Otitis media	**Abbreviations**
Aphonia	Otoscope	
Audiologist	Pertussis	AD
Audiometry	Pharyngitis	AS
Aural	Rhinitis	AU
Croup	Rhinoplasty	DPT
Decongestant	Rhinorrhea	EENT
Dysphonia	Sinusitis	ENT
Epiglottic	Tinnitus	ET
Laryngitis	Tonsillectomy	HEENT
Laryngospasm	Tracheotomy	OM
Nares	Tympanic membrane	T&A
Nasal cannula	Tympanotomy	URI
Nasogastric	Vertigo	
Otalgia		

Worksheet 17A
New Word Parts

Directions: Write out the meaning for each combining form, prefix, and suffix. Then locate a new term from the chapter that uses the word part.

Combining Forms	Meaning	Chapter Term	Meaning
1. adenoid/o	_____	_____	_____
2. audi/o	_____	_____	_____
3. audit/o	_____	_____	_____
4. aur/o	_____	_____	_____
5. cochle/o	_____	_____	_____
6. epiglott/o	_____	_____	_____
7. laryng/o	_____	_____	_____
8. myring/o	_____	_____	_____
9. nas/o	_____	_____	_____
10. ot/o	_____	_____	_____
11. pharyng/o	_____	_____	_____
12. rhin/o	_____	_____	_____
13. sinus/o	_____	_____	_____
14. tonsill/o	_____	_____	_____
15. trache/o	_____	_____	_____
16. tympan/o	_____	_____	_____

Prefixes

	Meaning	Chapter Term	Meaning
17. de-	_____	_____	_____
18. endo-	_____	_____	_____
19. pan-	_____	_____	_____
20. para-	_____	_____	_____

(Continued)

Suffixes	Meaning	Chapter Term	Meaning
21. -osmia	_____	_____	_____
22. -phonia	_____	_____	_____

Worksheet 17B
Word Part Review

Directions: Write out the meaning for each combining form, prefix, and suffix.

Combining Forms	Meaning
1. gastr/o	
2. myc/o	
3. neur/o	
4. py/o	

Prefixes

5. a- _____
6. an- _____
7. dys- _____

Suffixes

8. -algia _____
9. -ectomy _____
10. -gram _____
11. -itis _____
12. -logist _____
13. -logy _____
14. -megaly _____
15. -meter _____
16. -metry _____
17. -oma _____
18. -osis _____
19. -otomy _____
20. -plasty _____
21. -plegia _____

(Continued)

Suffixes	Meaning
22. -rrhea	_____
23. -rrhexis	_____
24. -sclerosis	_____
25. -scope	_____
26. -scopy	_____
27. -spasm	_____
28. -stenosis	_____

Worksheet 17C
Word Surgery

Directions: Below are terms built from word parts. Analyze each term by listing and defining the word parts used to build it.

Medical Term	Word Part Meanings
1. adenoiditis	
2. laryngoplegia	
3. otalgia	
4. anosmia	
5. pharyngoplasty	
6. endotracheal	
7. cochlear	
8. myringoplasty	
9. tracheomegaly	
10. dysphonia	
11. tympanorrhexis	

(*Continued*)

Medical Term	Word Part Meanings
12. audiogram	
13. tympanoplasty	
14. epiglottitis	
15. nasogastric	
16. rhinomycosis	
17. auditory	
18. pansinusitis	
19. myringosclerosis	
20. aural	
21. pharyngotomy	
22. audiology	
23. otopyorrhea	
24. laryngospasm	
25. tonsillectomy	

Worksheet 17D
Word Search

Directions: Find and circle the answer for each fill-in-the-blank question in the word search puzzle.

1. A(n) _____ neuroma is a benign tumor of the auditory nerve sheath.

2. A(n) _____ is a medication to reduce nasal and sinus stuffiness.

3. Endotracheal _____ involves placing a tube through the mouth and into the trachea.

4. The medical term for whooping cough is _____.

5. A(n) _____ implant is a hearing device surgically placed behind the ear.

6. The medical term for dizziness is _____.

7. _____ is the medical term for nose bleed.

8. The symptoms of _____ include a barking cough.

9. A nasal _____ is a two-pronged plastic device for delivering oxygen.

10. The medical term for ringing in the ears is _____.

```
T  D  S  I  X  A  T  S  I  P  E  N
N  E  P  T  W  P  N  D  V  J  O  C
C  C  K  Z  R  T  U  E  W  I  L  I
C  O  T  N  X  D  R  O  T  P  S  T
A  N  C  T  T  H  A  R  U  R  S
L  G  F  H  I  T  B  N  T  C  X  U
U  E  F  G  L  U  V  I  M  C  R  O
N  S  O  X  T  E  N  L  B  C  D  C
N  T  R  N  V  N  A  M  Q  L  N  A
A  A  I  M  I  C  X  R  K  K  J  B
C  N  X  T  K  Z  C  G  W  C  B  D
M  T  P  E  R  T  U  S  S  I  S  K
```

Worksheet 17E
Unscramble

Directions: Unscramble each medical term below. A definition for the term is given below each scrambled term.

1. p r a y l g o s n c e o _____

    instrument to view the voice box

2. s n i o m a a _____

    term meaning unable to smell

3. x m a p o t r h e n r i s y _____

    term meaning ruptured eardrum

4. s i n t t i u n _____

    ringing in the ears

5. n a c u n a l _____

    two-pronged plastic device for delivering oxygen

6. s p e i t a s i x _____

    nosebleed

7. h c r a e s o t e n i t o s s _____

    narrowing of the trachea

8. s t e u r s s i p _____

    whooping cough

9. h i n s r l p a o y t _____

    surgical repair of the nose

10. a o s n h r p a n e g a l y _____

    pertaining to the nose and throat

Worksheet 17F
Abbreviations

Directions: Write the full term that each abbreviation stands for.

1. AD _____
2. AS _____
3. AU _____
4. DPT _____
5. EENT _____
6. ENT _____
7. ET _____
8. HEENT _____
9. OE _____
10. OM _____
11. Oto _____
12. PE tube _____
13. T&A _____
14. URI _____

Worksheet 17G
Case Study

Directions: Below is a case study presentation of a patient with a condition covered in this chapter. Read the case study and answer the questions below. Some questions will ask for information not included within this chapter. Use your text, a medical dictionary, or any other reference material you choose to answer these questions.

This 35-year-old male musician was seen in the EENT clinic complaining of a progressive hearing loss over the past 15 years. He is now unable to hear what is being said if there is any environmental noise present. He states that he has played with a group of musicians using amplified instruments and no earplugs for the past 20 years. External ear structures appear normal bilaterally with otoscopy. Tympanometry is normal bilaterally. Audiometry reveals diminished hearing bilaterally. Rinne and Weber tuning-fork tests indicate that the patient's ears are unable to conduct sound waves to the inner ear, but rule out damage to the auditory nerves. Diagnosis is moderate bilateral conductive hearing loss as a result of prolonged exposure to loud noise. Patient is referred for evaluation for a hearing aid.

1. What specific type of hearing loss does this patient appear to have? Look this condition up in a reference source and include a short description of it.

   _____

   _____

2. What diagnostic tests did the physician perform? Describe them in your own words.

   _____

   _____

3. This patient's auditory nerves were undamaged. What do these nerves do?

   _____

   _____

4. Explain the difference between a hearing aid and a cochlear implant.

   _____

   _____

5. This case study uses the term bilateral several times. What does this term mean?

   _____

   _____

6. How do you think this patient could have avoided this hearing loss?

   _____

   _____

Worksheet 17H
Web Destinations

Ménière's Disease

The National Institute on Deafness and Other Communication Disorders (NIDCD) is one of the organizations in the National Institutes of Health (NIH). The NIH supports research to learn how to prevent, detect, diagnose, and treat diseases and disabilities. The NIDCD website at www.nidcd.nih.gov describes Ménière's disease as an abnormality of the inner ear causing a host of symptoms, including vertigo or severe dizziness, tinnitus or a roaring sound in the ears, fluctuating hearing loss, and the sensation of pressure or pain in the affected ear. Visit this website. Select the "Health Information" tab. Left click on the Ménière's under the Balance list. Scroll down to the bottom of this basic information page and left click on Read more about Ménière's disease. Use the information from this webpage to write a report on the causes, symptoms, diagnosis, treatment, and research for Ménière's disease.

Pressure Equalizing Tubes

The American Academy of Otolaryngology-Head and Neck Surgery website discusses ear infections and ear tubes. This website states:

> By the age of five, nearly every child has experienced at least one episode. Most ear infections either resolve on their own or are effectively treated by antibiotics. But sometimes, ear infections and/or fluid in the middle ear may become a chronic problem leading to other issues such as hearing loss, and behavior and speech problems. In these cases, insertion of an ear tube by an otolaryngologist may be considered.

Visit this website at www.entnet.org. Click on the Health Information link, then the Ears link. Select Ear Tubes from the list. Read the information provided and write a summary.

Worksheet 17I
Professional Profile and Journal

Professional Profile

Audiology

Audiology is the branch of healthcare devoted to the study, diagnosis, treatment, and prevention of communication disorders resulting from hearing loss. Audiologists provide a comprehensive array of services related to prevention, diagnosis, and treatment of hearing impairment and its associate communication disorders. Audiologists perform diagnostic hearing tests, fit and dispense hearing aid amplification devices, and rehabilitate persons with hearing loss. Audiology services work with clients of all ages from young children born with hearing impairment to the elderly who experience hearing loss as a part of the aging process. They practice in private offices, hospitals, and schools.

Doctor of Audiology (AuD)

- Also referred to as an audiologist
- Graduates from an accredited 4-year graduate program in audiology
- Completes an extensive clinical internship in a variety of practice settings
- Passes a national certification examination

For more information regarding these health careers, visit the following websites:

- American Academy of Audiology at www.audiology.org

Professional Journal

In this exercise you will now have an opportunity to put the words you have learned into practice. Imagine yourself in the role of an audiologist. If you refer back to the Professional Profile, you will see that this healthcare professional is responsible for the study, diagnosis, treatment, and prevention of communication disorders resulting from hearing loss. Use the 10 words listed below, or any other new terms from this chapter, to write sentences to describe the patients you saw today.

An example of a sentence is: Testing confirmed that damage to the *stapes* made it impossible for sound waves to cross the middle ear cavity.

1. audiometry _____

2. cochlea _____

3. auditory nerve _____

4. otoscope _____

5. tympanometry _____

6. acoustic neuroma _____

7. cochlear implant _____

8. deafness _____

9. hearing aid _____

10. Rinne and Weber tuning fork test _____

Name _____ Date _____ Score _____

Chapter 17 Word Parts Quiz

Directions: Define the combining form, prefix, or suffix in the spaces provided.

1. adenoid/o _____
2. audit/o _____
3. aur/o _____
4. cochle/o _____
5. epiglott/o _____
6. laryng/o _____
7. myc/o _____
8. myring/o _____
9. nas/o _____
10. ot/o _____
11. pharyng/o _____
12. py/o _____
13. rhin/o _____
14. sinus/o _____
15. tonsill/o _____
16. trache/o _____
17. tympan/o _____
18. -osmia _____
19. -phonia _____
20. -plegia _____
21. -rrhexis _____
22. -sclerosis _____
23. -stenosis _____
24. de- _____
25. para- _____

Name _____ Date _____ Score _____

Chapter 17 Spelling Quiz

Directions: Write each term as your instructor pronounces it.

1. _____
2. _____
3. _____
4. _____
5. _____
6. _____
7. _____
8. _____
9. _____
10. _____
11. _____
12. _____
13. _____
14. _____
15. _____
16. _____
17. _____
18. _____
19. _____
20. _____

Name _____ Date _____ Score _____

Chapter 17 Labeling Quiz 1

Directions: Label the structures of the ear.

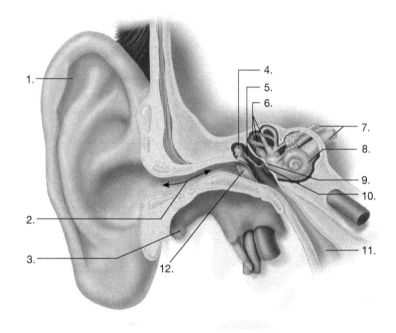

1. _____
2. _____
3. _____
4. _____
5. _____
6. _____

7. _____
8. _____
9. _____
10. _____
11. _____
12. _____

Name _____ Date _____ Score _____

Chapter 17 Labeling Quiz 2

Directions: Label the organs of the upper respiratory system.

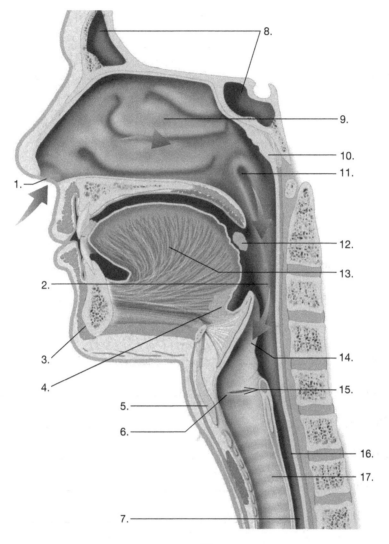

1. _____
2. _____
3. _____
4. _____
5. _____
6. _____
7. _____
8. _____
9. _____

10. _____
11. _____
12. _____
13. _____
14. _____
15. _____
16. _____
17. _____

© 2012 Pearson Education, Inc.   Chapter 17/OTORHINOLARYNGOLOGY: THE EAR, NOSE, AND THROAT   387

Name _____ Date _____ Score _____

Chapter 17 Word Building Quiz

Directions: Build a single medical term for each phrase below.

1. pertaining to the cochlea _____
2. hardening of eardrum _____
3. narrowing of trachea _____
4. surgical removal of adenoids _____
5. discharge of pus from ear _____
6. without smell _____
7. ear pain _____
8. cutting into pharynx _____
9. epiglottis inflammation _____
10. surgical repair of trachea _____
11. pertaining to nose and stomach _____
12. eardrum record _____
13. pertaining to the throat _____
14. record of hearing _____
15. abnormal condition of ear fungus _____
16. pertaining to the tonsils _____
17. process of viewing larynx _____
18. inflammation of all sinuses _____
19. eardrum rupture _____
20. paralysis of larynx _____
21. without voice _____
22. inflammation of nose _____
23. pertaining to hearing _____
24. surgical removal of larynx _____
25. involuntary contraction of pharynx _____

Name _____ Date _____ Score _____

Chapter 17 Quiz

Fill-in-the-Blank

1. The abbreviation ENT stands for the medical specialty of _____.

2. The function of the ears are _____ and _____.

3. The medical term for the throat is _____.

4. The adenoids are also called the _____ tonsils.

5. The three tiny bones in the middle ear are the _____, _____, and _____.

6. The _____ is a flap of cartilage that prevents food or drink from entering the larynx or trachea.

7. The term that means being unable to smell is _____.

8. The medical term for windpipe is _____.

9. The medical term for eardrum is _____ membrane.

10. The medical term for voice box is _____.

Word Building

Build a term that means:

1. cutting into eardrum _____

2. one who studies hearing _____

3. tonsil inflammation _____

4. narrowing of trachea _____

5. surgical repair of ear _____

6. instrument to view larynx _____

7. pertaining to the ear _____

8. without voice _____

9. discharge from nose _____

10. pertaining to the nose and throat _____

Matching

_____ 1. decongestant
_____ 2. falling test
_____ 3. pertussis
_____ 4. acoustic neuroma
_____ 5. tinnitus
_____ 6. OM
_____ 7. tonsils
_____ 8. diphtheria
_____ 9. dysphonia
_____ 10. hearing aid
_____ 11. pinna
_____ 12. croup
_____ 13. AU
_____ 14. semicircular canals
_____ 15. epistaxis
_____ 16. PE tubes
_____ 17. ossicles
_____ 18. nasal cannula
_____ 19. cochlea
_____ 20. deafness
_____ 21. vocal cords
_____ 22. vertigo
_____ 23. Ménière's disease
_____ 24. ET
_____ 25. otitis externa

a. amplification device
b. dizziness
c. chronic inner ear infection
d. both ears
e. infection with barking cough
f. swimmer's ear
g. middle ear bones
h. test for balance and equilibrium
i. organs for equilibrium
j. hearing impairment
k. plastic device to deliver oxygen
l. produce speech
m. medication to reduce nasal stuffiness
n. formation of thick membrane across throat
o. endotracheal
p. whooping cough
q. remove foreign invaders from air and food
r. ringing in the ears
s. benign turmor
t. auricle
u. speech problems
v. middle ear infection
w. drain trapped fluid from middle ear
x. nosebleed
y. shaped like a coiled snail shell

Chapter 17 Answer Keys

Worksheet 17A Answer Key

1. adenoids
2. hearing
3. hearing
4. ear
5. cochlea
6. epiglottis
7. larynx (voice box)
8. tympanic membrane (eardrum)
9. nose
10. ear
11. pharynx (throat)
12. nose
13. sinus
14. tonsils
15. trachea (windpipe)
16. tympanic membrane (eardrum)
17. without
18. within
19. all
20. alongside
21. smell
22. voice

Worksheet 17B Answer Key

1. stomach
2. fungus
3. nerve
4. pus
5. without
6. without
7. difficult
8. pain
9. surgical removal
10. record
11. inflammation
12. one who studies
13. study of
14. enlarged
15. instrument to measure
16. process of measuring
17. tumor
18. abnormal condition
19. cutting into
20. surgical repair
21. paralysis
22. discharge, flow
23. rupture
24. hardening
25. instrument for viewing
26. process of viewing
27. involuntary muscle contraction
28. narrowing

Worksheet 17C Answer Key

1. adenoid/o = adenoids; -itis = inflammation
2. laryng/o = larynx; -plegia = paralysis
3. ot/o = ear; -algia = pain
4. an- = without; -osmia = smell
5. pharyng/o = pharynx; -plasty = surgical repair
6. endo- = within; trache/o = trachea; -al = pertaining to
7. cochle/o = cochlea; -ar = pertaining to
8. myring/o = eardrum; -plasty = surgical repair
9. trache/o = trachea; -megaly = enlarged
10. dys- = difficult; -phonia = voice
11. tympan/o = eardrum; -rrhexis = rupture
12. audi/o = hearing; -gram = record
13. tympan/o = eardrum; -plasty = surgical repair
14. epiglott/o = epiglottis; -itis = inflammation
15. nas/o = nose; gastr/o = stomach; -ic = pertaining to
16. rhin/o = nose; myc/o = fungus; -osis = abnormal condition
17. audit/o = hearing; -ory = pertaining to
18. pan- = all; sinus/o = sinuses; -itis = inflammation
19. myring/o = eardrum; -sclerosis = hardening
20. aur/o = ear; -al = pertaining to
21. pharyng/o = pharynx; -otomy = cutting into
22. audi/o = hearing; -logy = study of
23. ot/o = ear; py/o = pus; -rrhea = flow/discharge
24. laryng/o = larynx; -spasm = involuntary muscle contraction
25. tonsill/o = tonsils; -ectomy = surgical removal

Worksheet 17D Answer Key

1. acoustic
2. decongestant
3. intubation
4. pertussis
5. cochlear
6. vertigo
7. epistaxis
8. croup
9. cannula
10. tinnitus

```
T D S I X A T S I P E N
N E P T W P N D V J O C
C C K Z R T U E W I L I
C O T N X D R O T P S T
A N C T T H A R U R S
L G F H I T B N T C X U
U E F G L U V I M C R O
N S O X T E N L B C D C
N T R N V N A M Q L N A
A A I M I C X R K K J B
C N X T K Z C G W C B D
M T P E R T U S S I S K
```

Worksheet 17E Answer Key

1. laryngoscope
2. anosmia
3. tympanorrhexis
4. tinnitus
5. cannula
6. epistaxis
7. tracheostenosis
8. pertussis
9. rhinoplasty
10. nasopharyngeal

Worksheet 17F Answer Key

1. right ear
2. left ear
3. both ears
4. diphtheria, pertussis, tetanus
5. eyes, ears, nose, throat
6. ear, nose, and throat
7. endotracheal
8. head, eyes, ears, nose, throat
9. otitis externa
10. otitis media
11. otology
12. pressure equalizing tube
13. tonsillectomy and adenoidectomy
14. upper respiratory infection

Worksheet 17G Answer Key

1. Conductive hearing loss-disease or malformation of the outer or middle ear; all sound is weaker because it is not conducted correctly to the inner ear.
2. Otoscopy—examination of the auditory canal and middle ear; Tympanometry—measurement of the movement of the tympanic membrane; audiometry—test for hearing ability; Rinne and Weber tuning-fork tests—assess both the nerve and bone conduction of sound
3. Auditory nerves carry sound impulses to the brain
4. Hearing aids or amplification devices amplify sound and will work best for conductive hearing loss; cochlear implant is a device that converts sound signals into magnetic impulses to stimulate the auditory nerve and is used to treat profound sensorineural hearing loss.
5. Bilateral refers to both sides
6. Protect his ears better during playing music by wearing earplugs

Worksheet 17H Answer Key

Essay activity, student answers will vary.

Worksheet 17I Answer Key

Student answers will vary.

Chapter 17 Word Parts Quiz Answer Key

1. adenoids
2. hearing
3. ear
4. cochlea
5. epiglottis
6. larynx (voice box)
7. fungus
8. tympanic membrane (eardrum)
9. nose
10. ear
11. pharynx (throat)
12. pus
13. nose
14. sinus
15. tonsils
16. trachea (windpipe)
17. tympanic membrane (eardrum)
18. smell
19. voice
20. paralysis
21. rupture
22. hardening
23. narrowing
24. without
25. alongside

Chapter 17 Spelling Quiz Answer Key

1. acoustic
2. cochlear
3. croup
4. diphtheria
5. endotracheal
6. Ménière
7. cannula
8. pertussis
9. tinnitus
10. vertigo
11. myringotomy
12. adenoidectomy
13. epiglottitis
14. laryngospasm
15. nasopharyngeal
16. otomycosis
17. dysphonia
18. anosmia
19. pansinusitis
20. tympanorrhexis

Chapter 17 Labeling Quiz 1 Answer Key

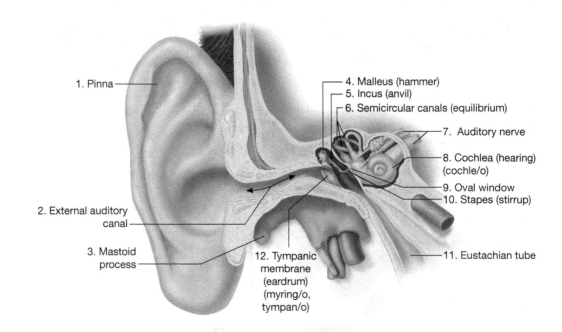

Chapter 17 Labeling Quiz 2 Answer Key

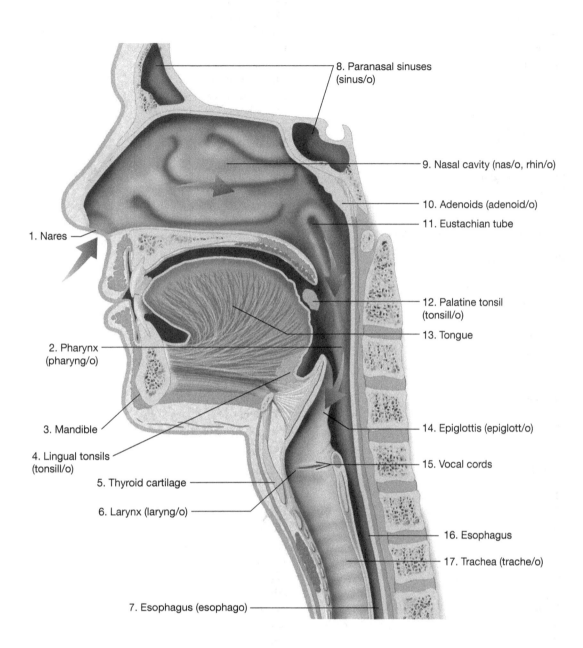

1. Nares
2. Pharynx (pharyng/o)
3. Mandible
4. Lingual tonsils (tonsill/o)
5. Thyroid cartilage
6. Larynx (laryng/o)
7. Esophagus (esophago)
8. Paranasal sinuses (sinus/o)
9. Nasal cavity (nas/o, rhin/o)
10. Adenoids (adenoid/o)
11. Eustachian tube
12. Palatine tonsil (tonsill/o)
13. Tongue
14. Epiglottis (epiglott/o)
15. Vocal cords
16. Esophagus
17. Trachea (trache/o)

Chapter 17 Word Building Quiz Answer Key

1. cochlear
2. myringosclerosis
3. tracheostenosis
4. adenoidectomy
5. otopyorrhea
6. anosmia
7. otalgia
8. pharyngotomy
9. epiglottitis
10. tracheoplasty
11. nasogastric
12. tympanogram
13. pharyngeal
14. audiogram
15. otomycosis
16. tonsillar
17. laryngoscopy
18. pansinusitis
19. tympanorrhexis
20. laryngoplegia
21. aphonia
22. rhinitis
23. auditory
24. laryngectomy
25. pharyngospasm

Chapter 17 Quiz Answer Key

Fill-in-the-Blank

1. otorhinolaryngology
2. hearing, equilibrium (balance)
3. pharynx
4. pharyngeal
5. stapes, malleus, incus
6. epiglottis
7. anosmia
8. trachea
9. tympanic
10. larynx

Word Building

1. tympanotomy or myringotomy
2. audiologist
3. tonsillitis
4. tracheostenosis
5. otoplasty
6. laryngoscope
7. otic or aural
8. aphonia
9. rhinorrhea
10. nasopharyngeal

Matching

1. m
2. h
3. p
4. s
5. r
6. v
7. q
8. n
9. u
10. a
11. t
12. e
13. d
14. i
15. x
16. w
17. g
18. k
19. y
20. j
21. l
22. b
23. c
24. o
25. f